THE WAR WITHIN

One Step at a Time

A Doonesbury Book
by G. B. TRUDEAU

Andrews McMeel
Publishing, LLC

Kansas City

DOONESBURY is distributed internationally by Universal Press Syndicate.

08 09 10 BBG 10 9 8 7 6 5 4 3

ISBN-13: 978-0-7407-6202-4
ISBN-10: 0-7407-6202-8

Library of Congress Control Number: 2006925237

DOONESBURY may be viewed on the Internet at www.doonesbury.com and www.GoComics.com.

If there are obstacles, the shortest line between two points may be the crooked one.
—Bertold Brecht

Foreword
by General Richard B. Myers, USAF, Retired,
Former Chairman of the Joint Chiefs of Staff

Our nation owes a great deal of gratitude to those Americans who serve their nation in this time of war. In calling on our troops to serve in combat and asking them to do what they have taken an oath to do, our nation's leaders have made the most difficult decision anyone can make. Such a decision, which will inevitably change the lives of our soldiers and the lives of their families, is a solemn responsibility. Some will make the ultimate sacrifice, some will live the rest of their lives with injuries, many will live with horrific memories of combat, and all will sacrifice to some degree.

As the Chairman of the Joint Chiefs of Staff, I met thousands of soldiers, sailors, airmen, and marines at bases around the world. And when I looked them in the eyes, I was inevitably met with the immense pride of those who have committed their lives to something bigger than themselves, who have made the decision for various reasons to serve their country—some protecting the homeland, some serving in bases in friendly and allied nations, and many serving on the front lines of the Global War on Terrorism. These Americans know the seriousness and magnitude of their leaders' decisions to fight for freedom.

As Chairman, I also met many wounded soldiers. Regular visits to the Walter Reed Army Medical Center and Bethesda Naval Hospital were important to me, providing an opportunity to meet and recognize service-members who had been injured. These visits also served as a reminder of the magnitude of our decisions. Leaders go into Walter Reed prepared to be depressed but come out absolutely inspired by the patients' overwhelmingly positive attitudes about their contributions to the country. I felt a tremendous sense of humility after every visit, and in a way I even felt ashamed for any sense of difficulty I had about my own challenges. There I met people who had experienced great pain and sacrifice, and they weren't complaining. I will never forget the soldier who looked at me from his hospital bed and said, "I was willing to give my life for my country, and I only had to give my leg."

Our battlefield medicine has improved so dramatically that we now give care to the wounded shortly after they sustain their injuries. Survival rates have improved tremendously, and long-term treatment improves future quality of life. We have people surviving and recovering from severe traumatic wounds, and I am proud of our nation's commitment to the treatment of those injured in combat. The series about B.D. has accurately recognized the tremendous advancements of the military medical profession and the service of the doctors, nurses, medical technicians, therapists, and counselors—whether in the Defense Department hospitals or Veterans Affairs (VA) hospitals—who help our troops deal with their injuries.

Any time we put people into combat, there's going to be physical and emotional injury. Both are serious and both need treatment. Today we have a much better understanding of this than we did in the past. The counselor Elias, a Vietnam vet who has been helping B.D. come to grips with his Post-Traumatic Stress Disorder (PTSD), is a terrific example of something we've seen: veterans from previous conflicts working in our Vet Centers to help those who have served during the current conflict. Many servicemembers who have been wounded won't be able to, or won't choose to, continue their military service. But I hope that many of them will say, "I'd like to go to the VA and contribute," and come back into the system to help others. They've been there, they've been through it, and they know what issues need to be addressed. Fortunately PTSD is losing the stigma it once had, and I hope Garry Trudeau's *The War Within* will help soldiers in B.D.'s situation find their way to the help they need and deserve.

Garry's done his research and engaged wounded soldiers, and his portrayal of their experiences is right on the mark. The troops genuinely appreciate that America is reading about their service and getting a realistic feel for what it's all about. Garry has also managed to find humor in their experiences, a lot of it, while using his artistic touch to look at some very serious issues.

What our servicemembers want very much is to get on with the rest of their lives. I ask America to appreciate what they have done and recognize their sacrifices. And Garry Trudeau, with his series on B.D.'s wounding and recovery, does exactly that.

THE WAR WITHIN

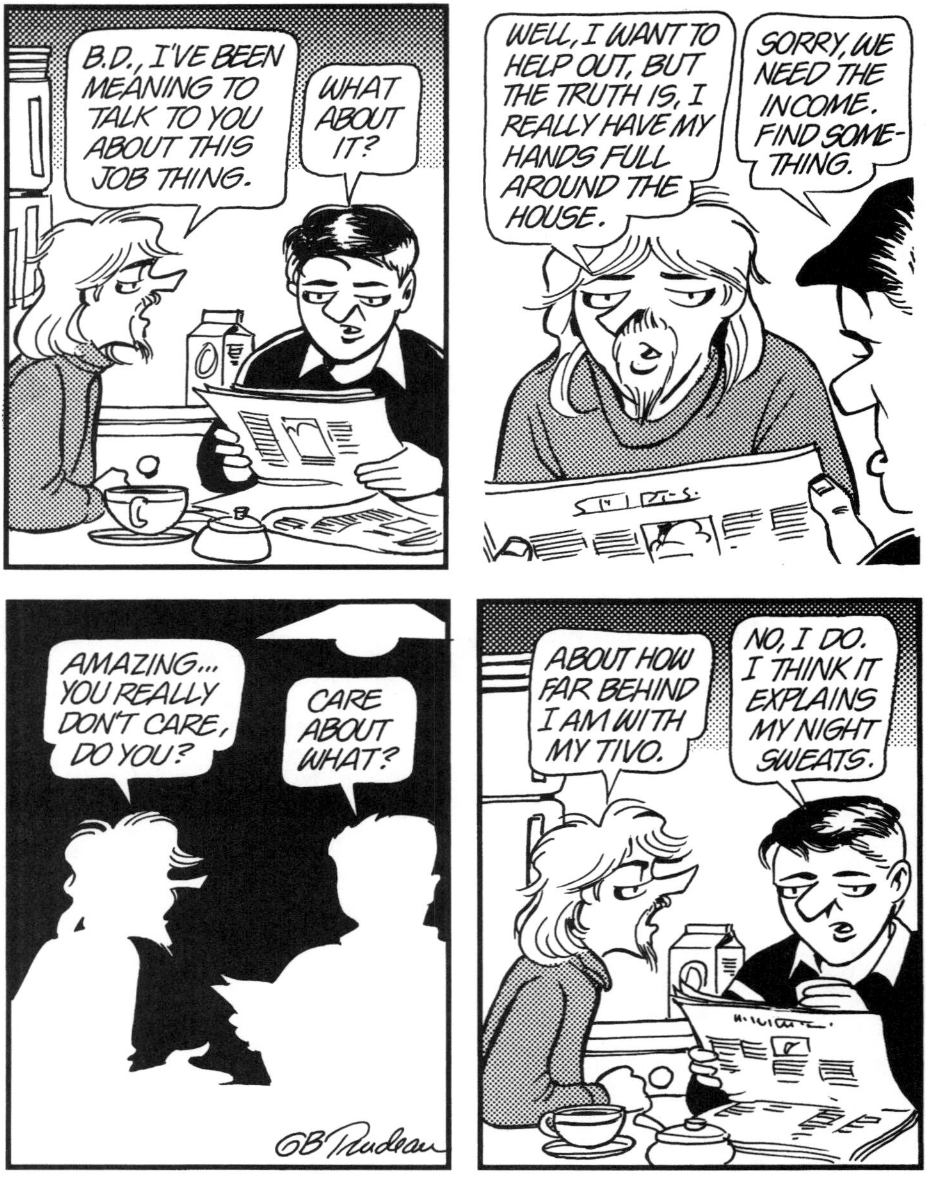
B.D., I'VE BEEN MEANING TO TALK TO YOU ABOUT THIS JOB THING.
WHAT ABOUT IT?
WELL, I WANT TO HELP OUT, BUT THE TRUTH IS, I REALLY HAVE MY HANDS FULL AROUND THE HOUSE.
SORRY, WE NEED THE INCOME. FIND SOMETHING.
AMAZING... YOU REALLY DON'T CARE, DO YOU?
CARE ABOUT WHAT?
ABOUT HOW FAR BEHIND I AM WITH MY TIVO.
NO, I DO. I THINK IT EXPLAINS MY NIGHT SWEATS.
GBTrudeau

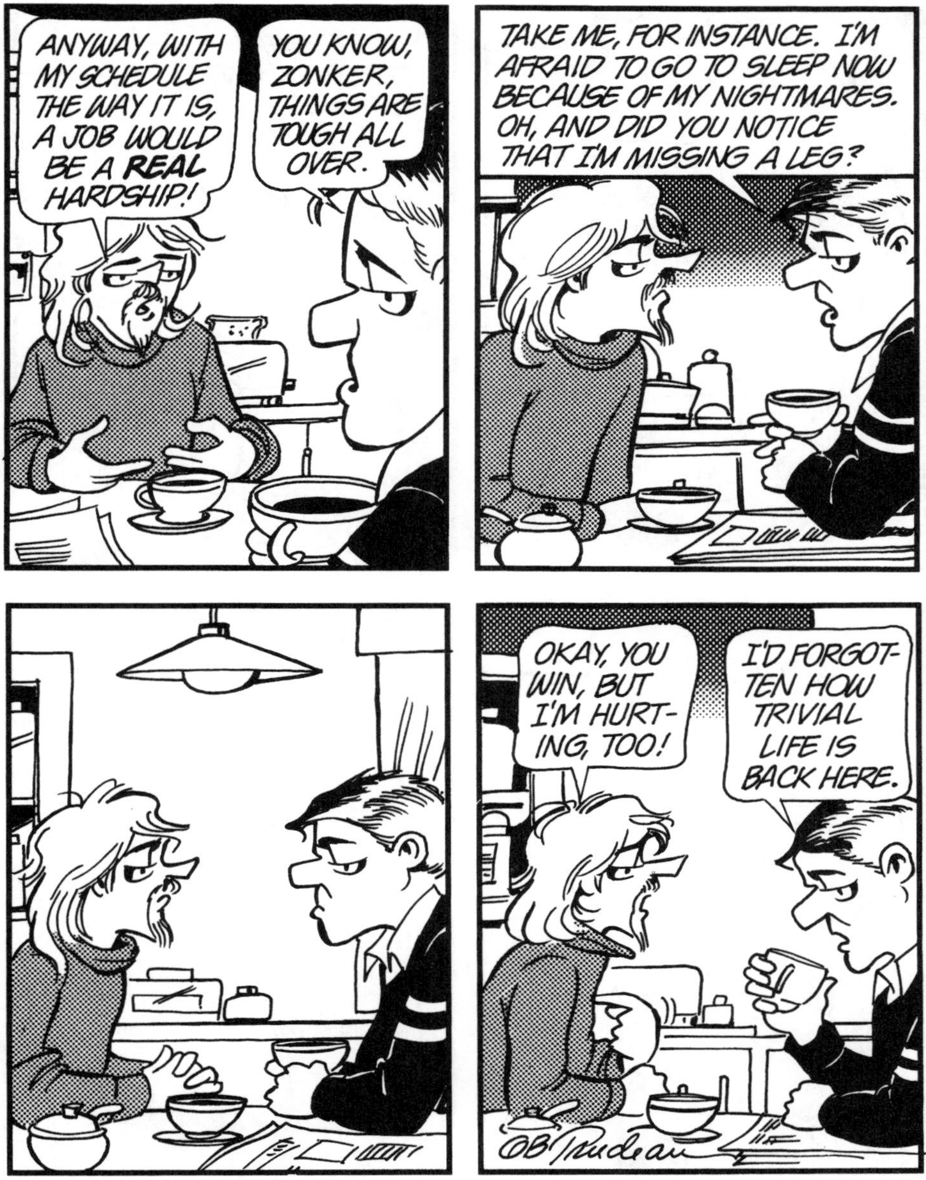
ANYWAY, WITH MY SCHEDULE THE WAY IT IS, A JOB WOULD BE A **REAL** HARDSHIP!
YOU KNOW, ZONKER, THINGS ARE TOUGH ALL OVER.
TAKE ME, FOR INSTANCE. I'M AFRAID TO GO TO SLEEP NOW BECAUSE OF MY NIGHTMARES. OH, AND DID YOU NOTICE THAT I'M MISSING A LEG?
OKAY, YOU WIN, BUT I'M HURTING, TOO!
I'D FORGOTTEN HOW TRIVIAL LIFE IS BACK HERE.
GB Trudeau

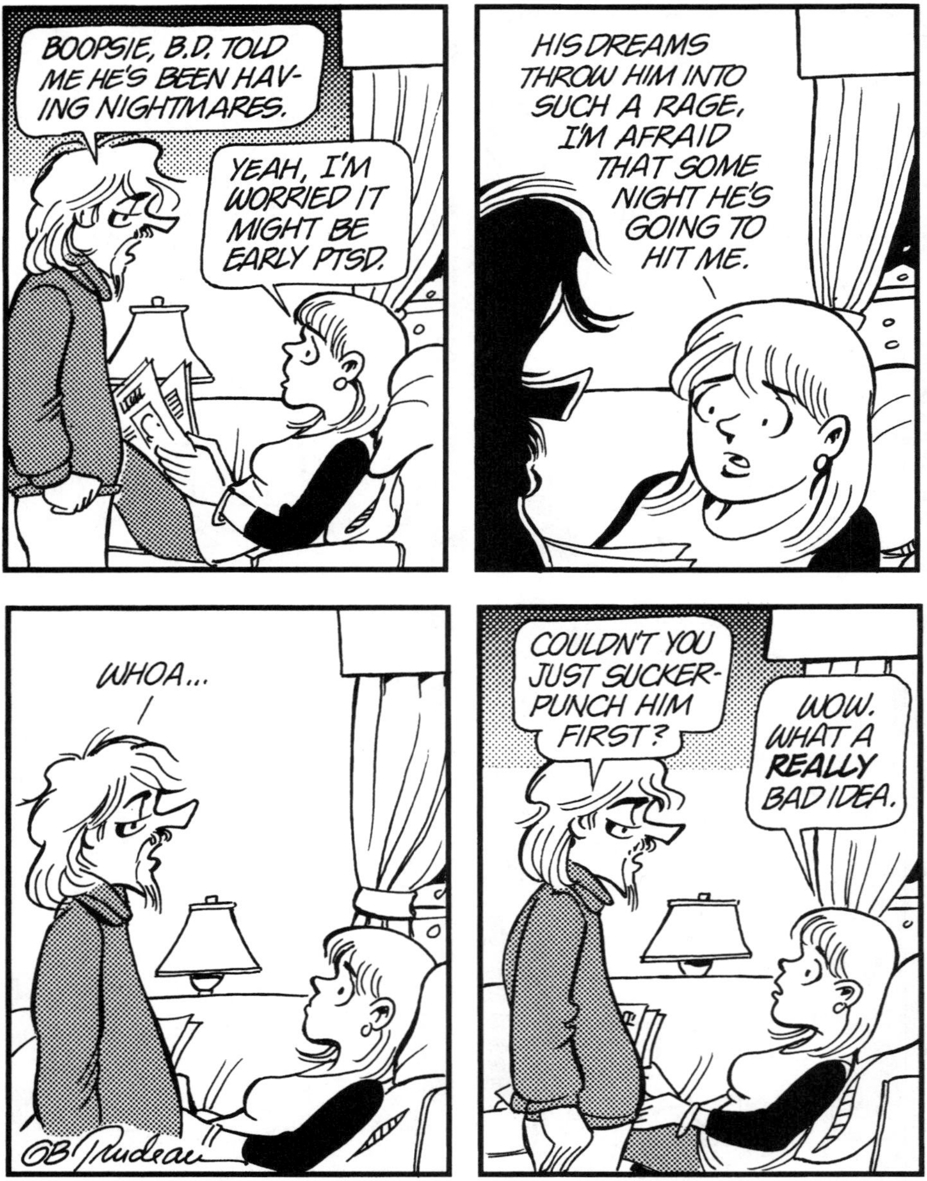
BOOPSIE, B.D. TOLD ME HE'S BEEN HAV-ING NIGHTMARES.
YEAH, I'M WORRIED IT MIGHT BE EARLY PTSD.
HIS DREAMS THROW HIM INTO SUCH A RAGE, I'M AFRAID THAT SOME NIGHT HE'S GOING TO HIT ME.
WHOA...
COULDN'T YOU JUST SUCKER-PUNCH HIM FIRST?
WOW. WHAT A **REALLY** BAD IDEA.
©B Trudeau

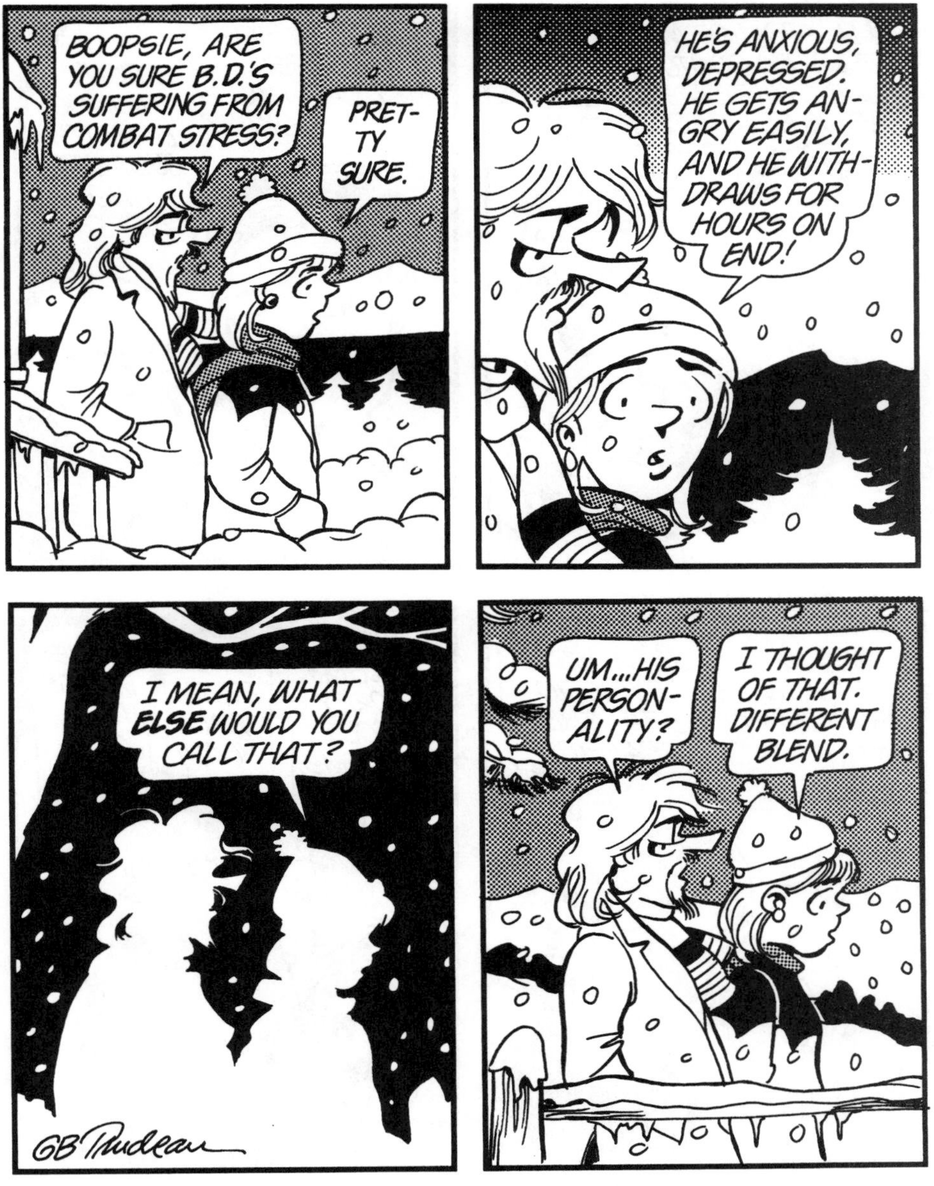
BOOPSIE, ARE YOU SURE B.D.'S SUFFERING FROM COMBAT STRESS?
PRETTY SURE.
HE'S ANXIOUS, DEPRESSED. HE GETS ANGRY EASILY, AND HE WITHDRAWS FOR HOURS ON END!
I MEAN, WHAT ELSE WOULD YOU CALL THAT?
GB Trudeau
UM...HIS PERSONALITY?
I THOUGHT OF THAT. DIFFERENT BLEND.

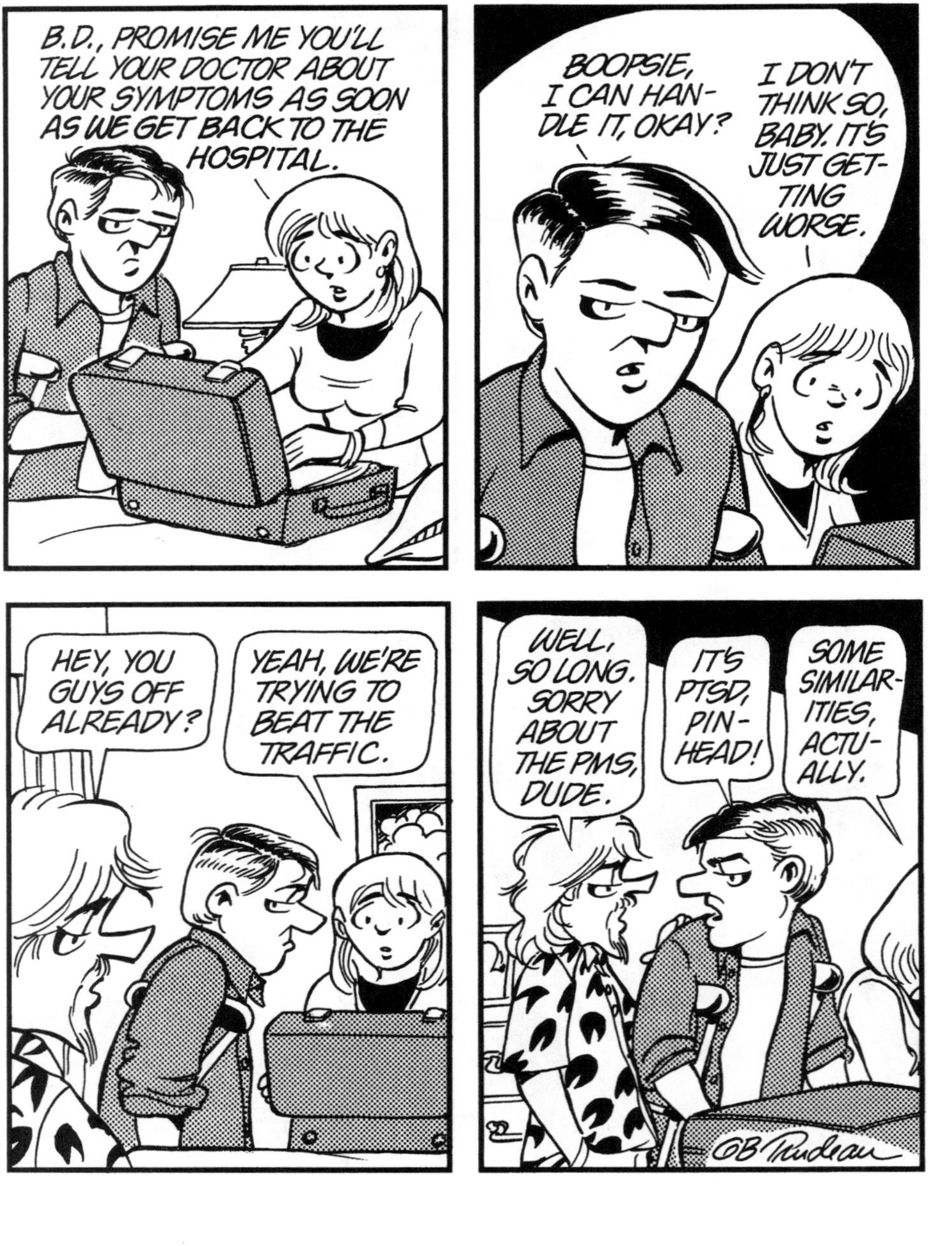
B.D., PROMISE ME YOU'LL TELL YOUR DOCTOR ABOUT YOUR SYMPTOMS AS SOON AS WE GET BACK TO THE HOSPITAL.
BOOPSIE, I CAN HANDLE IT, OKAY?
I DON'T THINK SO, BABY. IT'S JUST GETTING WORSE.
HEY, YOU GUYS OFF ALREADY?
YEAH, WE'RE TRYING TO BEAT THE TRAFFIC.
WELL, SO LONG. SORRY ABOUT THE PMS, DUDE.
IT'S PTSD, PINHEAD!
SOME SIMILARITIES, ACTUALLY.
©B Trudeau

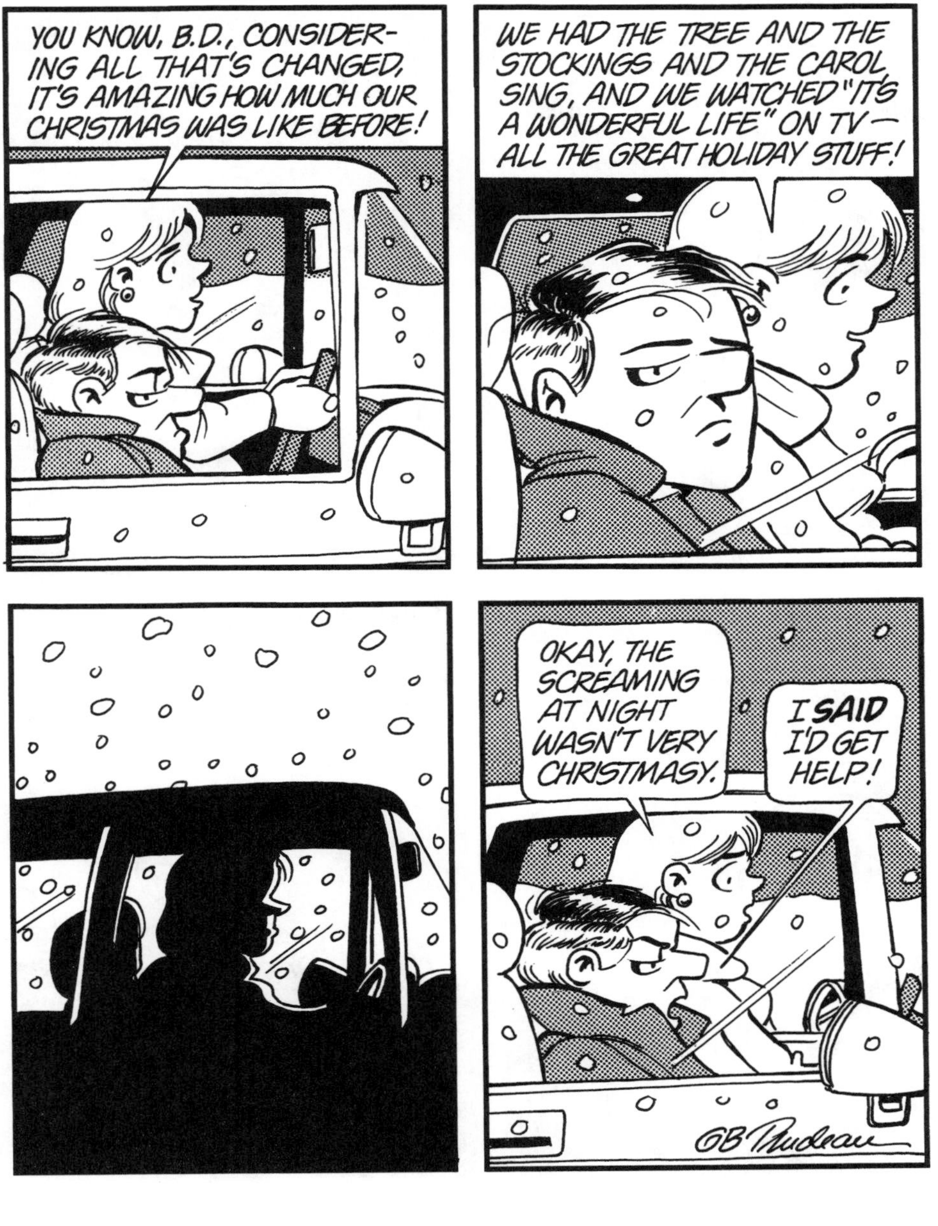
YOU KNOW, B.D., CONSIDERING ALL THAT'S CHANGED, IT'S AMAZING HOW MUCH OUR CHRISTMAS WAS LIKE BEFORE!
WE HAD THE TREE AND THE STOCKINGS AND THE CAROL SING, AND WE WATCHED "IT'S A WONDERFUL LIFE" ON TV — ALL THE GREAT HOLIDAY STUFF!
OKAY, THE SCREAMING AT NIGHT WASN'T VERY CHRISTMASY.
I **SAID** I'D GET HELP!
GB Trudeau

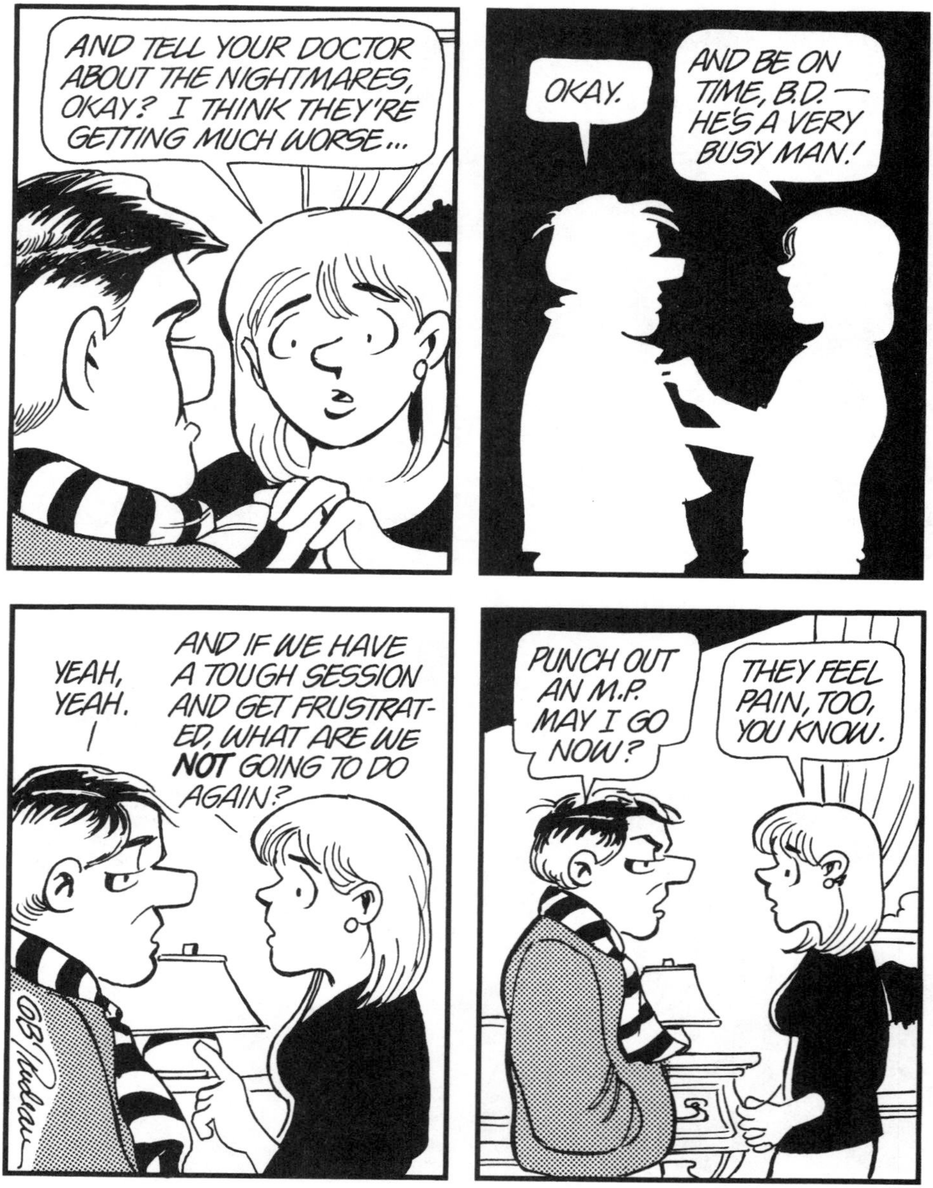
AND TELL YOUR DOCTOR ABOUT THE NIGHTMARES, OKAY? I THINK THEY'RE GETTING MUCH WORSE...
OKAY.
AND BE ON TIME, B.D.— HE'S A VERY BUSY MAN!
YEAH, YEAH.
AND IF WE HAVE A TOUGH SESSION AND GET FRUSTRATED, WHAT ARE WE **NOT** GOING TO DO AGAIN?
PUNCH OUT AN M.P. MAY I GO NOW?
THEY FEEL PAIN, TOO, YOU KNOW.
GB Trudeau

SO TELL ME ABOUT THE NEW NIGHT-MARE, B.D.
IT'S LIKE THE OLD ONES, DOC, ONLY MORE VIOLENT.
THIS TIME THE WHOLE CITY IS UNDER ATTACK, NOT JUST MY PLATOON. I RUN FROM BLOCK TO BLOCK, BUT THERE ARE CORPSES EVERYWHERE. THE CARNAGE IS INESCAPABLE!
I SEE...
ARE YOU SURE YOU WEREN'T JUST WATCHING THE NEWS?
POSITIVE. MY TV'S GRAINY, AND THIS WAS HI-DEF.
GB Trudeau

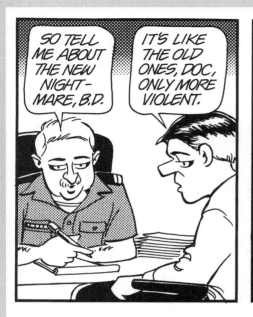

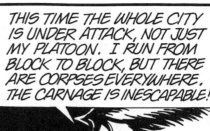

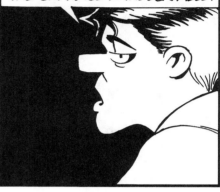

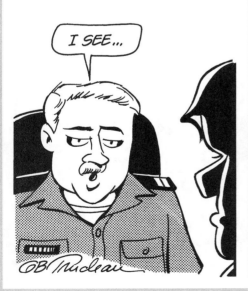

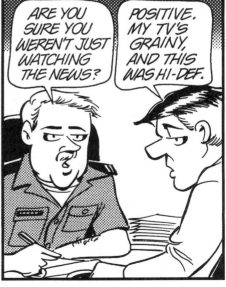

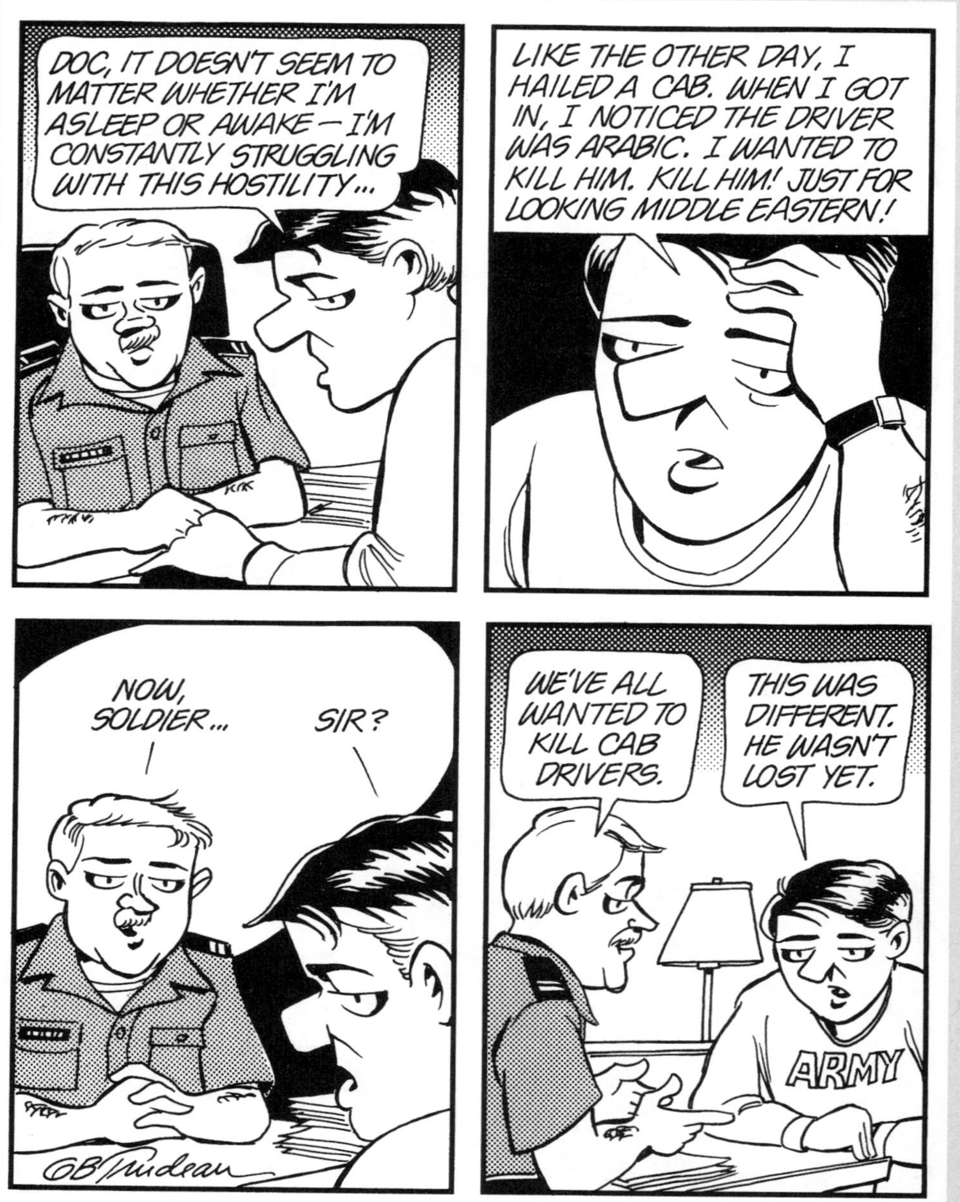
DOC, IT DOESN'T SEEM TO MATTER WHETHER I'M ASLEEP OR AWAKE — I'M CONSTANTLY STRUGGLING WITH THIS HOSTILITY...
LIKE THE OTHER DAY, I HAILED A CAB. WHEN I GOT IN, I NOTICED THE DRIVER WAS ARABIC. I WANTED TO KILL HIM. KILL HIM! JUST FOR LOOKING MIDDLE EASTERN!
NOW, SOLDIER...
SIR?
WE'VE ALL WANTED TO KILL CAB DRIVERS.
THIS WAS DIFFERENT. HE WASN'T LOST YET.
ARMY
GB Trudeau

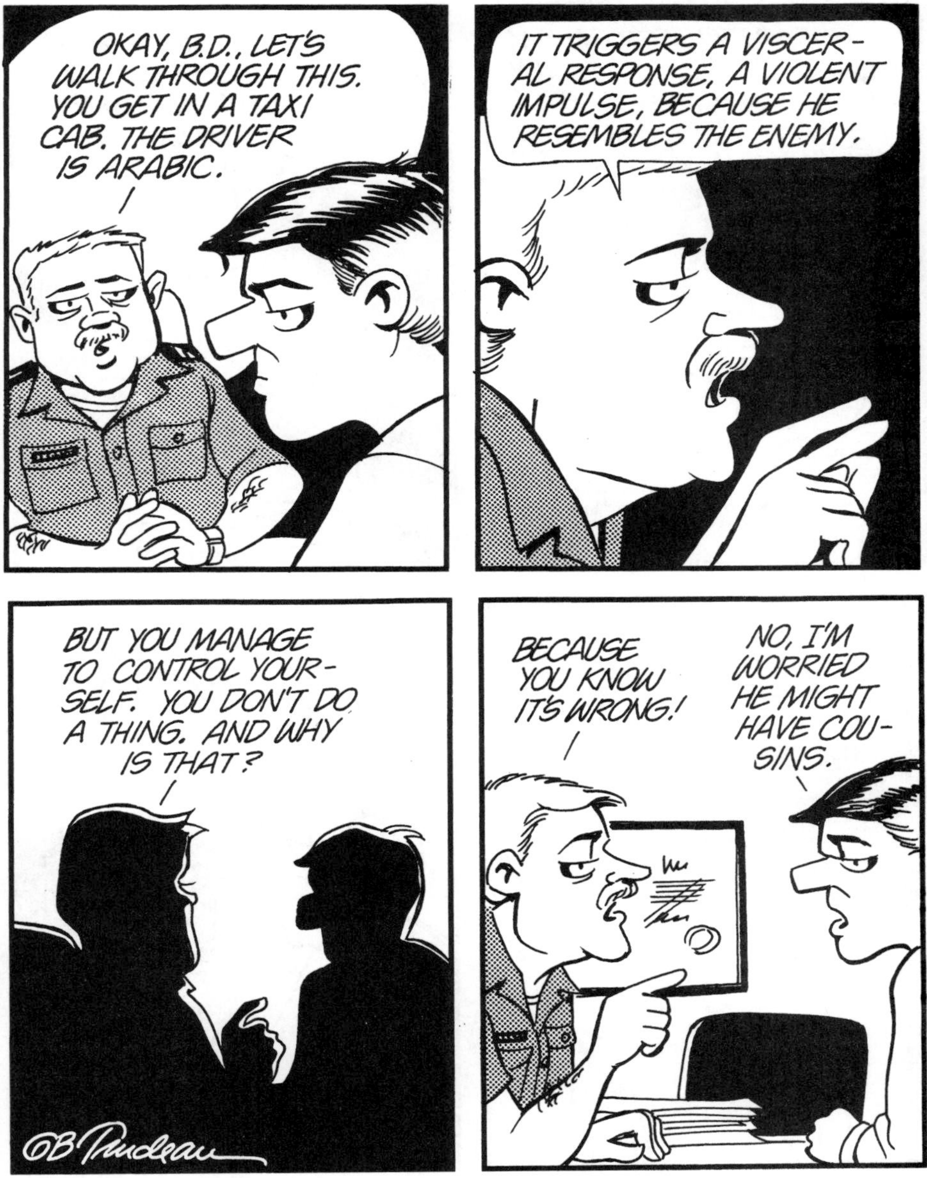
OKAY, B.D., LET'S WALK THROUGH THIS. YOU GET IN A TAXI CAB. THE DRIVER IS ARABIC.
IT TRIGGERS A VISCERAL RESPONSE, A VIOLENT IMPULSE, BECAUSE HE RESEMBLES THE ENEMY.
BUT YOU MANAGE TO CONTROL YOURSELF. YOU DON'T DO A THING. AND WHY IS THAT?
BECAUSE YOU KNOW IT'S WRONG!
NO, I'M WORRIED HE MIGHT HAVE COUSINS.
©B. Trudeau

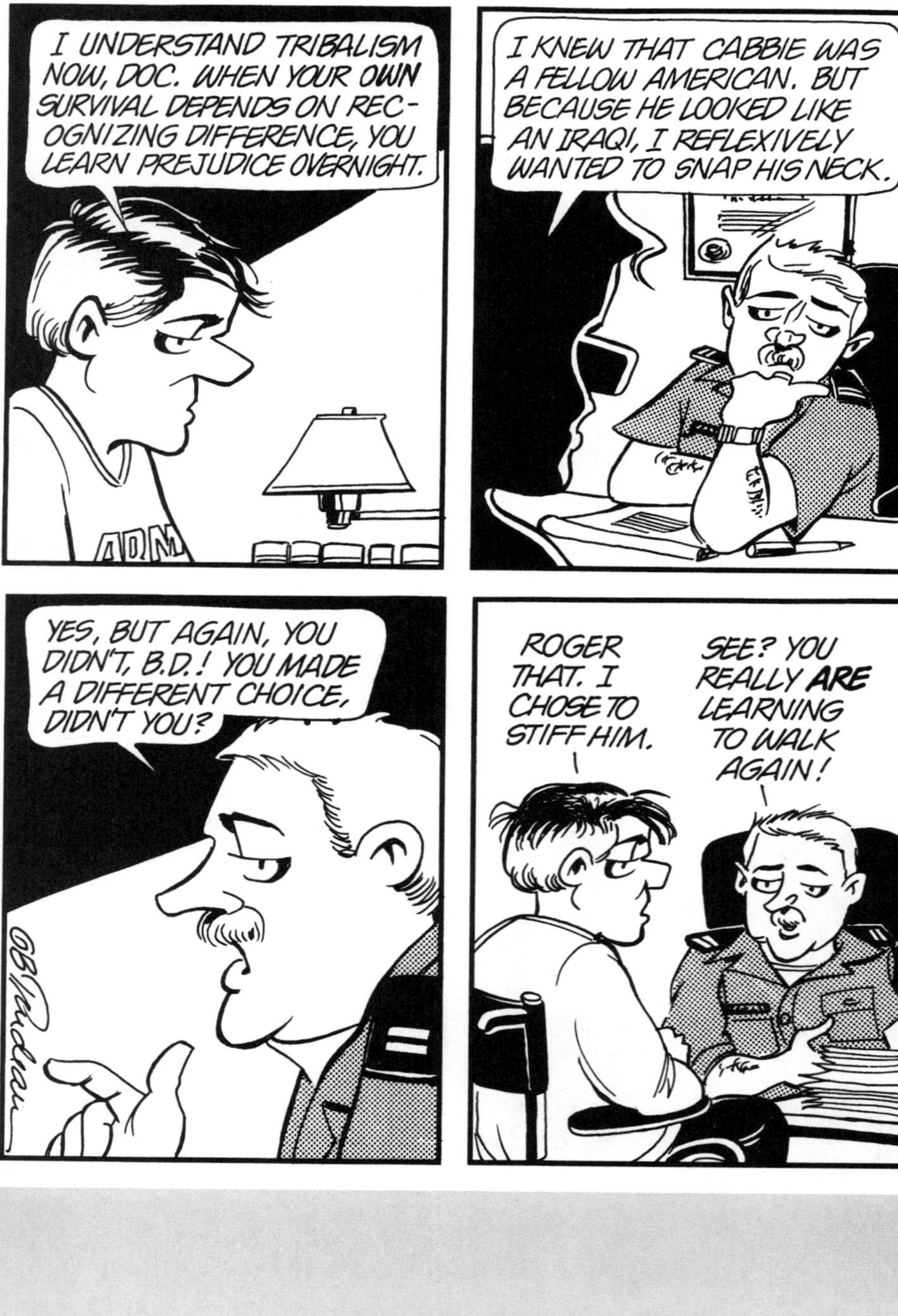
I UNDERSTAND TRIBALISM NOW, DOC. WHEN YOUR OWN SURVIVAL DEPENDS ON REC-OGNIZING DIFFERENCE, YOU LEARN PREJUDICE OVERNIGHT.
I KNEW THAT CABBIE WAS A FELLOW AMERICAN. BUT BECAUSE HE LOOKED LIKE AN IRAQI, I REFLEXIVELY WANTED TO SNAP HIS NECK.
YES, BUT AGAIN, YOU DIDN'T, B.D.! YOU MADE A DIFFERENT CHOICE, DIDN'T YOU?
ROGER THAT. I CHOSE TO STIFF HIM.
SEE? YOU REALLY ARE LEARNING TO WALK AGAIN!

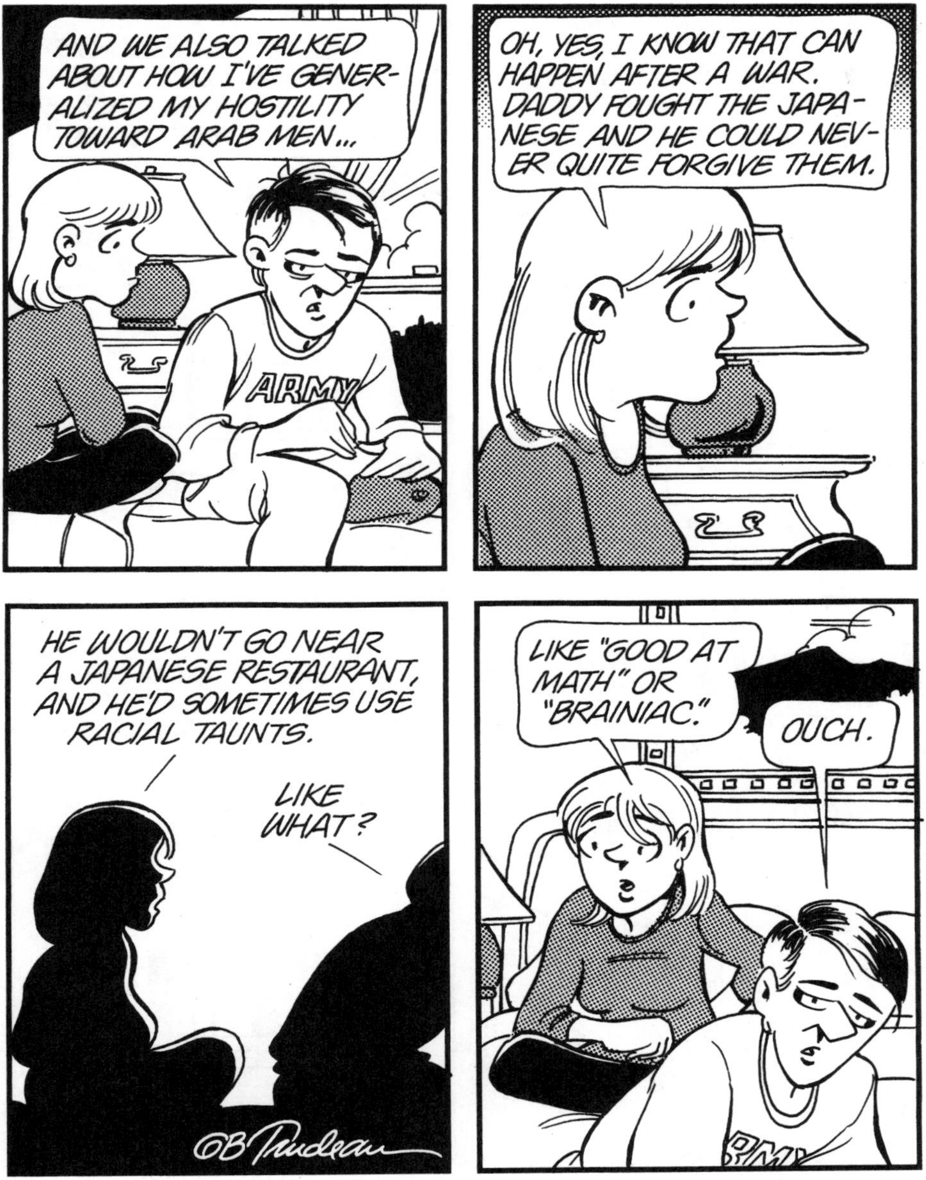
AND WE ALSO TALKED ABOUT HOW I'VE GENERALIZED MY HOSTILITY TOWARD ARAB MEN...
ARMY
OH, YES, I KNOW THAT CAN HAPPEN AFTER A WAR. DADDY FOUGHT THE JAPANESE AND HE COULD NEVER QUITE FORGIVE THEM.
HE WOULDN'T GO NEAR A JAPANESE RESTAURANT, AND HE'D SOMETIMES USE RACIAL TAUNTS.
LIKE WHAT?
©B Trudeau
LIKE "GOOD AT MATH" OR "BRAINIAC."
OUCH.

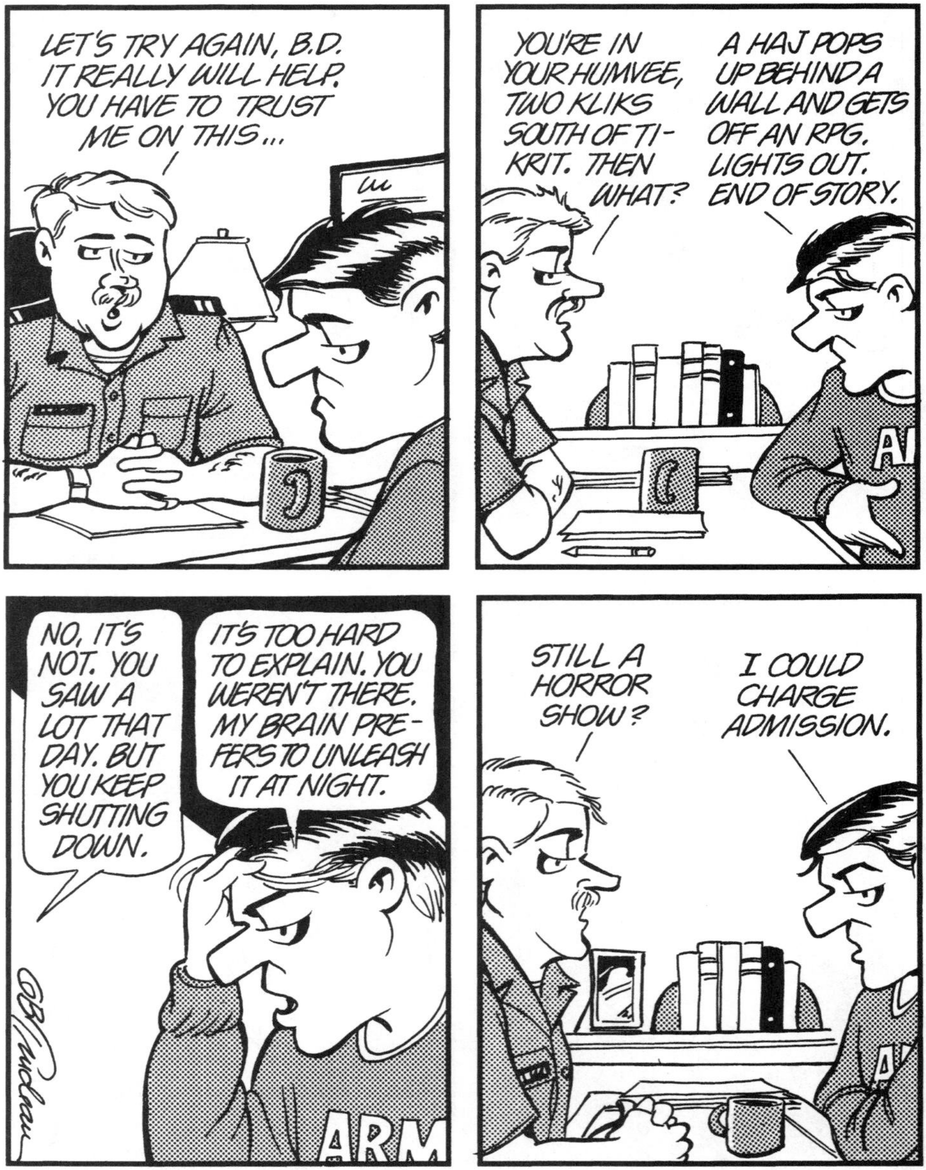
LET'S TRY AGAIN, B.D. IT REALLY WILL HELP. YOU HAVE TO TRUST ME ON THIS...
YOU'RE IN YOUR HUMVEE, TWO KLIKS SOUTH OF TI-KRIT. THEN WHAT?
A HAJ POPS UP BEHIND A WALL AND GETS OFF AN RPG. LIGHTS OUT. END OF STORY.
NO, IT'S NOT. YOU SAW A LOT THAT DAY. BUT YOU KEEP SHUTTING DOWN.
IT'S TOO HARD TO EXPLAIN. YOU WEREN'T THERE. MY BRAIN PRE-FERS TO UNLEASH IT AT NIGHT.
STILL A HORROR SHOW?
I COULD CHARGE ADMISSION.

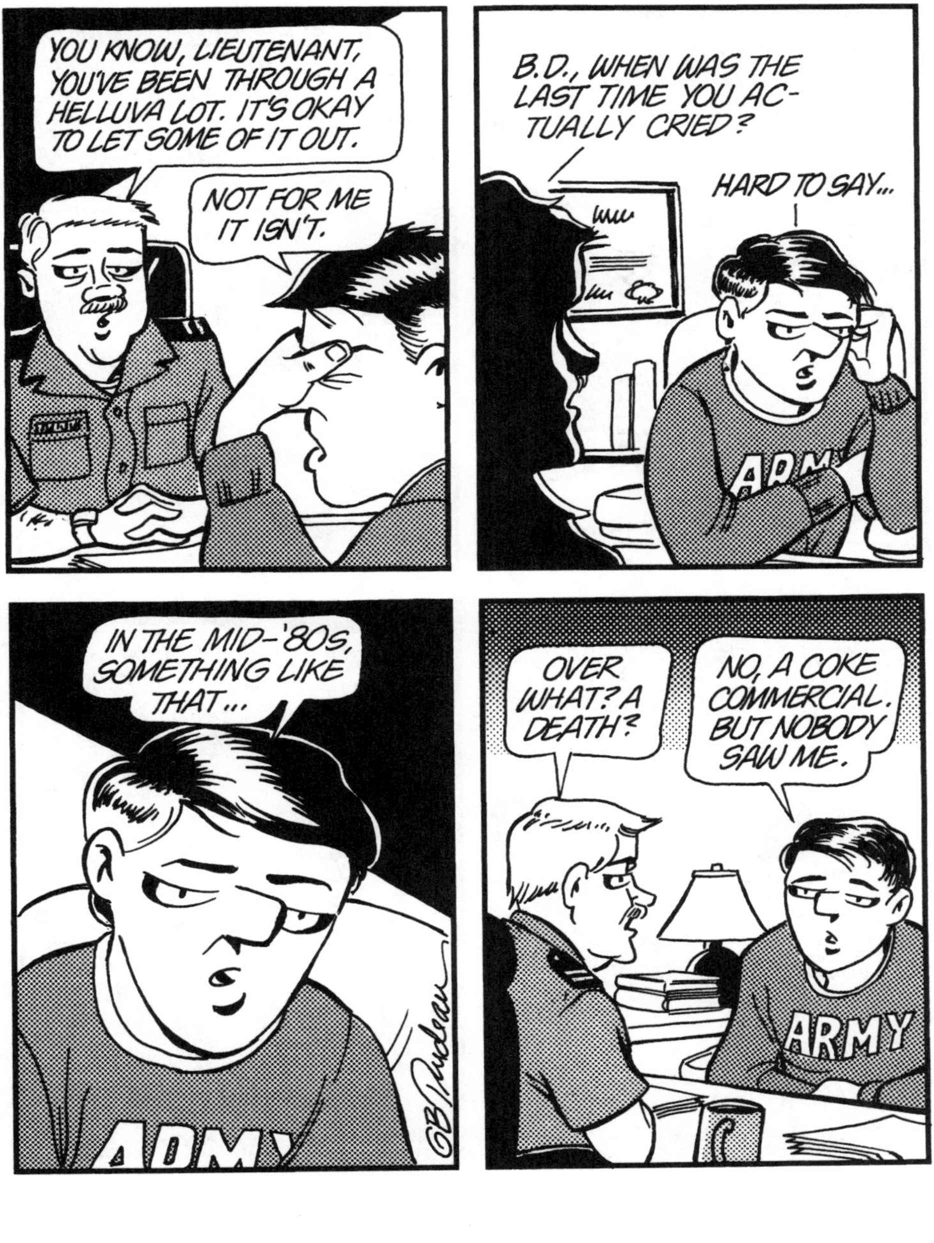
YOU KNOW, LIEUTENANT, YOU'VE BEEN THROUGH A HELLUVA LOT. IT'S OKAY TO LET SOME OF IT OUT.
NOT FOR ME IT ISN'T.
B.D., WHEN WAS THE LAST TIME YOU ACTUALLY CRIED?
HARD TO SAY...
ARMY
IN THE MID-'80s, SOMETHING LIKE THAT...
©B.Trudeau
OVER WHAT? A DEATH?
NO, A COKE COMMERCIAL. BUT NOBODY SAW ME.
ARMY

OKAY, HERE'S WHERE WE'RE AT, B.D.—FROM A TREATMENT STANDPOINT, THERE'S NO REASON YOU CAN'T GO HOME.

YOU HAVE EXCELLENT MOBILITY WITH YOUR C-LEG, AND WHILE YOU STILL HAVE PSYCHOLOGICAL ISSUES, IN MY JUDGMENT, YOU'RE READY TO TRANSITION TO THE V.A. SYSTEM.

THE V.A. SYSTEM? *THERE'S* MUSIC TO THE EARS. YOU ARE NOW ENTERING THE V.A. SYSTEM.

WELL, IT'S HOW WE SUPPORT OUR VETERANS. WHY SO CYNICAL?

I DUNNO. YOU HEAR STORIES.

OF WHAT? LIKE THEY'LL SWITCH YOU TO A PEG?

@BTrudeau

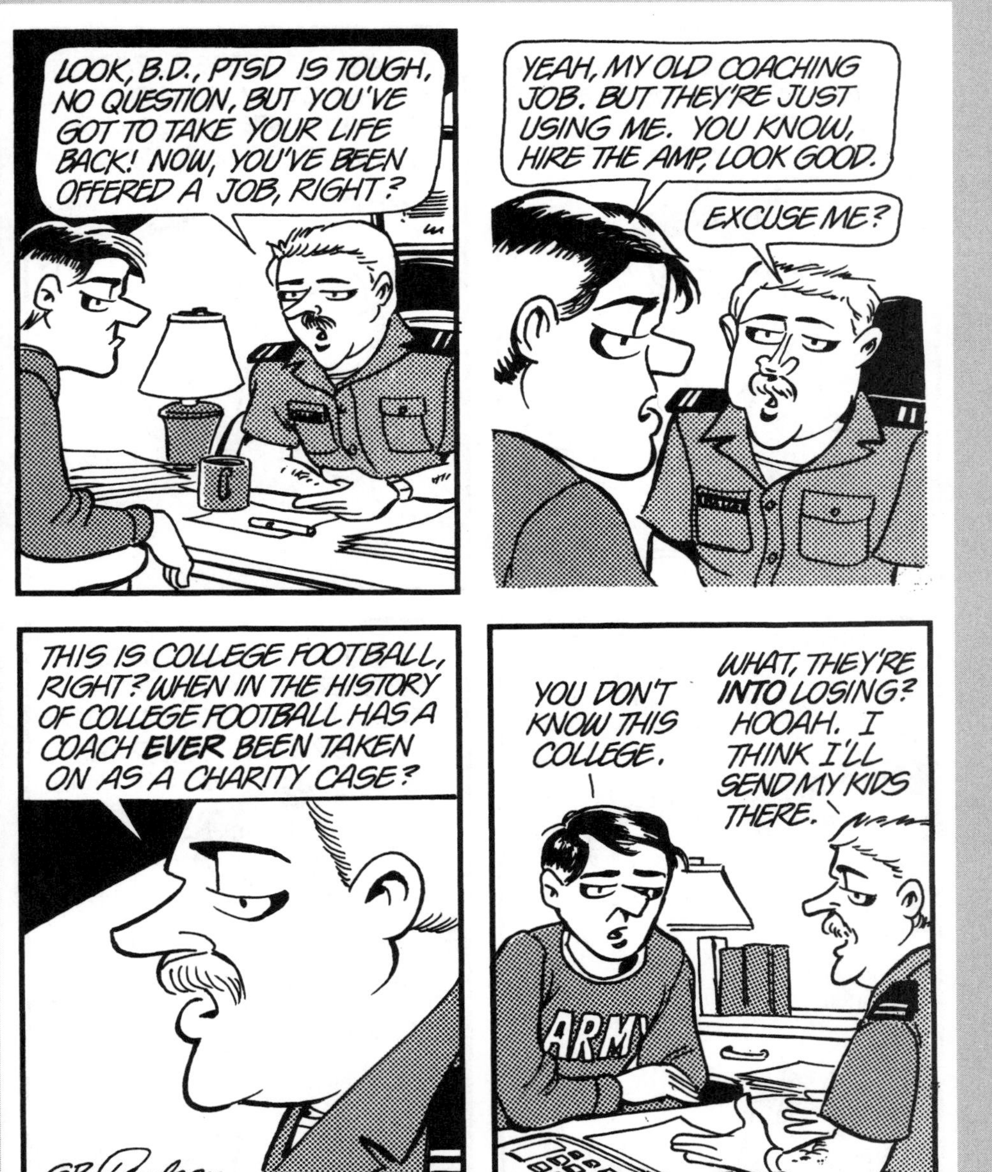
LOOK, B.D., PTSD IS TOUGH, NO QUESTION, BUT YOU'VE GOT TO TAKE YOUR LIFE BACK! NOW, YOU'VE BEEN OFFERED A JOB, RIGHT?
YEAH, MY OLD COACHING JOB. BUT THEY'RE JUST USING ME. YOU KNOW, HIRE THE AMP, LOOK GOOD.
EXCUSE ME?
THIS IS COLLEGE FOOTBALL, RIGHT? WHEN IN THE HISTORY OF COLLEGE FOOTBALL HAS A COACH **EVER** BEEN TAKEN ON AS A CHARITY CASE?
YOU DON'T KNOW THIS COLLEGE.
WHAT, THEY'RE **INTO** LOSING? HOOAH. I THINK I'LL SEND MY KIDS THERE.
ARMY
GB Trudeau

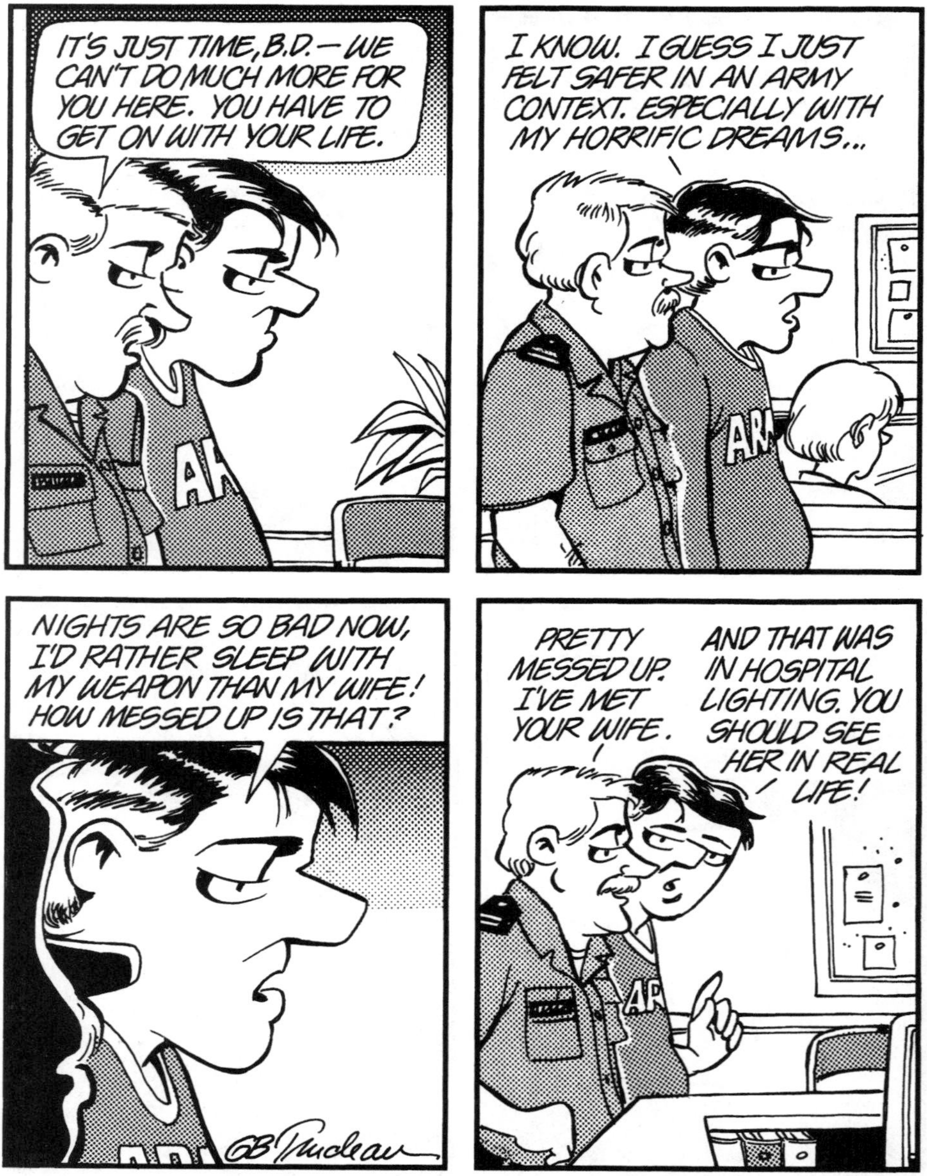
IT'S JUST TIME, B.D.— WE CAN'T DO MUCH MORE FOR YOU HERE. YOU HAVE TO GET ON WITH YOUR LIFE.
I KNOW. I GUESS I JUST FELT SAFER IN AN ARMY CONTEXT. ESPECIALLY WITH MY HORRIFIC DREAMS...
NIGHTS ARE SO BAD NOW, I'D RATHER SLEEP WITH MY WEAPON THAN MY WIFE! HOW MESSED UP IS THAT?
PRETTY MESSED UP. I'VE MET YOUR WIFE.
AND THAT WAS IN HOSPITAL LIGHTING. YOU SHOULD SEE HER IN REAL LIFE!
GB Trudeau

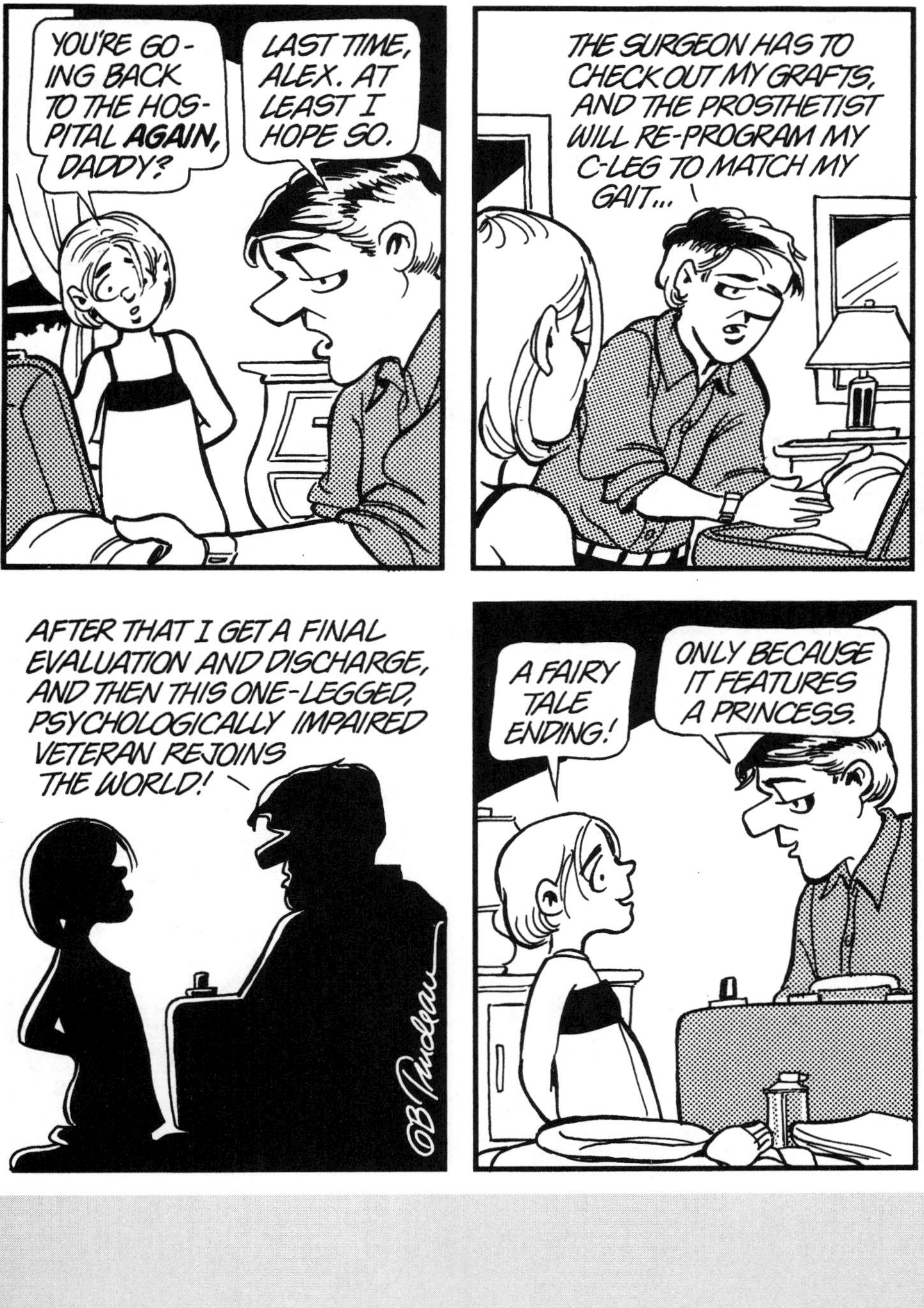
YOU'RE GO-ING BACK TO THE HOS-PITAL **AGAIN**, DADDY?
LAST TIME, ALEX. AT LEAST I HOPE SO.
THE SURGEON HAS TO CHECK OUT MY GRAFTS, AND THE PROSTHETIST WILL RE-PROGRAM MY C-LEG TO MATCH MY GAIT...
AFTER THAT I GET A FINAL EVALUATION AND DISCHARGE, AND THEN THIS ONE-LEGGED, PSYCHOLOGICALLY IMPAIRED VETERAN REJOINS THE WORLD!
A FAIRY TALE ENDING!
ONLY BECAUSE IT FEATURES A PRINCESS.

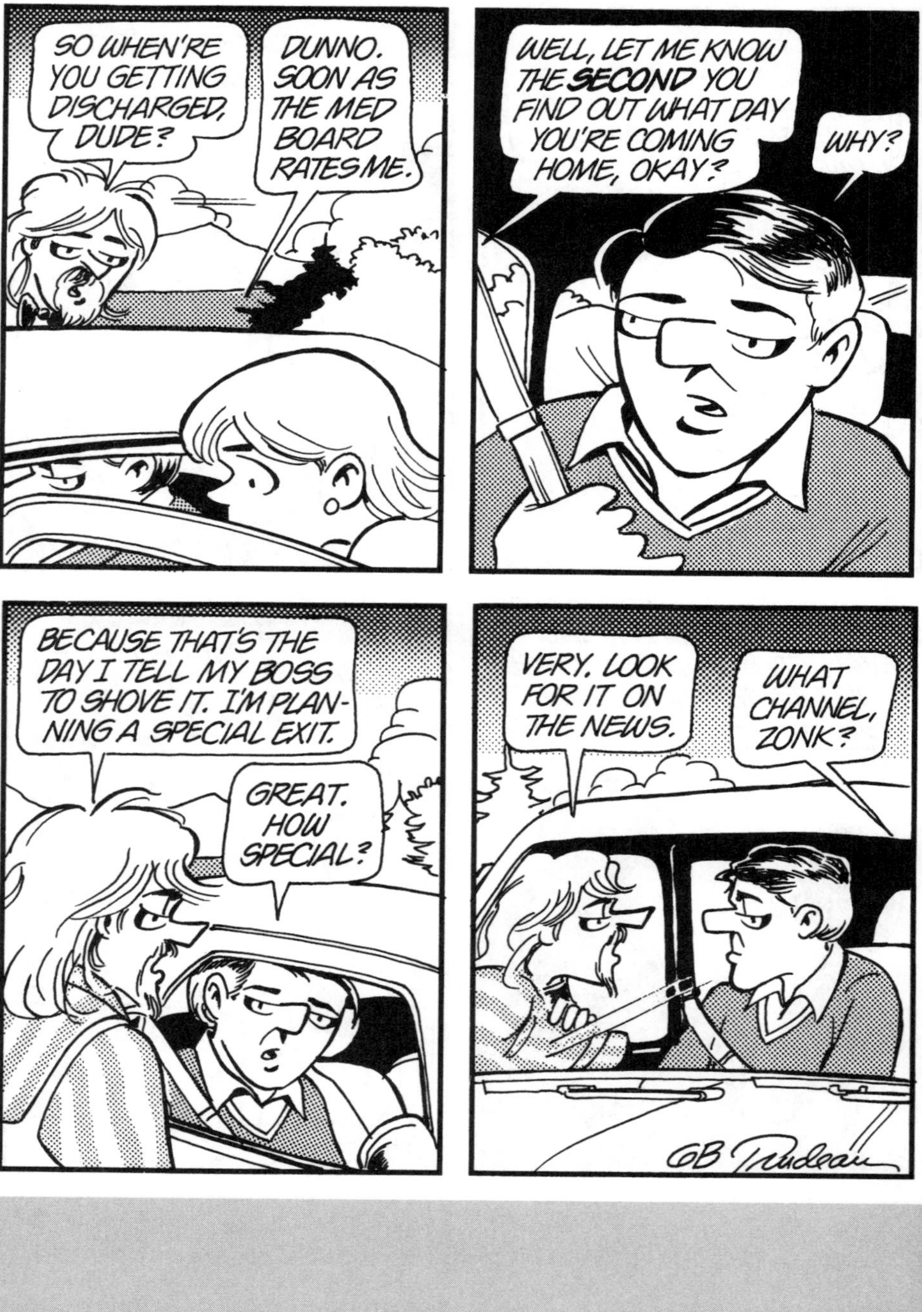
SO WHEN'RE YOU GETTING DISCHARGED, DUDE?
DUNNO. SOON AS THE MED BOARD RATES ME.
WELL, LET ME KNOW THE **SECOND** YOU FIND OUT WHAT DAY YOU'RE COMING HOME, OKAY?
WHY?
BECAUSE THAT'S THE DAY I TELL MY BOSS TO SHOVE IT. I'M PLANNING A SPECIAL EXIT.
GREAT. HOW SPECIAL?
VERY. LOOK FOR IT ON THE NEWS.
WHAT CHANNEL, ZONK?
GB Trudeau

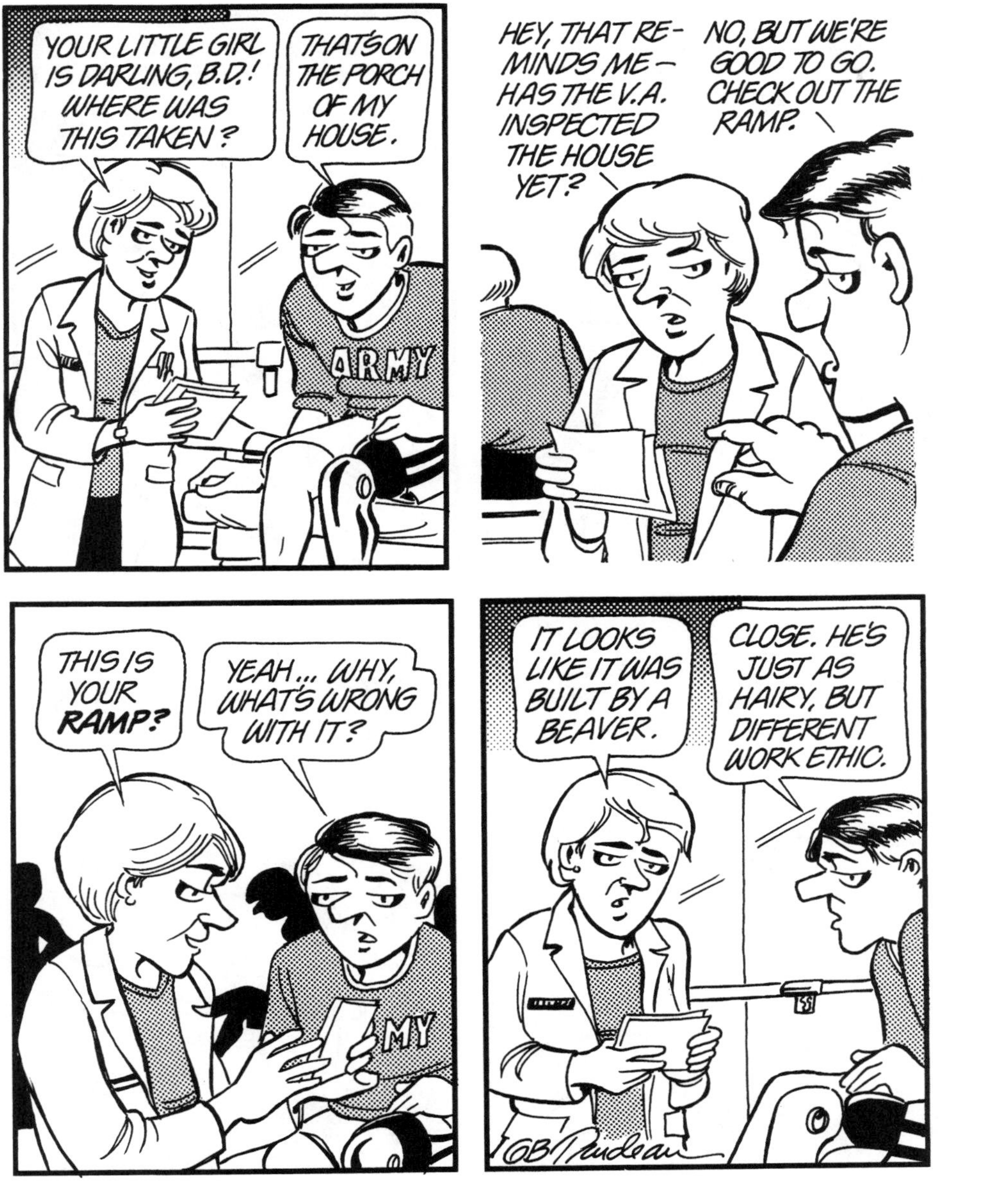
YOUR LITTLE GIRL IS DARLING, B.D.! WHERE WAS THIS TAKEN?
THAT'S ON THE PORCH OF MY HOUSE.
ARMY
HEY, THAT RE-MINDS ME — HAS THE V.A. INSPECTED THE HOUSE YET?
NO, BUT WE'RE GOOD TO GO. CHECK OUT THE RAMP.
THIS IS YOUR RAMP?
YEAH... WHY, WHAT'S WRONG WITH IT?
IT LOOKS LIKE IT WAS BUILT BY A BEAVER.
CLOSE. HE'S JUST AS HAIRY, BUT DIFFERENT WORK ETHIC.
©GB Trudeau

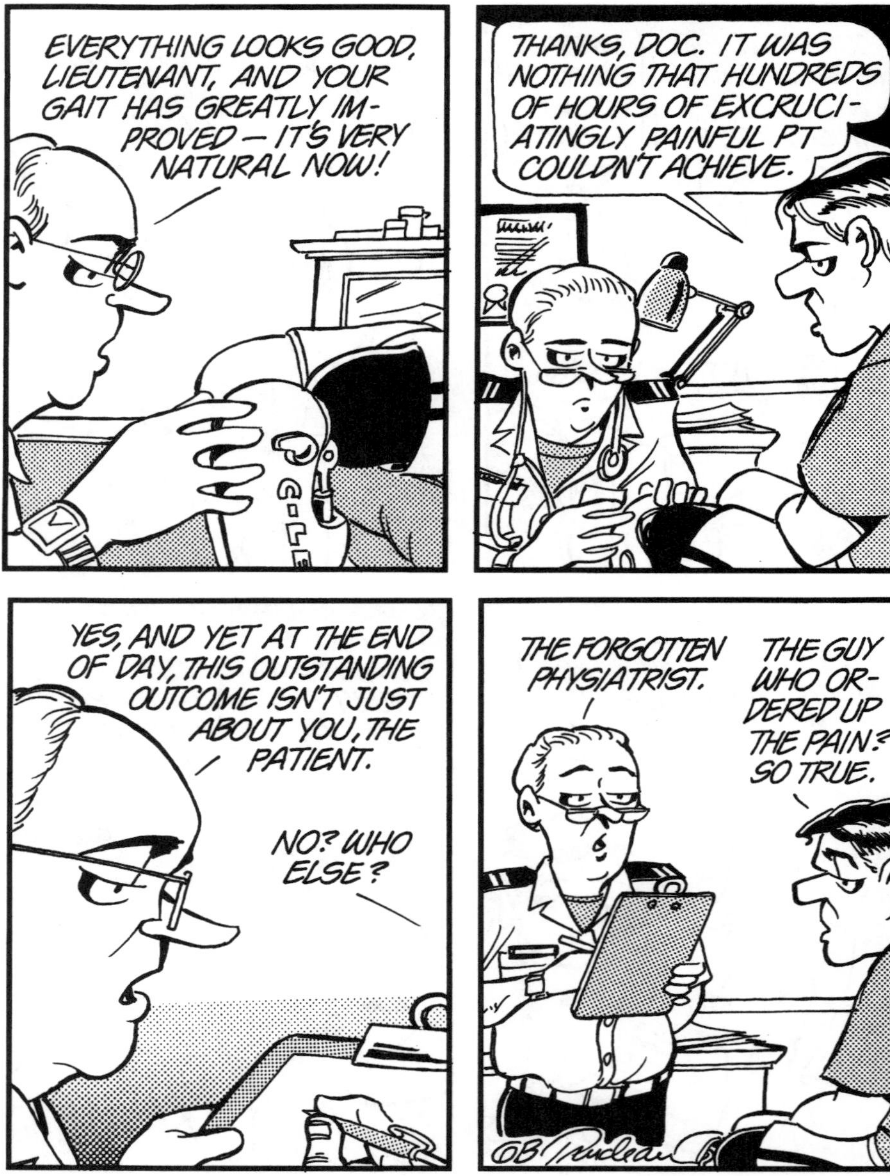
EVERYTHING LOOKS GOOD, LIEUTENANT, AND YOUR GAIT HAS GREATLY IM-PROVED — IT'S VERY NATURAL NOW!
THANKS, DOC. IT WAS NOTHING THAT HUNDREDS OF HOURS OF EXCRUCI-ATINGLY PAINFUL PT COULDN'T ACHIEVE.
YES, AND YET AT THE END OF DAY, THIS OUTSTANDING OUTCOME ISN'T JUST ABOUT YOU, THE PATIENT.
NO? WHO ELSE?
THE FORGOTTEN PHYSIATRIST.
THE GUY WHO OR-DERED UP THE PAIN? SO TRUE.
GB Trudeau

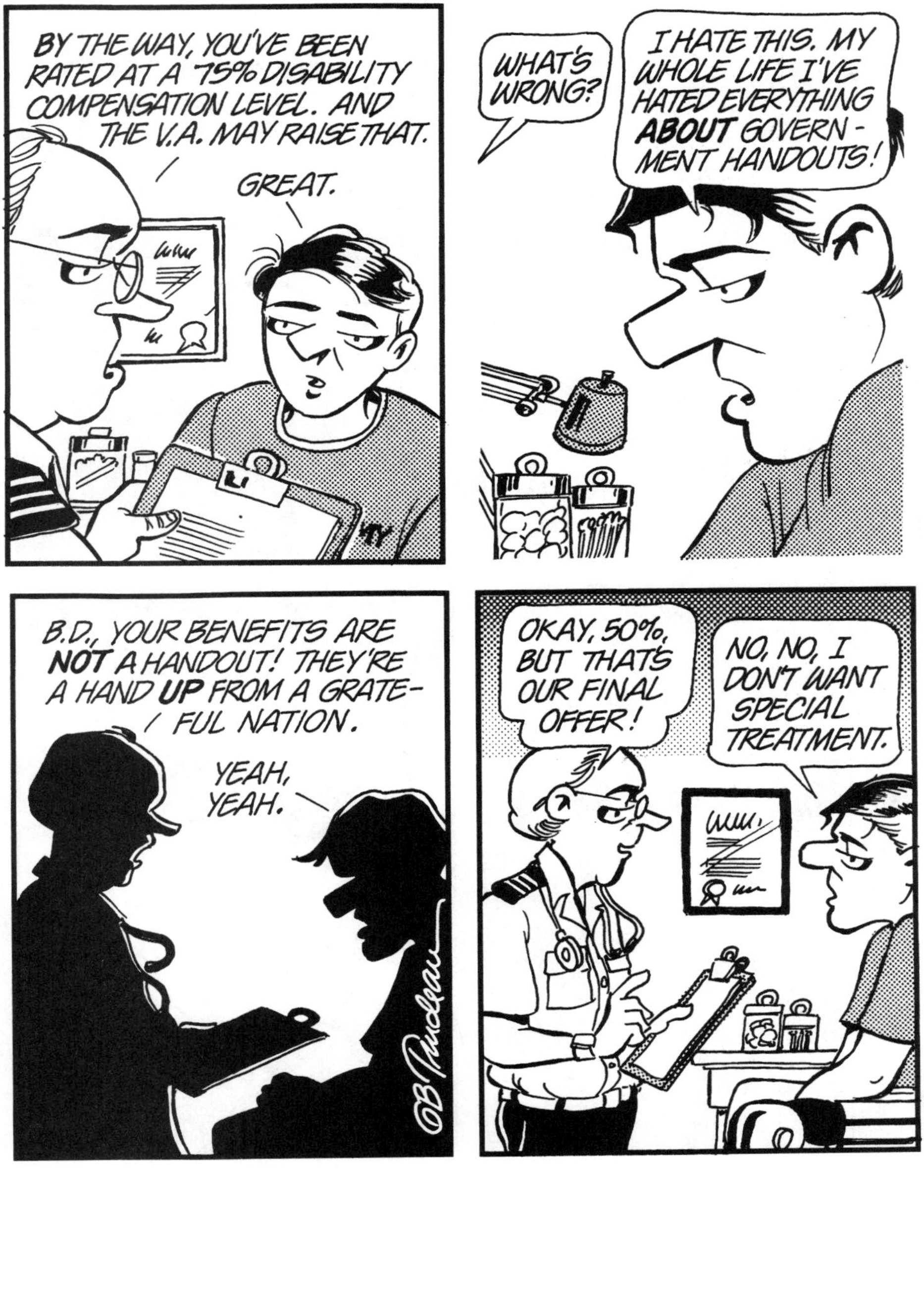
BY THE WAY, YOU'VE BEEN RATED AT A 75% DISABILITY COMPENSATION LEVEL. AND THE V.A. MAY RAISE THAT.
GREAT.
WHAT'S WRONG?
I HATE THIS. MY WHOLE LIFE I'VE HATED EVERYTHING **ABOUT** GOVERNMENT HANDOUTS!
B.D., YOUR BENEFITS ARE **NOT** A HANDOUT! THEY'RE A HAND **UP** FROM A GRATEFUL NATION.
YEAH, YEAH.
OKAY, 50%, BUT THAT'S OUR FINAL OFFER!
NO, NO, I DON'T WANT SPECIAL TREATMENT.

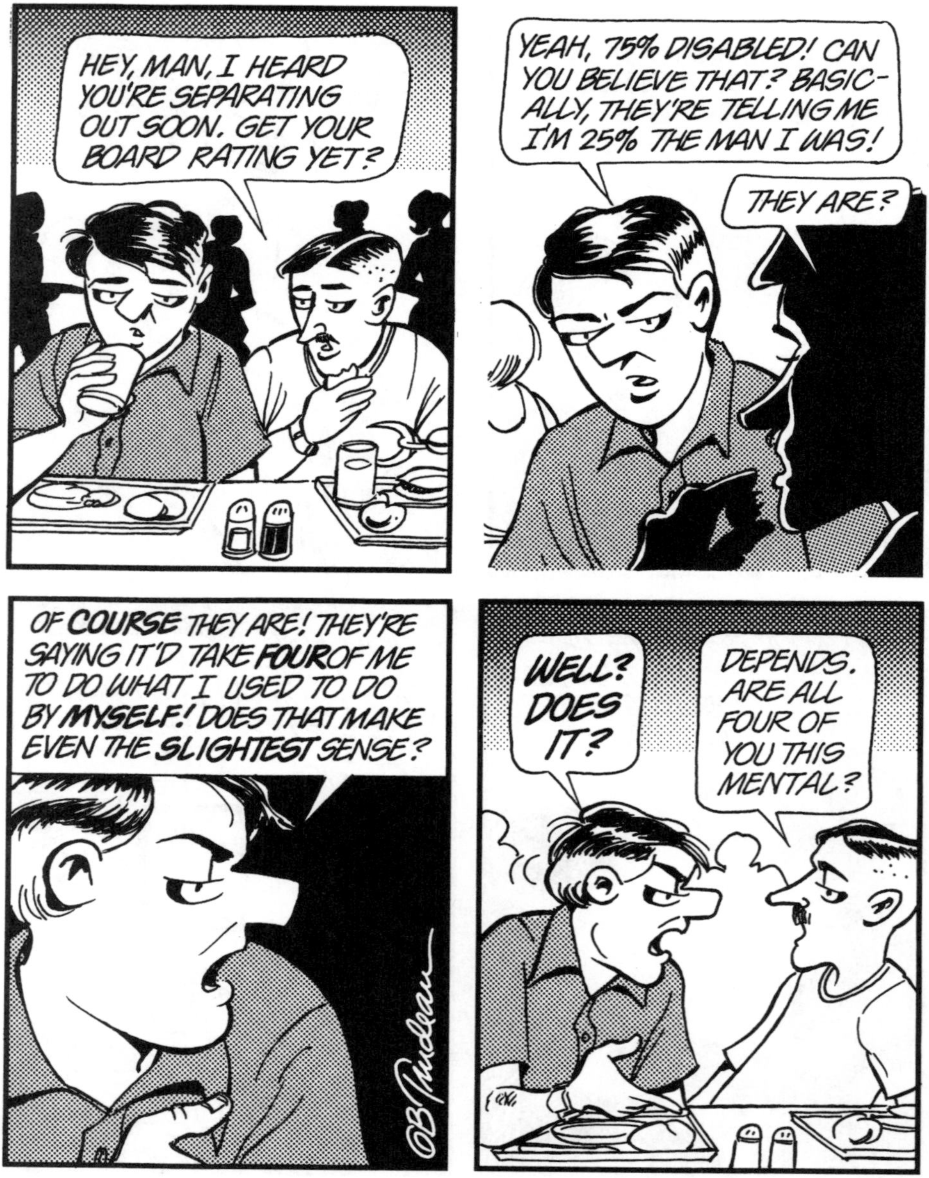
HEY, MAN, I HEARD YOU'RE SEPARATING OUT SOON. GET YOUR BOARD RATING YET?
YEAH, 75% DISABLED! CAN YOU BELIEVE THAT? BASICALLY, THEY'RE TELLING ME I'M 25% THE MAN I WAS!
THEY ARE?
OF **COURSE** THEY ARE! THEY'RE SAYING IT'D TAKE **FOUR** OF ME TO DO WHAT I USED TO DO BY **MYSELF!** DOES THAT MAKE EVEN THE **SLIGHTEST** SENSE?
WELL? DOES IT?
DEPENDS. ARE ALL FOUR OF YOU THIS MENTAL?

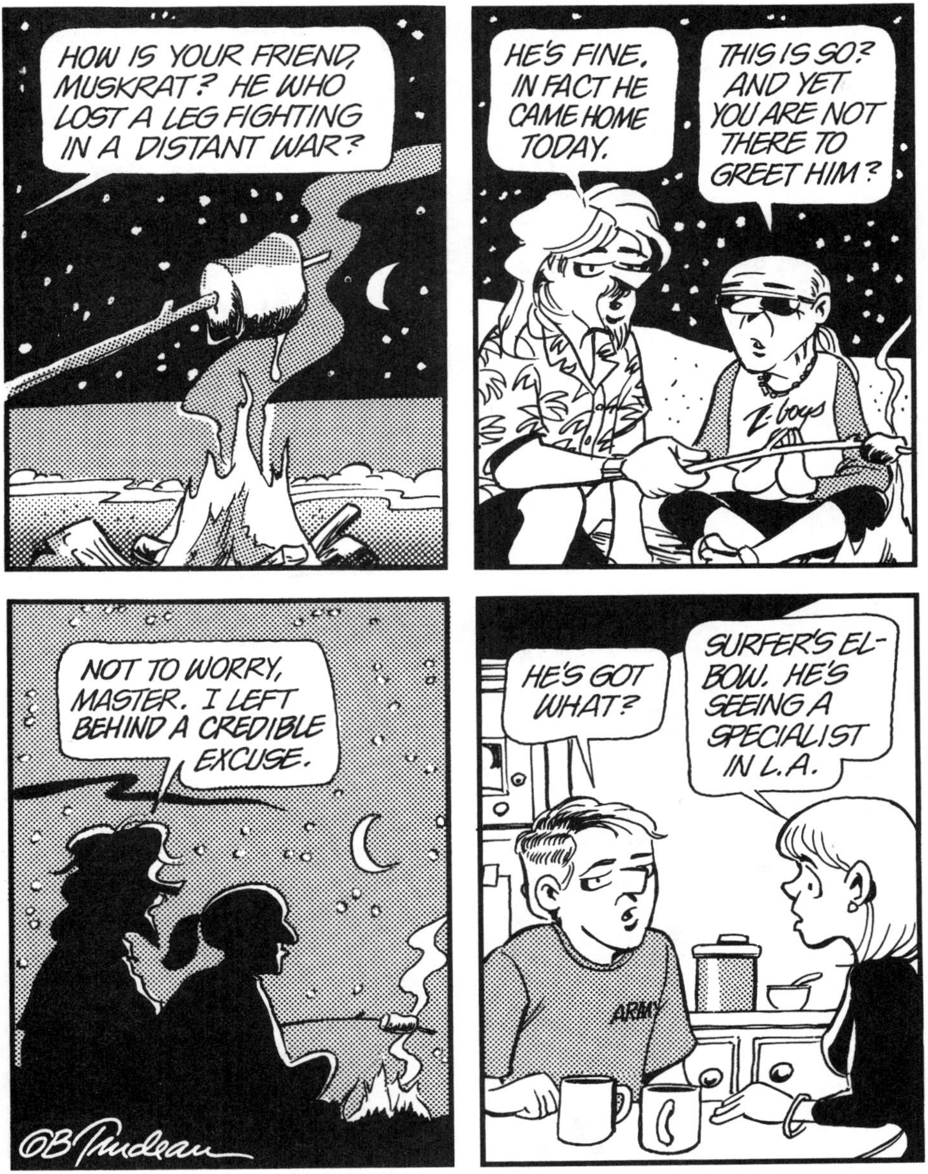
HOW IS YOUR FRIEND, MUSKRAT? HE WHO LOST A LEG FIGHTING IN A DISTANT WAR?
HE'S FINE. IN FACT HE CAME HOME TODAY.
THIS IS SO? AND YET YOU ARE NOT THERE TO GREET HIM?
Z-boys
NOT TO WORRY, MASTER. I LEFT BEHIND A CREDIBLE EXCUSE.
©B Trudeau
HE'S GOT WHAT?
SURFER'S EL-BOW. HE'S SEEING A SPECIALIST IN L.A.
ARMY

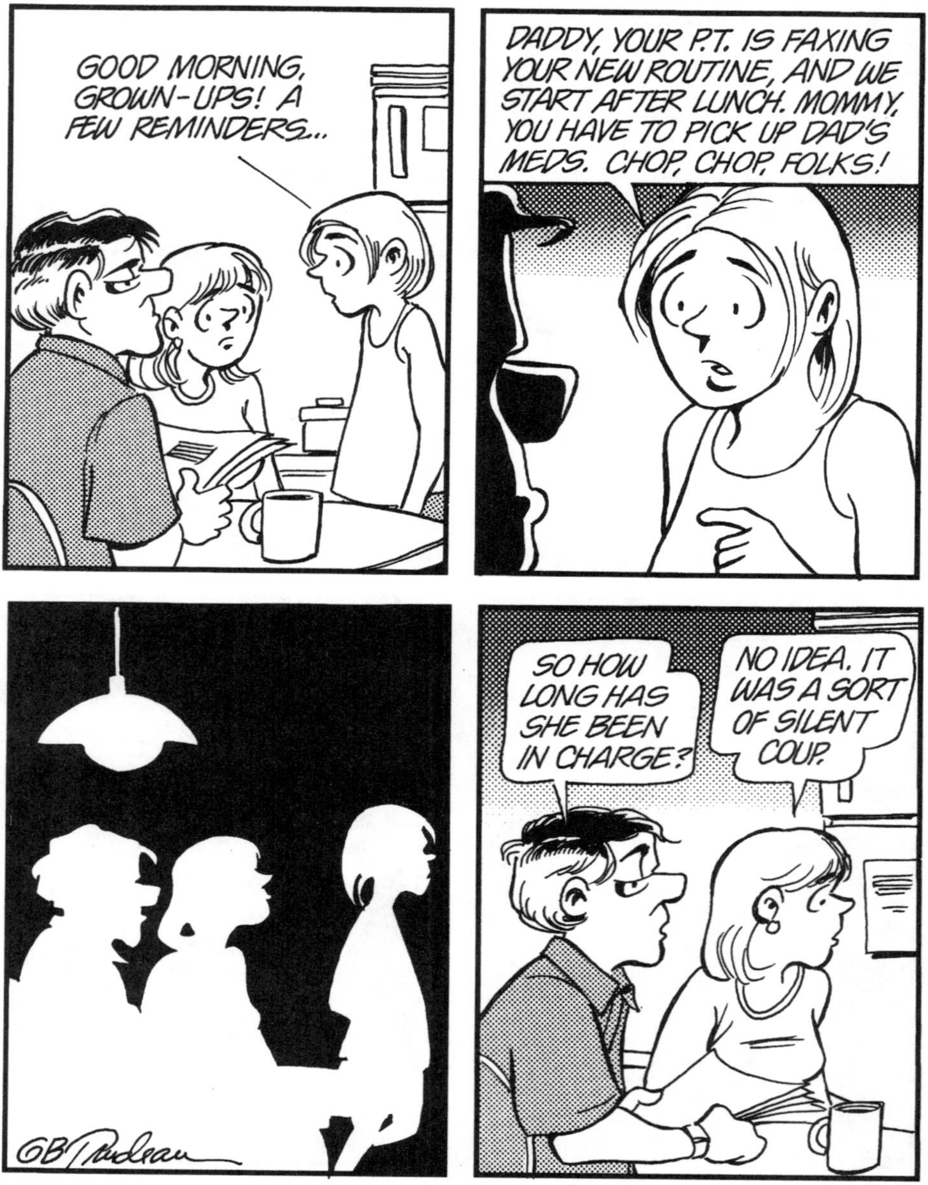
GOOD MORNING, GROWN-UPS! A FEW REMINDERS...
DADDY, YOUR P.T. IS FAXING YOUR NEW ROUTINE, AND WE START AFTER LUNCH. MOMMY, YOU HAVE TO PICK UP DAD'S MEDS. CHOP, CHOP, FOLKS!
GB Trudeau
SO HOW LONG HAS SHE BEEN IN CHARGE?
NO IDEA. IT WAS A SORT OF SILENT COUP.

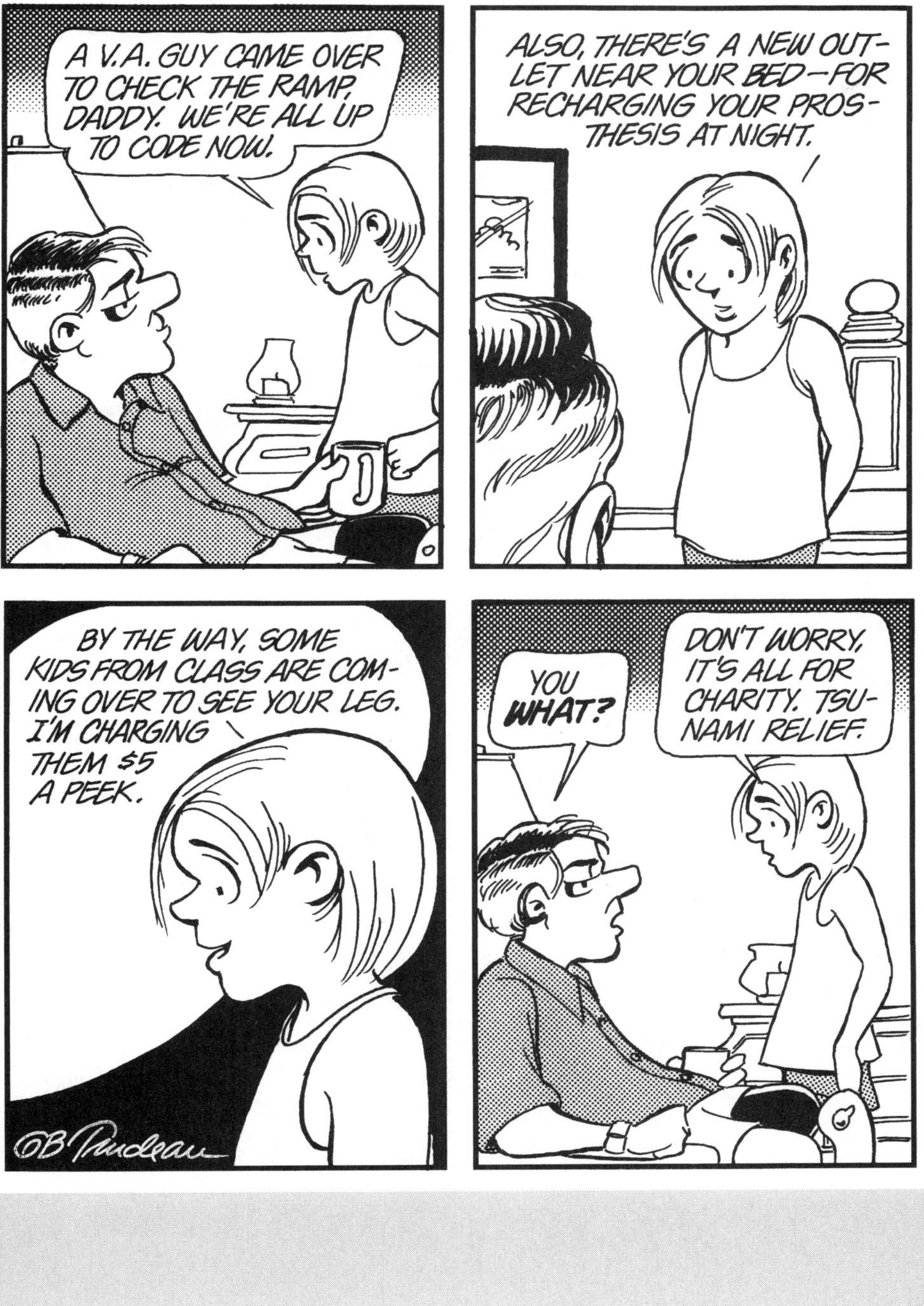
A V.A. GUY CAME OVER TO CHECK THE RAMP, DADDY. WE'RE ALL UP TO CODE NOW.
ALSO, THERE'S A NEW OUT-LET NEAR YOUR BED—FOR RECHARGING YOUR PROS-THESIS AT NIGHT.
BY THE WAY, SOME KIDS FROM CLASS ARE COM-ING OVER TO SEE YOUR LEG. I'M CHARGING THEM $5 A PEEK.
YOU WHAT?
DON'T WORRY, IT'S ALL FOR CHARITY. TSU-NAMI RELIEF.
©B Trudeau

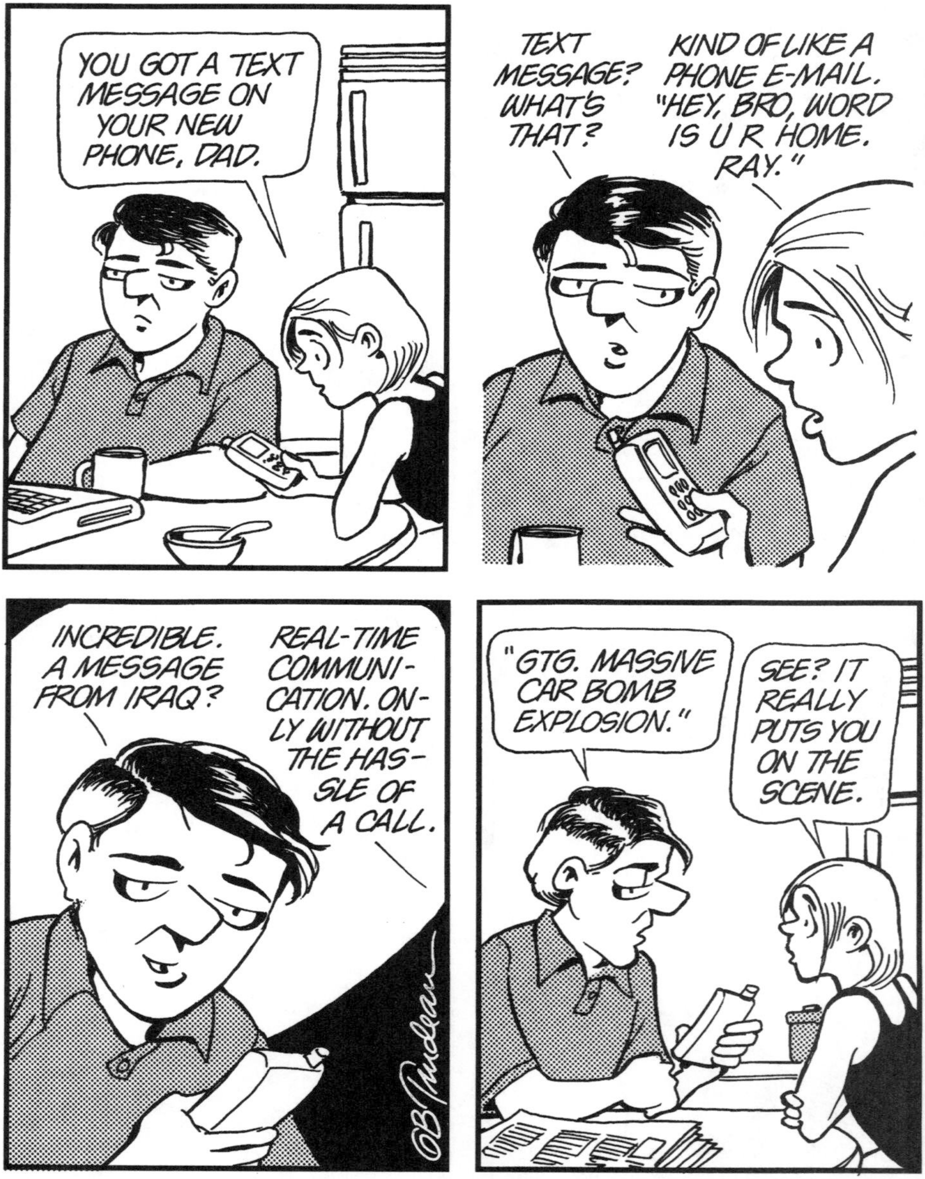
YOU GOT A TEXT MESSAGE ON YOUR NEW PHONE, DAD.
TEXT MESSAGE? WHAT'S THAT?
KIND OF LIKE A PHONE E-MAIL. "HEY, BRO, WORD IS U R HOME. RAY."
INCREDIBLE. A MESSAGE FROM IRAQ?
REAL-TIME COMMUNI-CATION. ON-LY WITHOUT THE HAS-SLE OF A CALL.
"GTG. MASSIVE CAR BOMB EXPLOSION."
SEE? IT REALLY PUTS YOU ON THE SCENE.
GBTrudeau

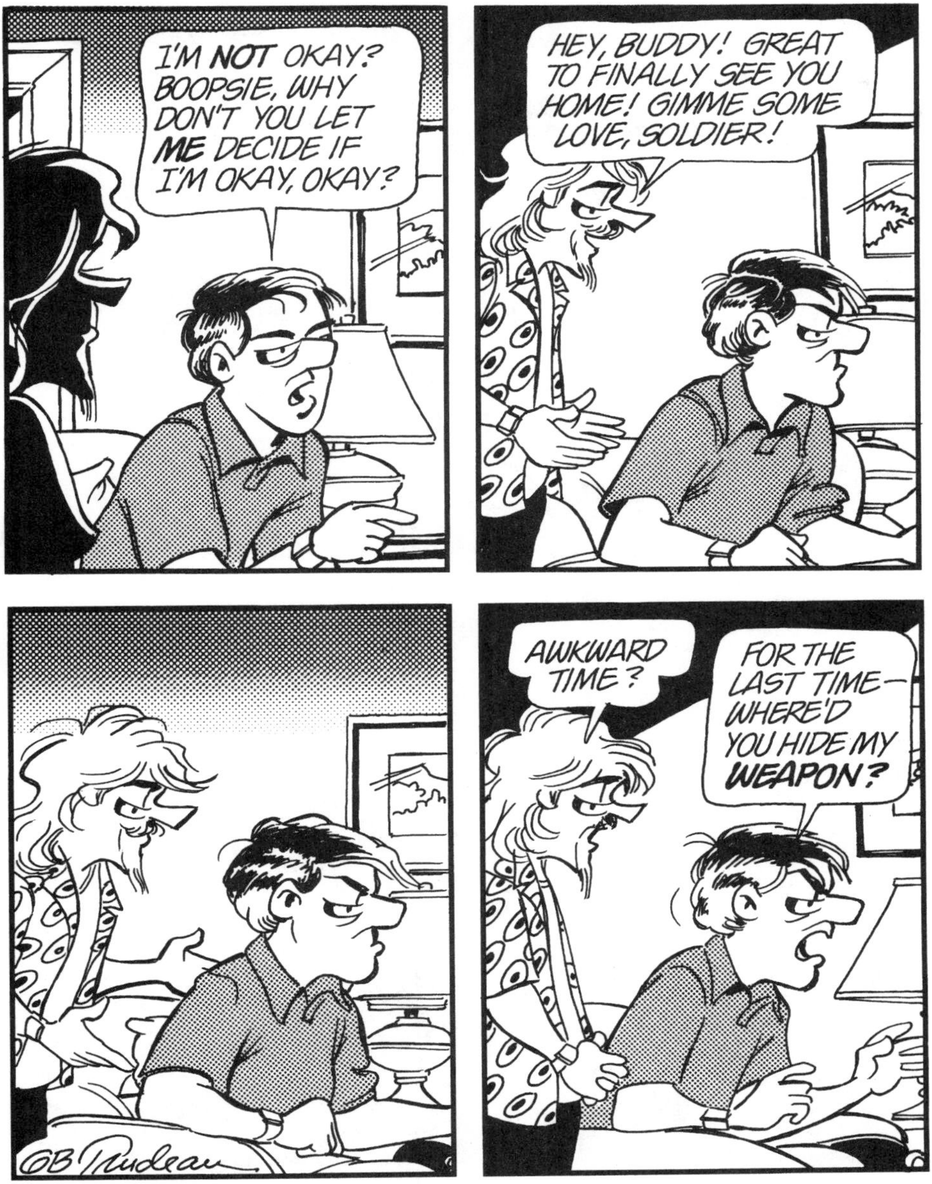
I'M NOT OKAY? BOOPSIE, WHY DON'T YOU LET ME DECIDE IF I'M OKAY, OKAY?
HEY, BUDDY! GREAT TO FINALLY SEE YOU HOME! GIMME SOME LOVE, SOLDIER!
AWKWARD TIME?
FOR THE LAST TIME— WHERE'D YOU HIDE MY WEAPON?
©B Trudeau

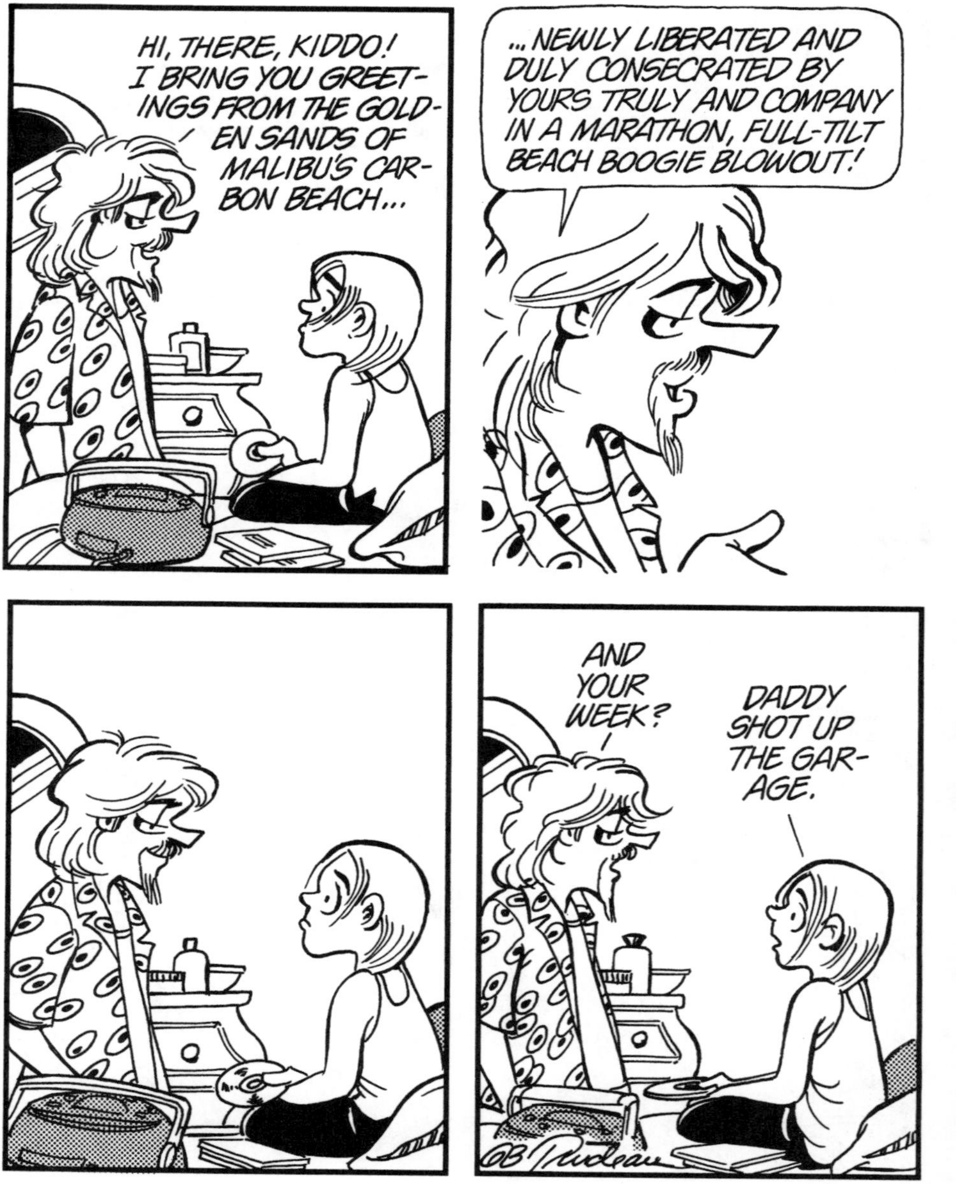
HI, THERE, KIDDO! I BRING YOU GREETINGS FROM THE GOLDEN SANDS OF MALIBU'S CARBON BEACH...
...NEWLY LIBERATED AND DULY CONSECRATED BY YOURS TRULY AND COMPANY IN A MARATHON, FULL-TILT BEACH BOOGIE BLOWOUT!
AND YOUR WEEK?
DADDY SHOT UP THE GARAGE.
GB Trudeau

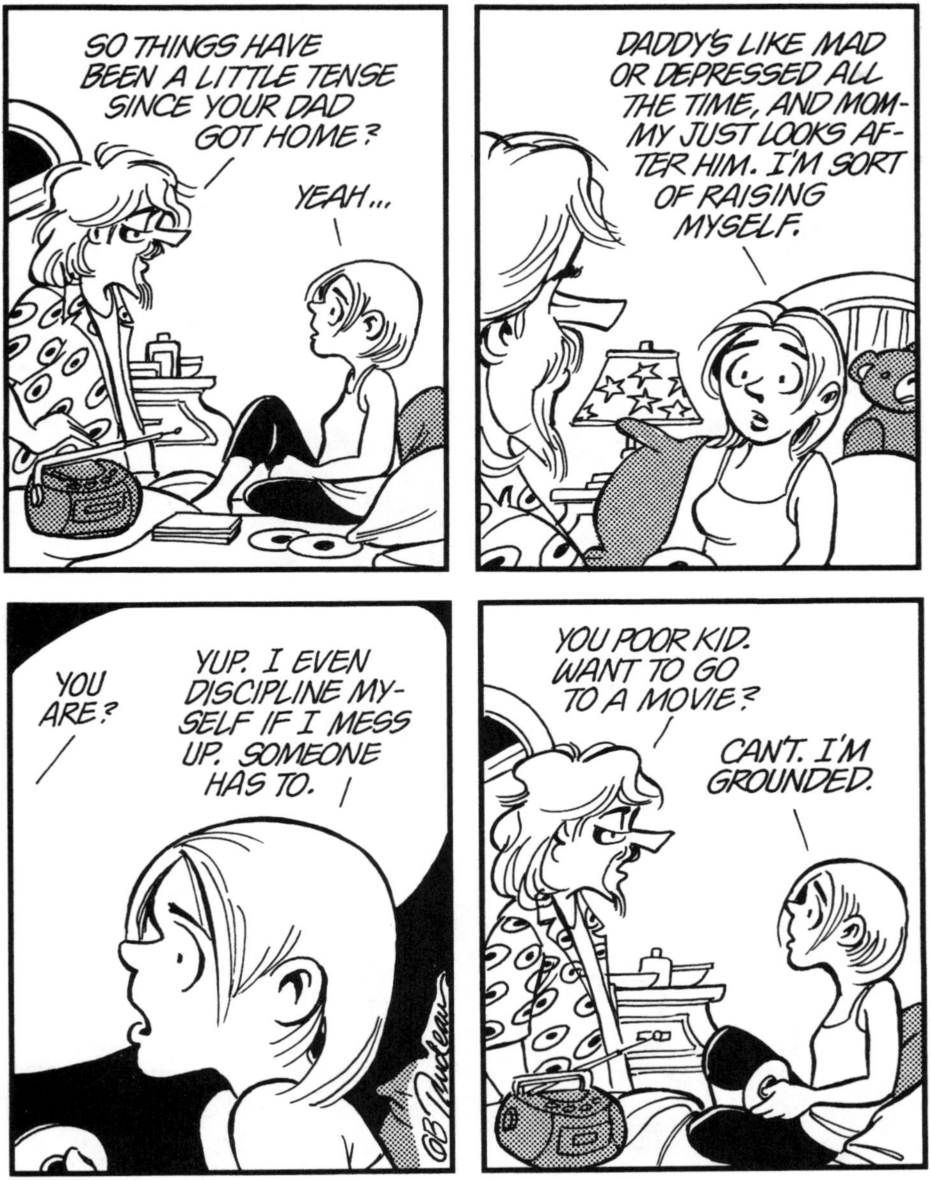
SO THINGS HAVE BEEN A LITTLE TENSE SINCE YOUR DAD GOT HOME?
YEAH...
DADDY'S LIKE MAD OR DEPRESSED ALL THE TIME, AND MOMMY JUST LOOKS AFTER HIM. I'M SORT OF RAISING MYSELF.
YOU ARE?
YUP. I EVEN DISCIPLINE MYSELF IF I MESS UP. SOMEONE HAS TO.
YOU POOR KID. WANT TO GO TO A MOVIE?
CAN'T. I'M GROUNDED.

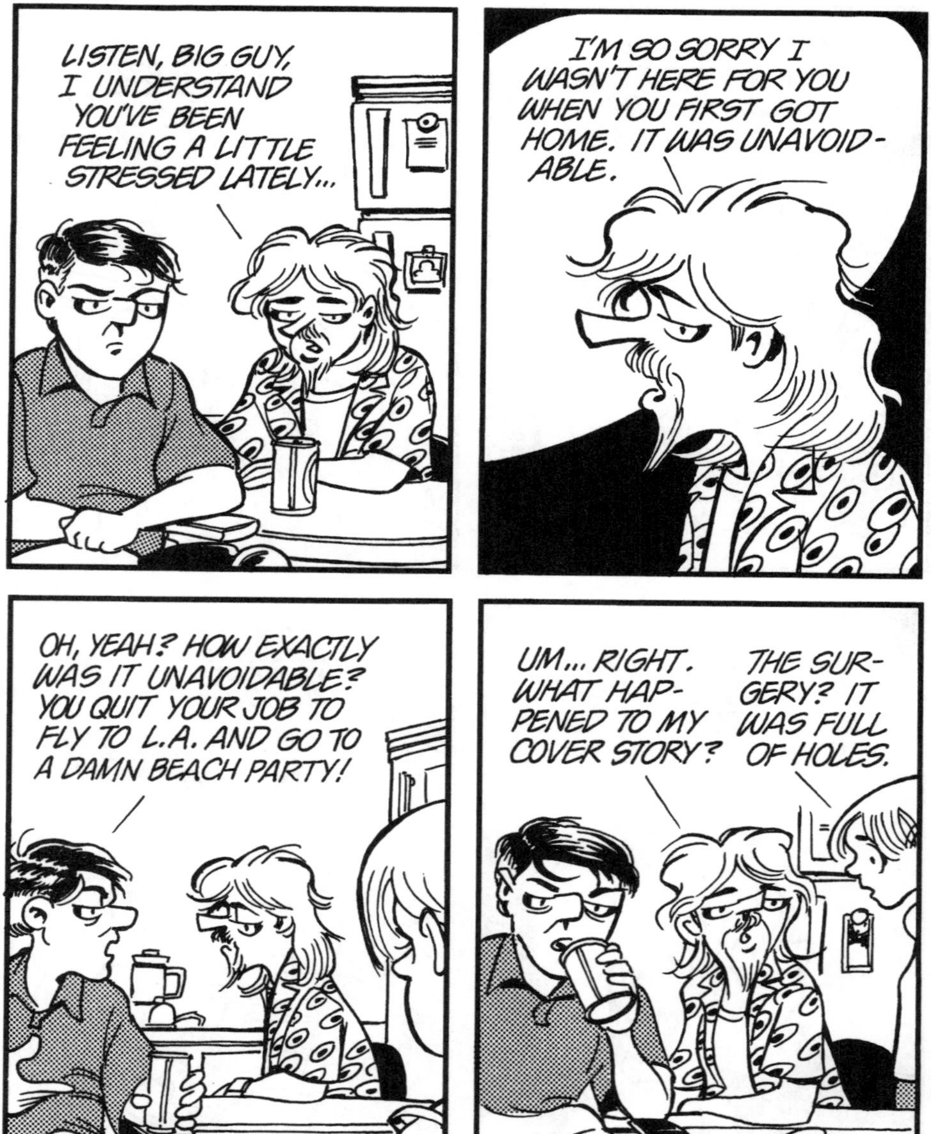
LISTEN, BIG GUY, I UNDERSTAND YOU'VE BEEN FEELING A LITTLE STRESSED LATELY...
I'M SO SORRY I WASN'T HERE FOR YOU WHEN YOU FIRST GOT HOME. IT WAS UNAVOID-ABLE.
OH, YEAH? HOW EXACTLY WAS IT UNAVOIDABLE? YOU QUIT YOUR JOB TO FLY TO L.A. AND GO TO A DAMN BEACH PARTY!
UM... RIGHT. WHAT HAP-PENED TO MY COVER STORY?
THE SUR-GERY? IT WAS FULL OF HOLES.
GB Trudeau

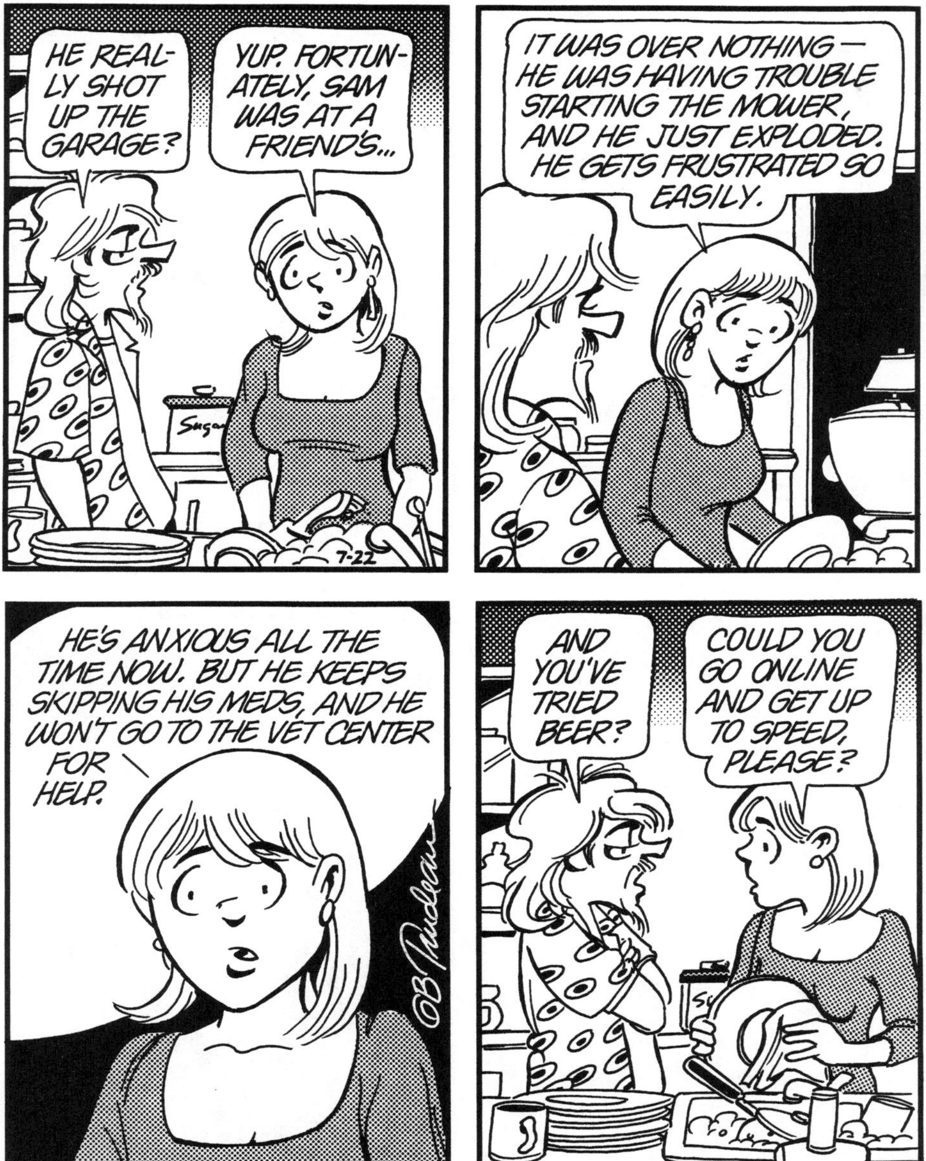
HE REALLY SHOT UP THE GARAGE?
YUP. FORTUNATELY, SAM WAS AT A FRIEND'S...
7-22
IT WAS OVER NOTHING— HE WAS HAVING TROUBLE STARTING THE MOWER, AND HE JUST EXPLODED. HE GETS FRUSTRATED SO EASILY.
HE'S ANXIOUS ALL THE TIME NOW. BUT HE KEEPS SKIPPING HIS MEDS, AND HE WON'T GO TO THE VET CENTER FOR HELP.
AND YOU'VE TRIED BEER?
COULD YOU GO ONLINE AND GET UP TO SPEED, PLEASE?

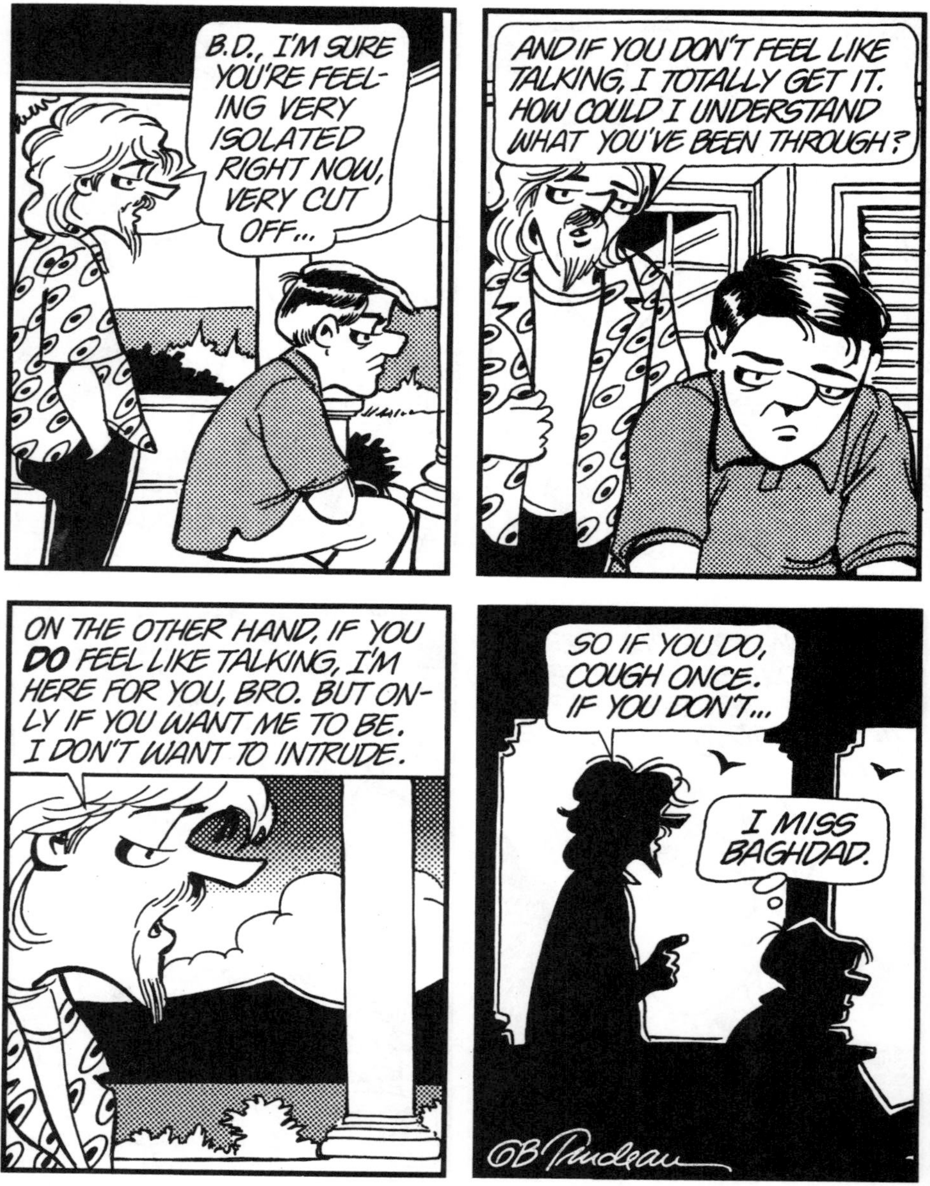
B.D., I'M SURE YOU'RE FEEL-ING VERY ISOLATED RIGHT NOW, VERY CUT OFF...
AND IF YOU DON'T FEEL LIKE TALKING, I TOTALLY GET IT. HOW COULD I UNDERSTAND WHAT YOU'VE BEEN THROUGH?
ON THE OTHER HAND, IF YOU DO FEEL LIKE TALKING, I'M HERE FOR YOU, BRO. BUT ON-LY IF YOU WANT ME TO BE. I DON'T WANT TO INTRUDE.
SO IF YOU DO, COUGH ONCE. IF YOU DON'T...
I MISS BAGHDAD.
©B Trudeau

WELL, LET ME START WITH THE SUBJECT THAT'S DEAREST TO THE HEARTS OF **ALL** WALDEN ALUMNI—THE FOOTBALL TEAM!

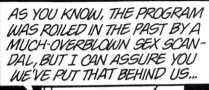

AS YOU KNOW, THE PROGRAM WAS ROILED IN THE PAST BY A MUCH-OVERBLOWN SEX SCANDAL, BUT I CAN ASSURE YOU WE'VE PUT THAT BEHIND US...

...WITH THE RE-HIRING OF RETURNING IRAQI WAR VETERAN B.D.! WE LOOK FORWARD TO A **GREAT** YEAR UNDER COACH B.D.'S SEASONED LEADERSHIP!

D.C. WALDEN CLUB

GB Trudeau

KING, I HEARD HE SHOT UP HIS GARAGE.

SO HE'S AGGRESSIVE. DO WE WANT SOME TOUCHY-FEELY TYPE?

D.C. WALDEN CLUB

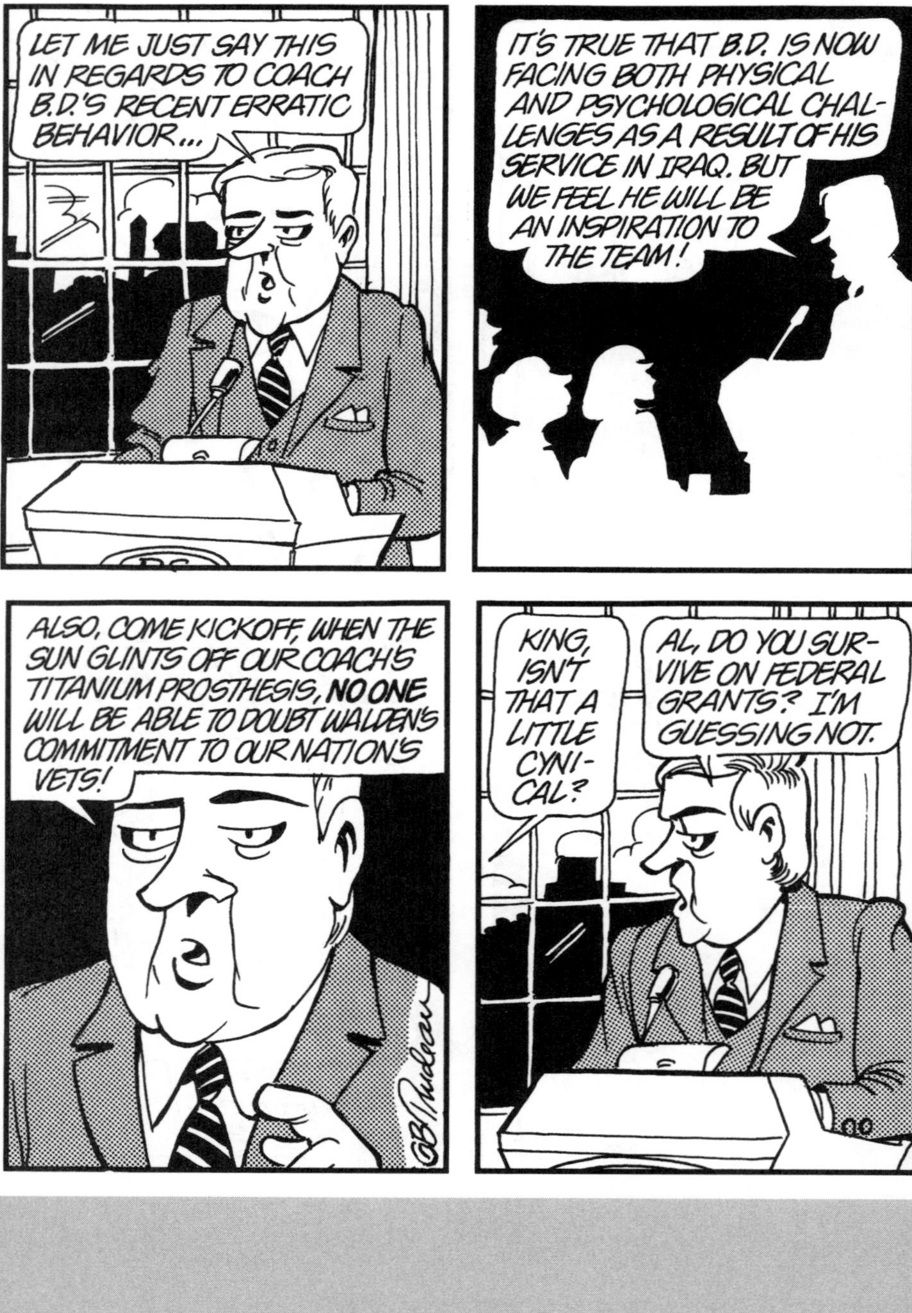
LET ME JUST SAY THIS IN REGARDS TO COACH B.D.'S RECENT ERRATIC BEHAVIOR...
IT'S TRUE THAT B.D. IS NOW FACING BOTH PHYSICAL AND PSYCHOLOGICAL CHALLENGES AS A RESULT OF HIS SERVICE IN IRAQ. BUT WE FEEL HE WILL BE AN INSPIRATION TO THE TEAM!
ALSO, COME KICKOFF, WHEN THE SUN GLINTS OFF OUR COACH'S TITANIUM PROSTHESIS, **NO ONE** WILL BE ABLE TO DOUBT WALDEN'S COMMITMENT TO OUR NATION'S VETS!
KING, ISN'T THAT A LITTLE CYNICAL?
AL, DO YOU SURVIVE ON FEDERAL GRANTS? I'M GUESSING NOT.
GB Trudeau

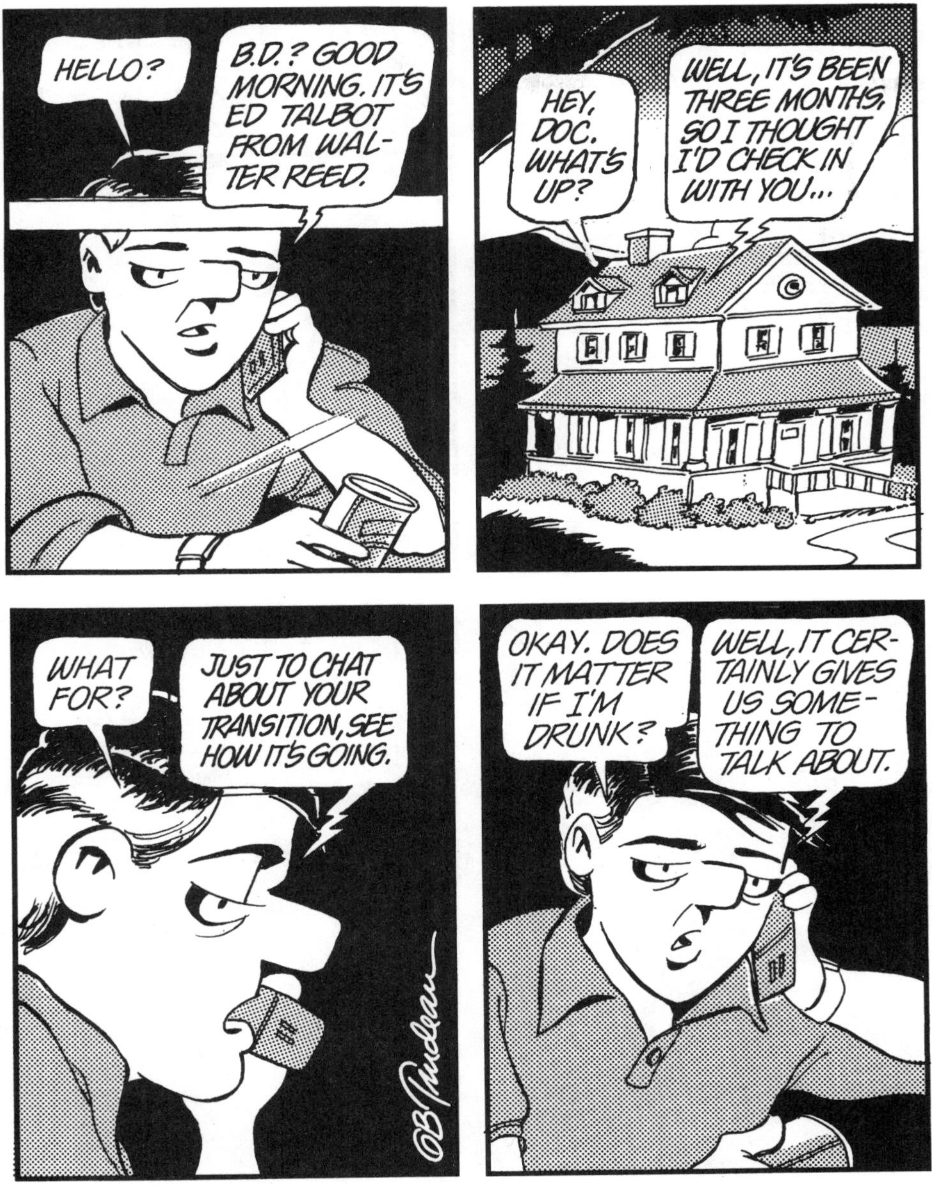
HELLO?
B.D.? GOOD MORNING. IT'S ED TALBOT FROM WALTER REED.
HEY, DOC. WHAT'S UP?
WELL, IT'S BEEN THREE MONTHS, SO I THOUGHT I'D CHECK IN WITH YOU...
WHAT FOR?
JUST TO CHAT ABOUT YOUR TRANSITION, SEE HOW IT'S GOING.
OKAY. DOES IT MATTER IF I'M DRUNK?
WELL, IT CERTAINLY GIVES US SOMETHING TO TALK ABOUT.

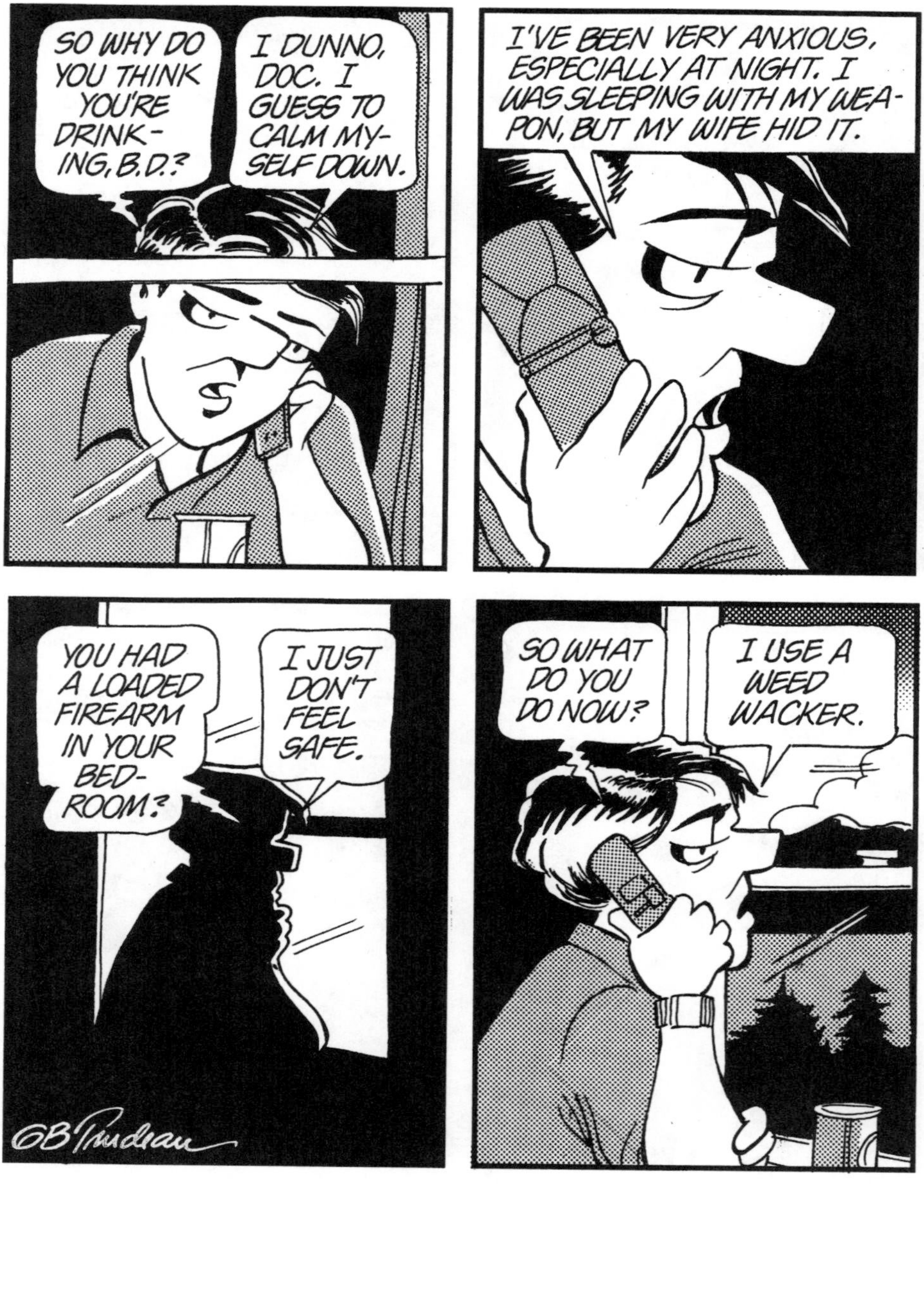
SO WHY DO YOU THINK YOU'RE DRINKING, B.D.?
I DUNNO, DOC. I GUESS TO CALM MYSELF DOWN.
I'VE BEEN VERY ANXIOUS, ESPECIALLY AT NIGHT. I WAS SLEEPING WITH MY WEAPON, BUT MY WIFE HID IT.
YOU HAD A LOADED FIREARM IN YOUR BEDROOM?
I JUST DON'T FEEL SAFE.
SO WHAT DO YOU DO NOW?
I USE A WEED WACKER.
GB Trudeau

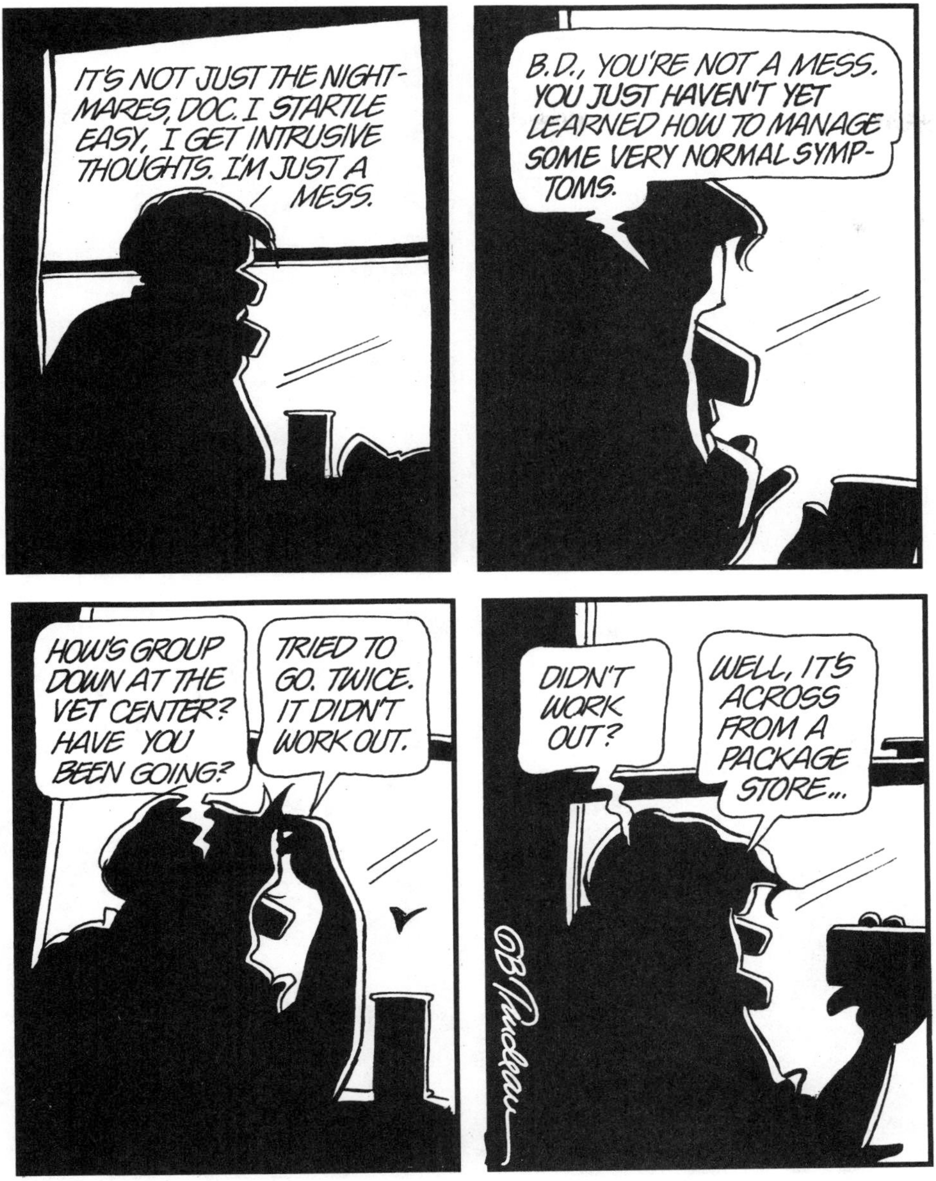
IT'S NOT JUST THE NIGHTMARES, DOC. I STARTLE EASY, I GET INTRUSIVE THOUGHTS. I'M JUST A MESS.
B.D., YOU'RE NOT A MESS. YOU JUST HAVEN'T YET LEARNED HOW TO MANAGE SOME VERY NORMAL SYMPTOMS.
HOW'S GROUP DOWN AT THE VET CENTER? HAVE YOU BEEN GOING?
TRIED TO GO. TWICE. IT DIDN'T WORK OUT.
DIDN'T WORK OUT?
WELL, IT'S ACROSS FROM A PACKAGE STORE...
GBTrudeau

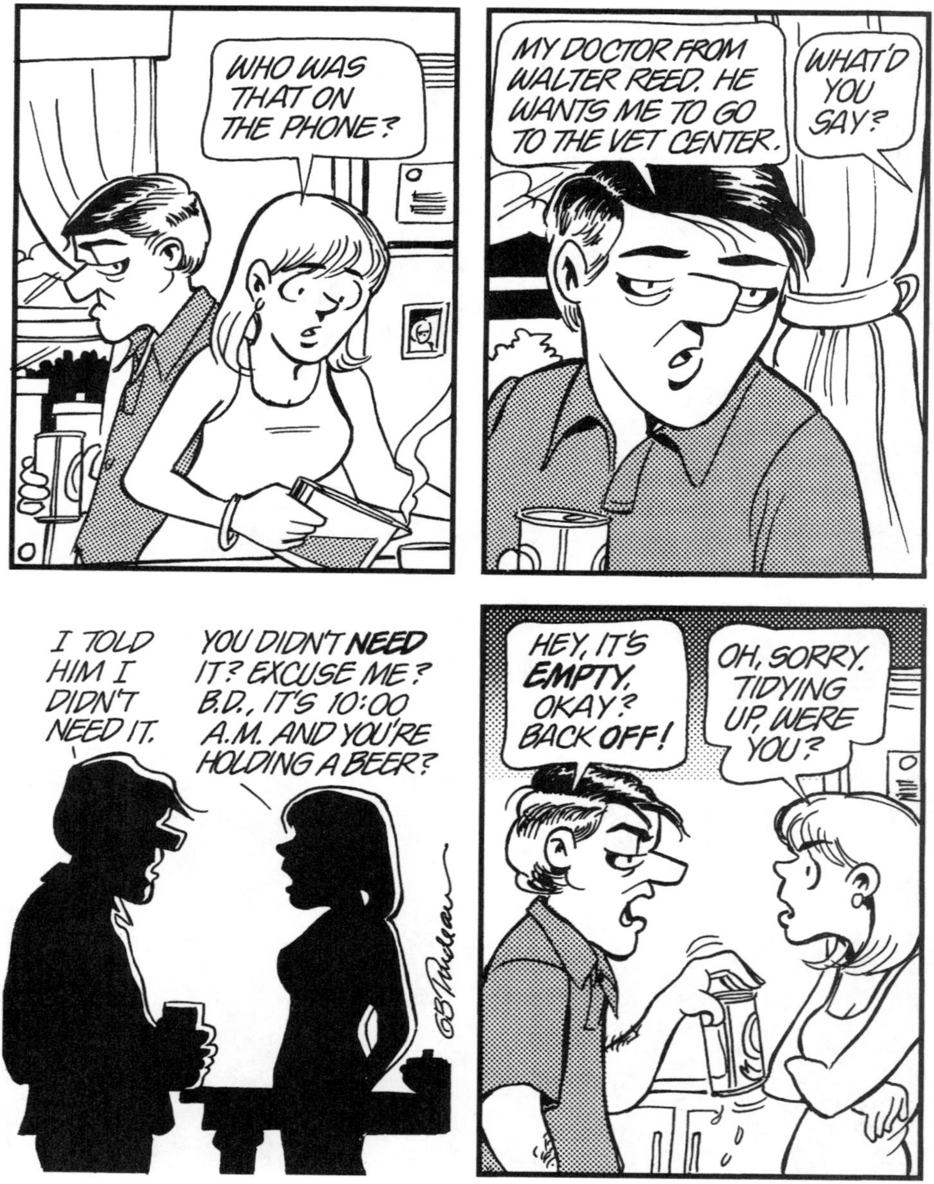
WHO WAS THAT ON THE PHONE?
MY DOCTOR FROM WALTER REED. HE WANTS ME TO GO TO THE VET CENTER.
WHAT'D YOU SAY?
I TOLD HIM I DIDN'T NEED IT.
YOU DIDN'T **NEED** IT? EXCUSE ME? B.D., IT'S 10:00 A.M. AND YOU'RE HOLDING A BEER?
HEY, IT'S **EMPTY**, OKAY? BACK **OFF**!
OH, SORRY. TIDYING UP, WERE YOU?

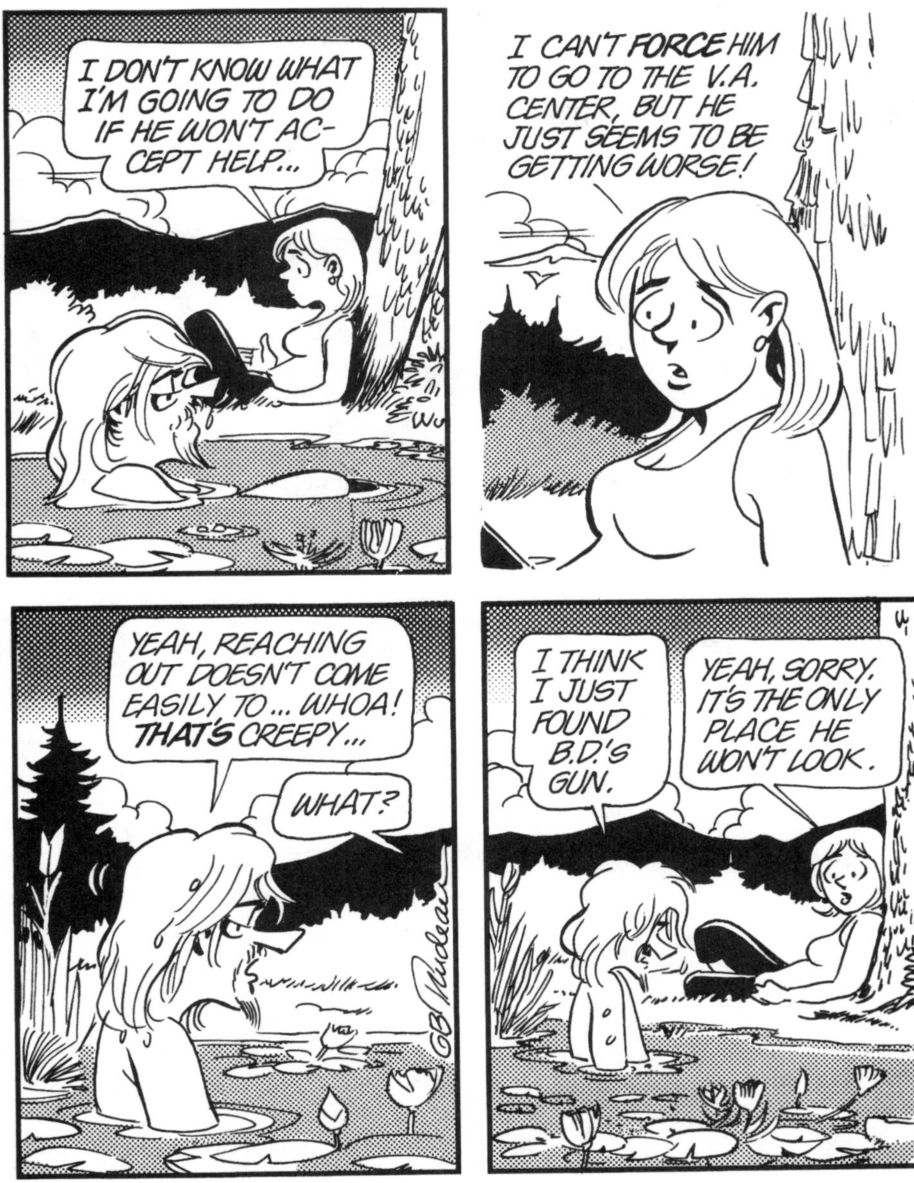
I DON'T KNOW WHAT I'M GOING TO DO IF HE WON'T ACCEPT HELP...
I CAN'T FORCE HIM TO GO TO THE V.A. CENTER, BUT HE JUST SEEMS TO BE GETTING WORSE!
YEAH, REACHING OUT DOESN'T COME EASILY TO ... WHOA! THAT'S CREEPY...
WHAT?
I THINK I JUST FOUND B.D.'s GUN.
YEAH, SORRY. IT'S THE ONLY PLACE HE WON'T LOOK.

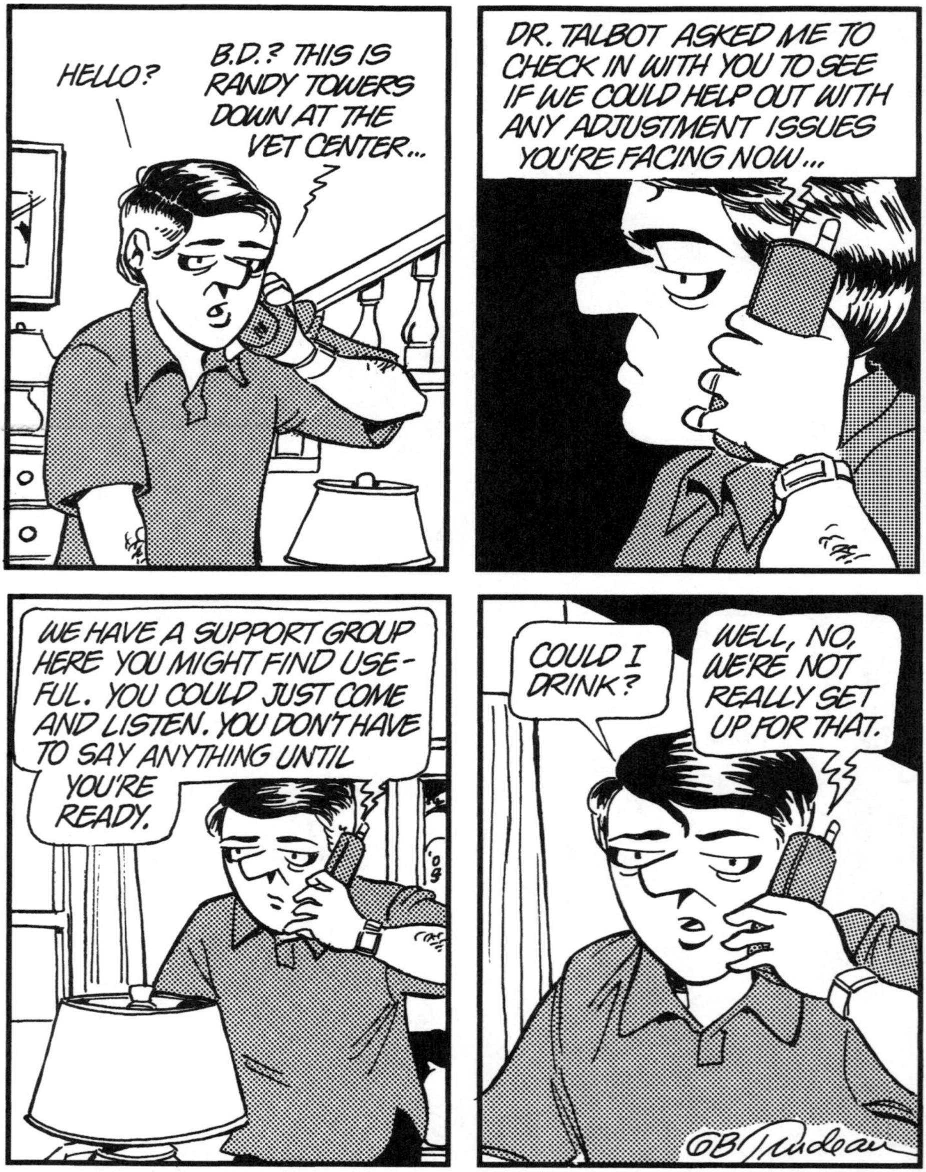
HELLO?
B.D.? THIS IS RANDY TOWERS DOWN AT THE VET CENTER...
DR. TALBOT ASKED ME TO CHECK IN WITH YOU TO SEE IF WE COULD HELP OUT WITH ANY ADJUSTMENT ISSUES YOU'RE FACING NOW...
WE HAVE A SUPPORT GROUP HERE YOU MIGHT FIND USE-FUL. YOU COULD JUST COME AND LISTEN. YOU DON'T HAVE TO SAY ANYTHING UNTIL YOU'RE READY.
COULD I DRINK?
WELL, NO, WE'RE NOT REALLY SET UP FOR THAT.
GBTrudeau

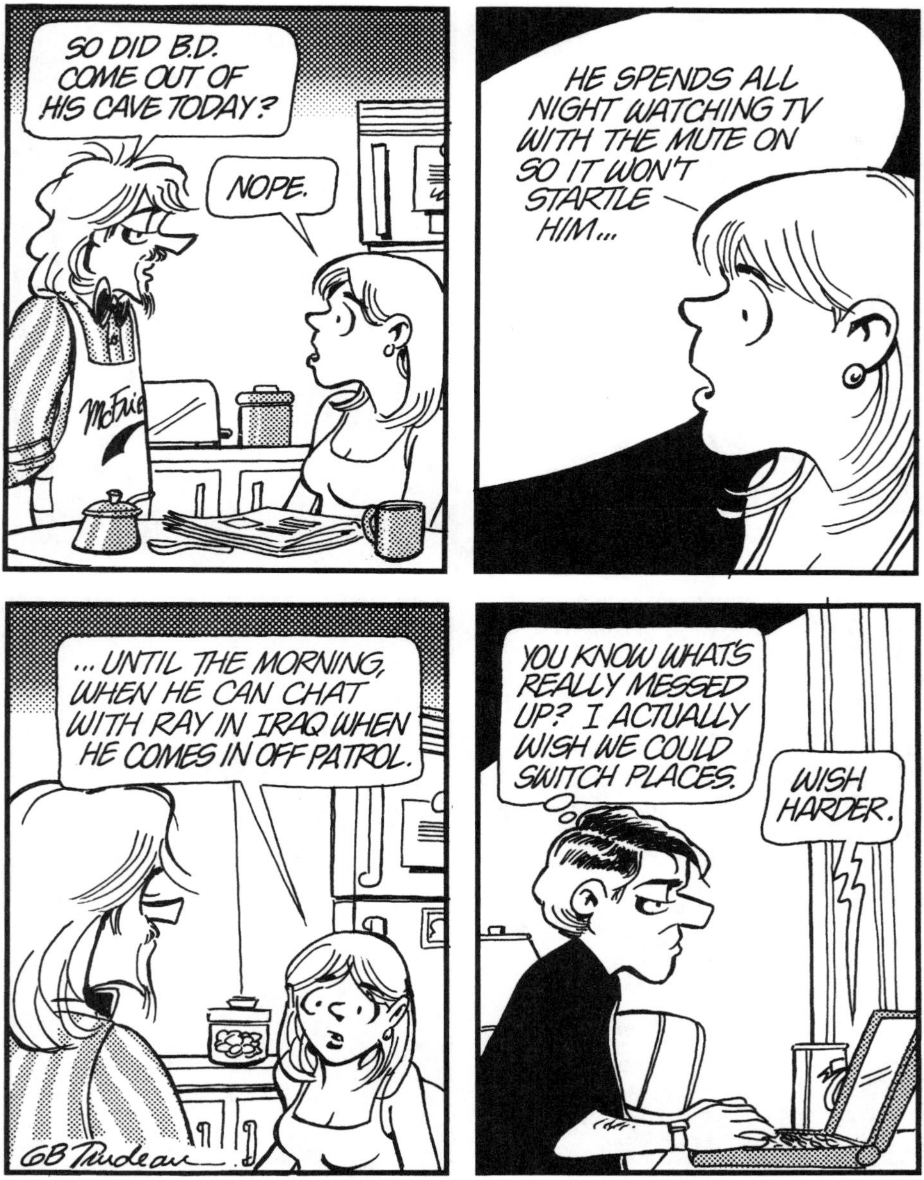
SO DID B.D. COME OUT OF HIS CAVE TODAY?
NOPE.
HE SPENDS ALL NIGHT WATCHING TV WITH THE MUTE ON SO IT WON'T STARTLE HIM...
...UNTIL THE MORNING, WHEN HE CAN CHAT WITH RAY IN IRAQ WHEN HE COMES IN OFF PATROL.
GB Trudeau
YOU KNOW WHAT'S REALLY MESSED UP? I ACTUALLY WISH WE COULD SWITCH PLACES.
WISH HARDER.

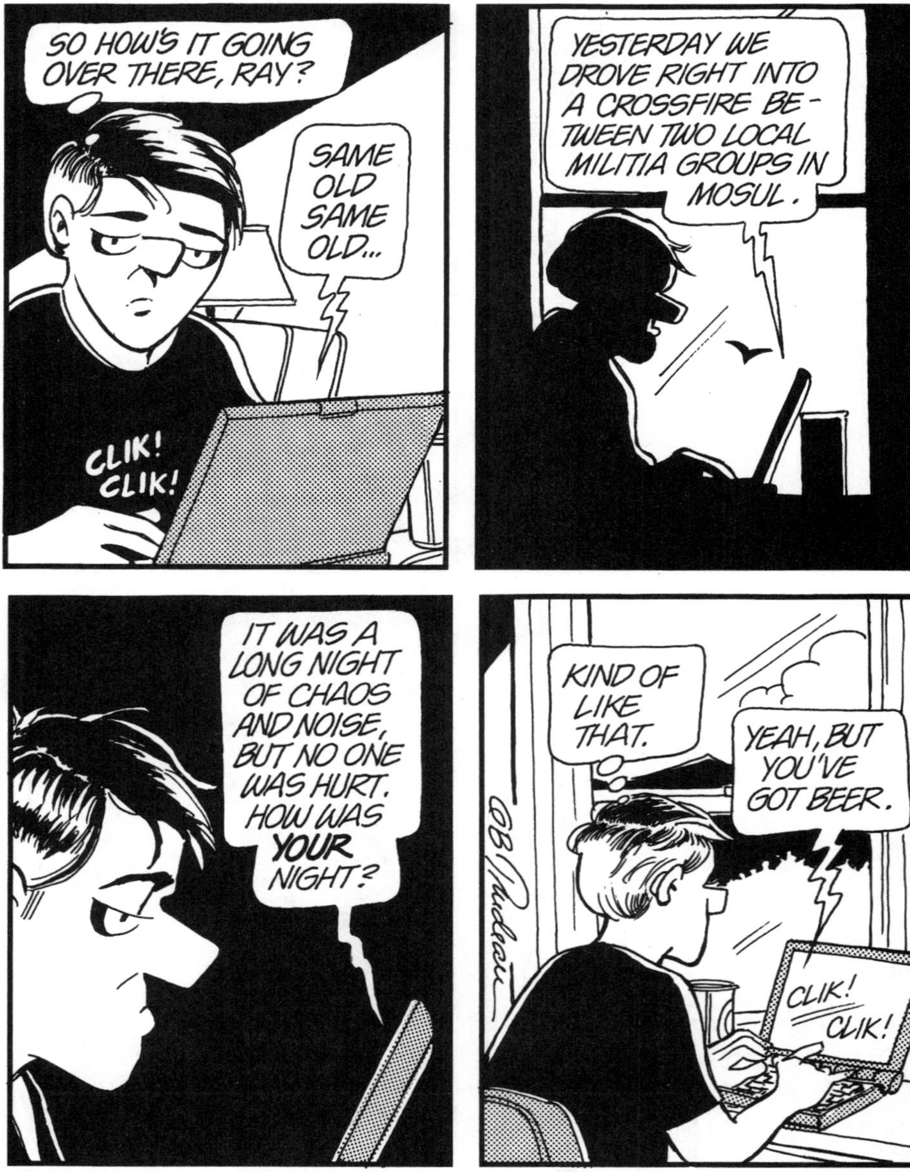
SO HOW'S IT GOING OVER THERE, RAY?
SAME OLD SAME OLD...
CLIK! CLIK!
YESTERDAY WE DROVE RIGHT INTO A CROSSFIRE BE-TWEEN TWO LOCAL MILITIA GROUPS IN MOSUL.
IT WAS A LONG NIGHT OF CHAOS AND NOISE, BUT NO ONE WAS HURT. HOW WAS **YOUR** NIGHT?
KIND OF LIKE THAT.
YEAH, BUT YOU'VE GOT BEER.
CLIK! CLIK!

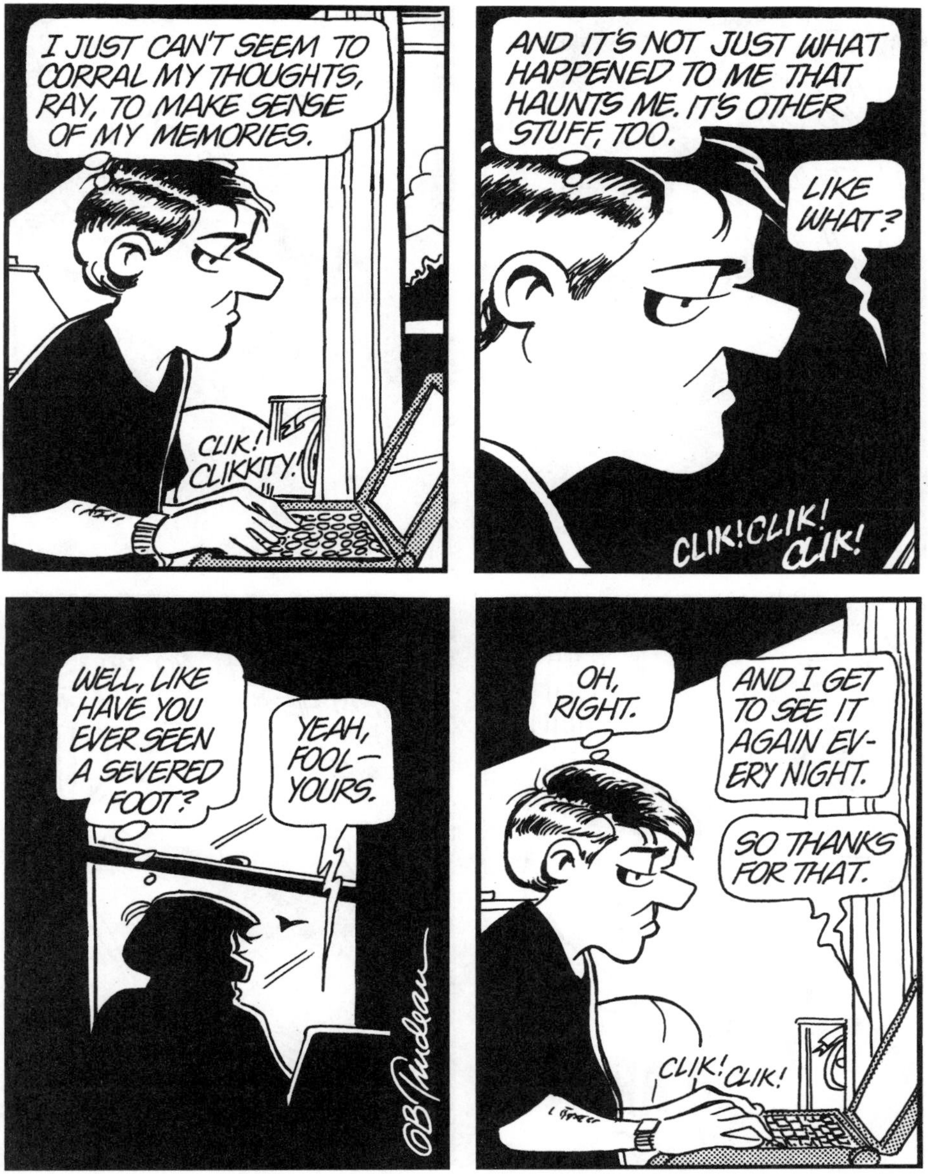
I JUST CAN'T SEEM TO CORRAL MY THOUGHTS, RAY, TO MAKE SENSE OF MY MEMORIES.
CLIK! CLIKKITY!
AND IT'S NOT JUST WHAT HAPPENED TO ME THAT HAUNTS ME. IT'S OTHER STUFF, TOO.
LIKE WHAT?
CLIK! CLIK! CLIK!
WELL, LIKE HAVE YOU EVER SEEN A SEVERED FOOT?
YEAH, FOOL— YOURS.
OH, RIGHT.
AND I GET TO SEE IT AGAIN EV-ERY NIGHT.
SO THANKS FOR THAT.
CLIK! CLIK!

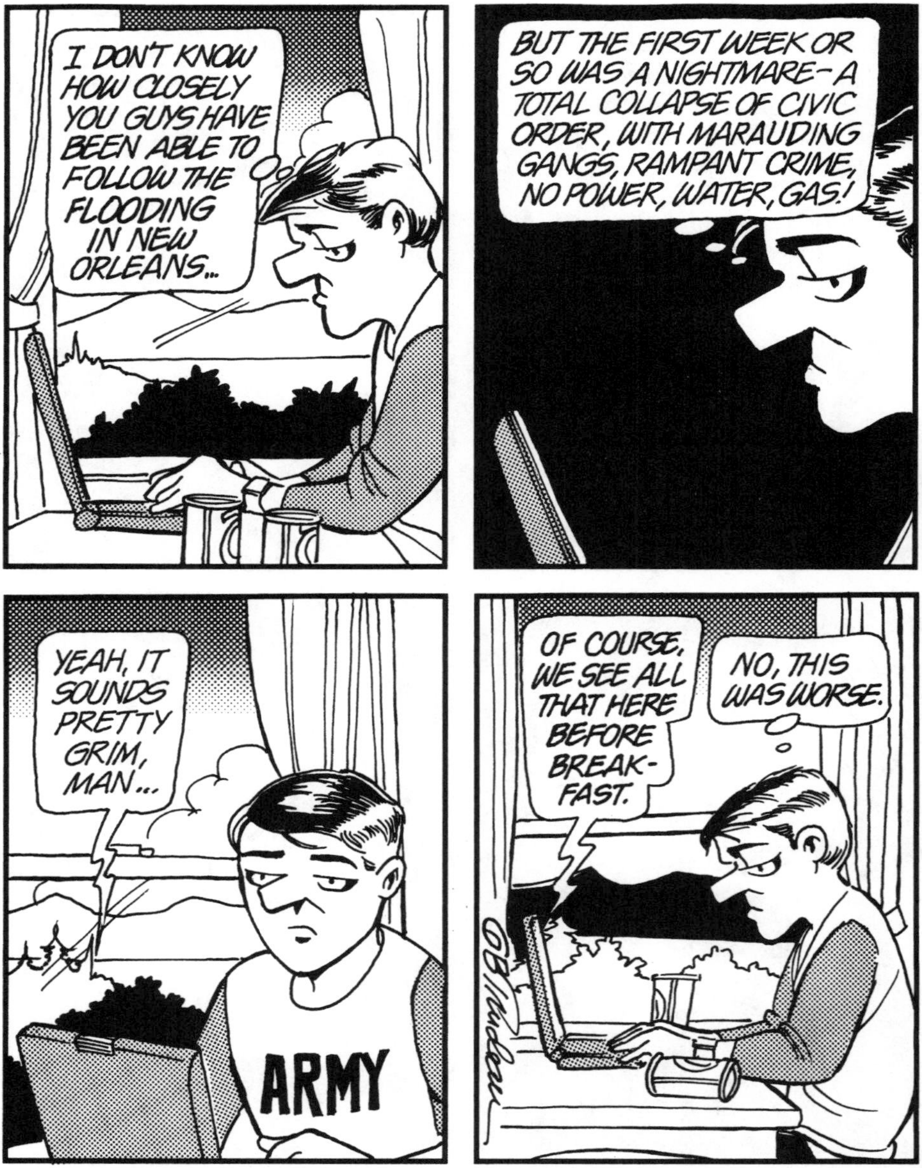
I DON'T KNOW HOW CLOSELY YOU GUYS HAVE BEEN ABLE TO FOLLOW THE FLOODING IN NEW ORLEANS...
BUT THE FIRST WEEK OR SO WAS A NIGHTMARE—A TOTAL COLLAPSE OF CIVIC ORDER, WITH MARAUDING GANGS, RAMPANT CRIME, NO POWER, WATER, GAS!
YEAH, IT SOUNDS PRETTY GRIM, MAN...
ARMY
OF COURSE, WE SEE ALL THAT HERE BEFORE BREAK-FAST.
NO, THIS WAS WORSE.

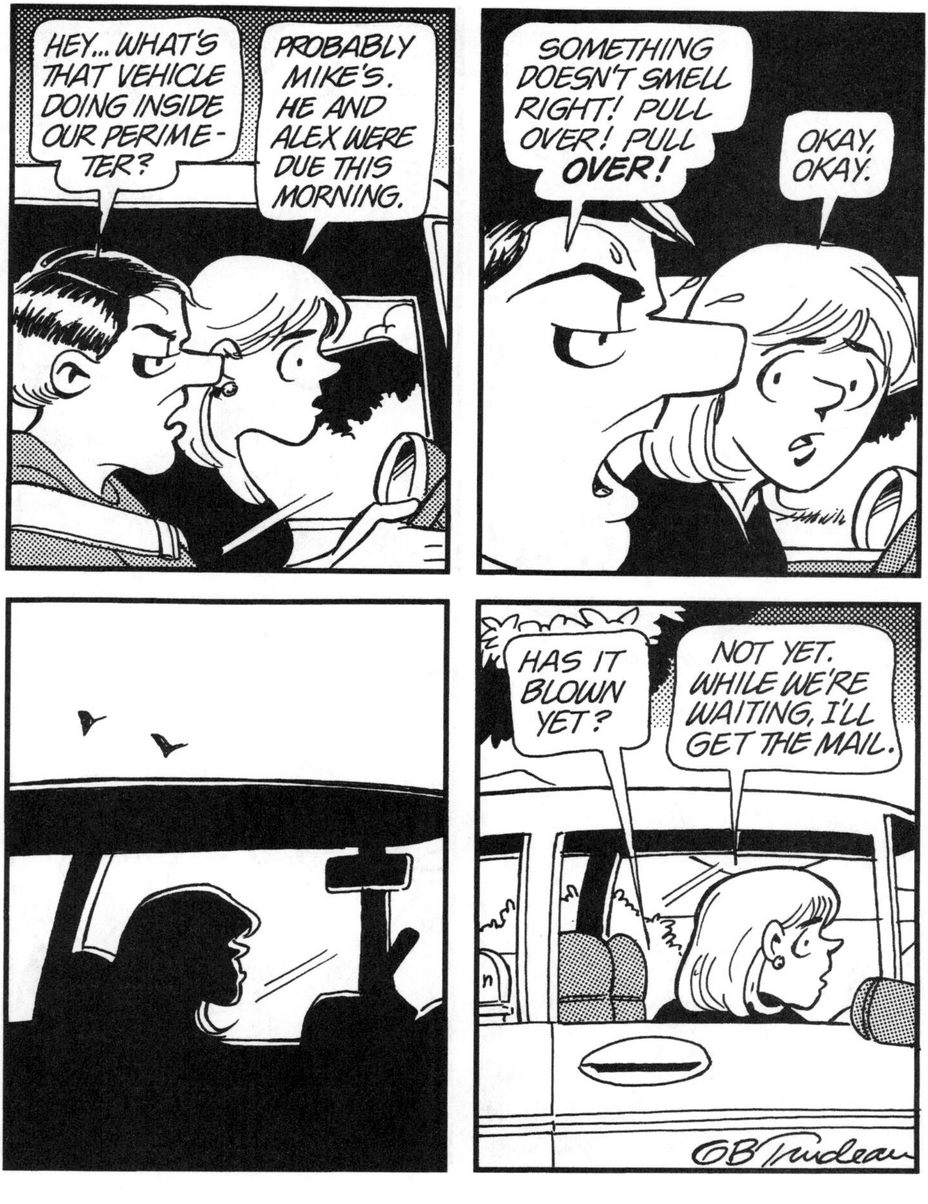
HEY... WHAT'S THAT VEHICLE DOING INSIDE OUR PERIME-TER?
PROBABLY MIKE'S. HE AND ALEX WERE DUE THIS MORNING.
SOMETHING DOESN'T SMELL RIGHT! PULL OVER! PULL OVER!
OKAY, OKAY.
HAS IT BLOWN YET?
NOT YET. WHILE WE'RE WAITING, I'LL GET THE MAIL.
GB Trudeau

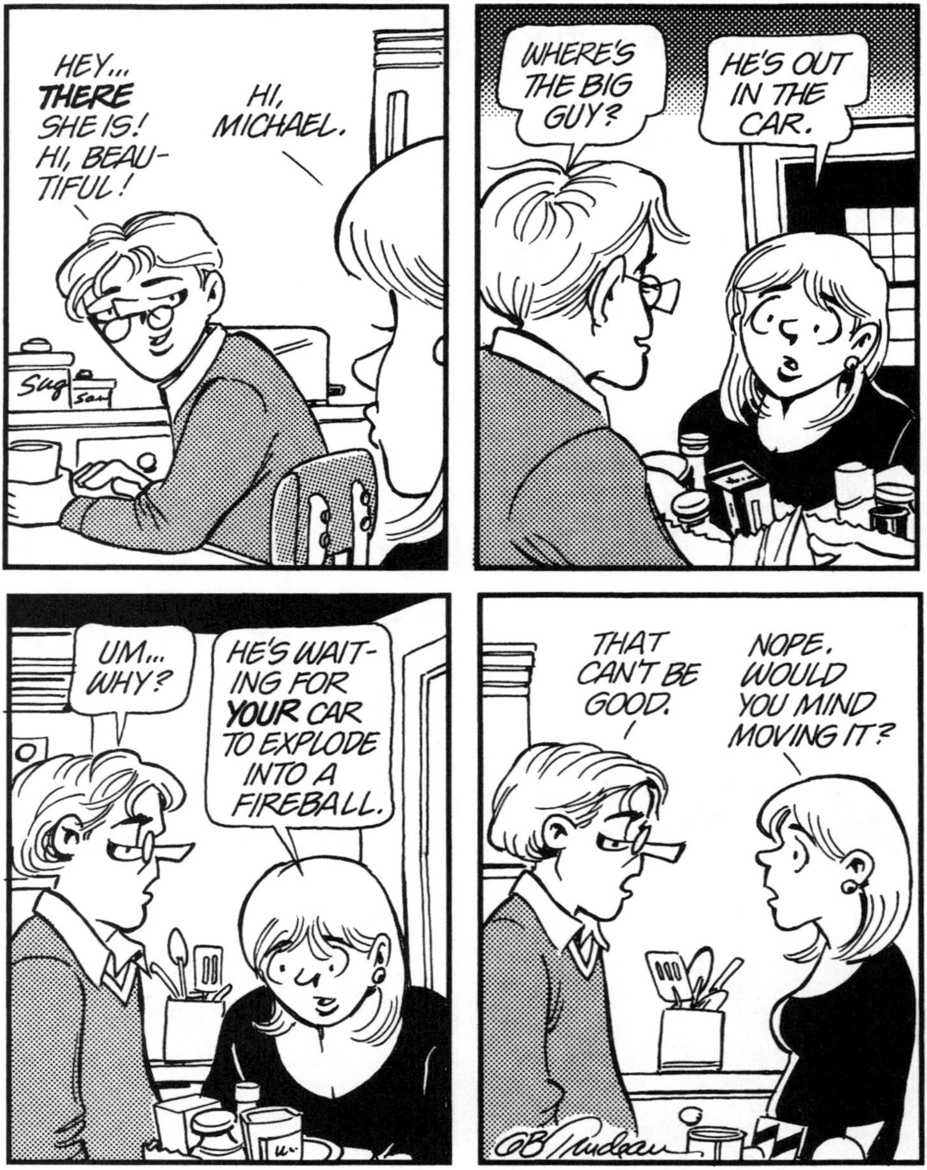
HEY... **THERE** SHE IS! HI, BEAU-TIFUL!
HI, MICHAEL.
WHERE'S THE BIG GUY?
HE'S OUT IN THE CAR.
UM... WHY?
HE'S WAIT-ING FOR **YOUR** CAR TO EXPLODE INTO A FIREBALL.
THAT CAN'T BE GOOD.
NOPE. WOULD YOU MIND MOVING IT?
GB Trudeau

THANKS FOR MOVING YOUR CAR, MIKE.
SURE. WHY DID IT UP-SET B.D.?
NOT SURE. MAYBE SOME CONNECTION BETWEEN TOYOTAS AND IED'S...
HE'LL BE IN SOON. JUST WAVE AND WELCOME HIM HOME.
B.D.? IT'S ME, MIKE! WELCOME HOME, BRO!
COULD BE SOMEONE DRESSED LIKE MIKE...
THAT'S CRAZY!
IS IT?
©B Trudeau

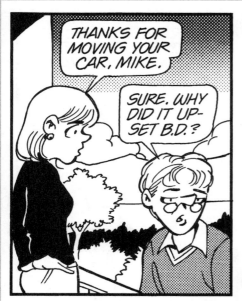

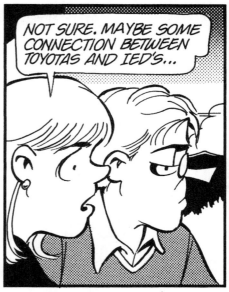

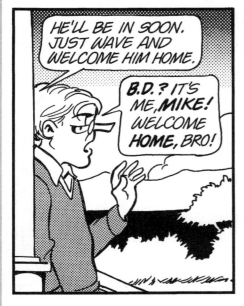

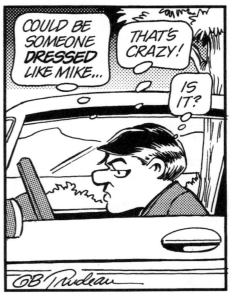

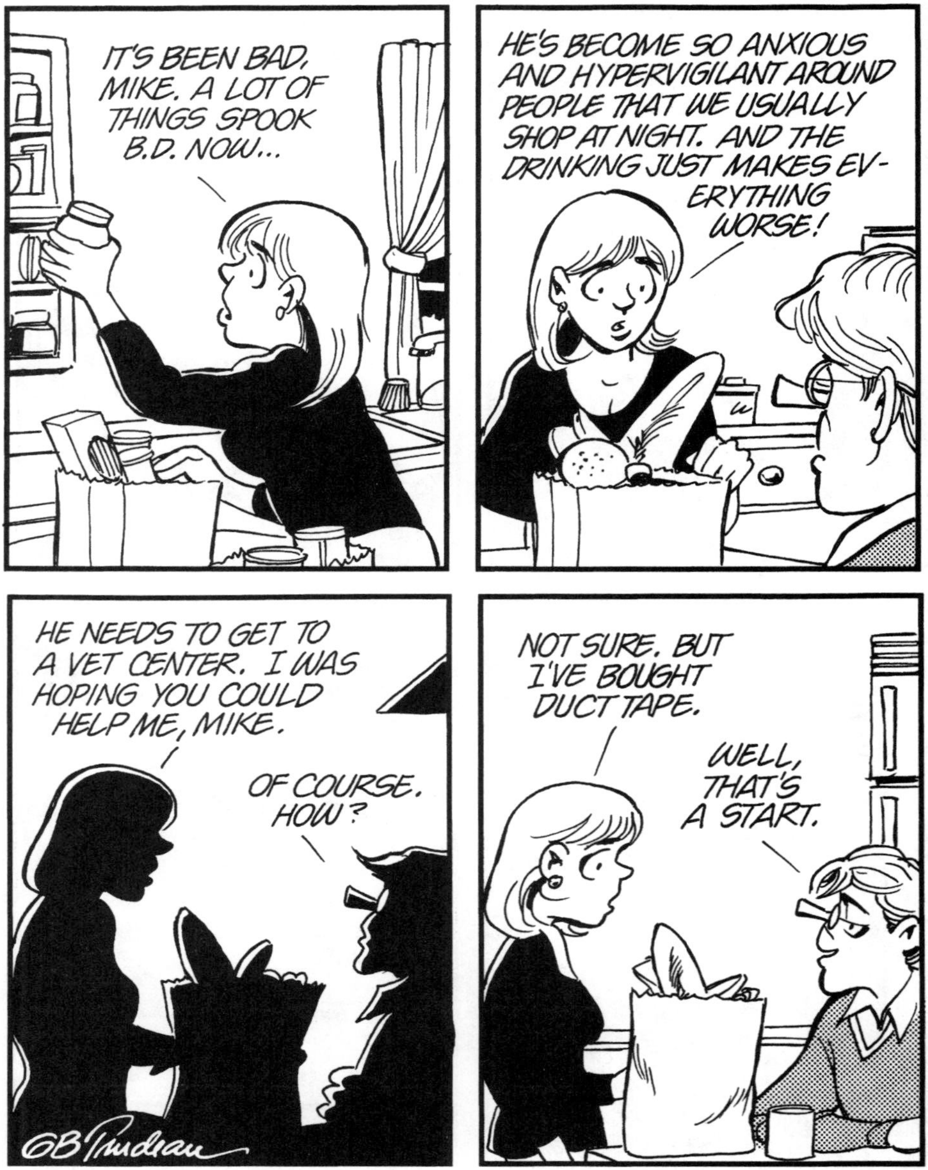
IT'S BEEN BAD, MIKE. A LOT OF THINGS SPOOK B.D. NOW...
HE'S BECOME SO ANXIOUS AND HYPERVIGILANT AROUND PEOPLE THAT WE USUALLY SHOP AT NIGHT. AND THE DRINKING JUST MAKES EVERYTHING WORSE!
HE NEEDS TO GET TO A VET CENTER. I WAS HOPING YOU COULD HELP ME, MIKE.
OF COURSE. HOW?
NOT SURE. BUT I'VE BOUGHT DUCT TAPE.
WELL, THAT'S A START.
GB Trudeau

ESPECIALLY WITH HIS DRINKING, I'M HAVING A HARD TIME COPING, MIKE. I'M TIRED AND ANXIOUS AND TOTALLY DEMORALIZED...
BASICALLY, I'M A COMPLETE MESS!
WELL, YOU DON'T LOOK LIKE A MESS. YOU LOOK AS LOVELY AS EVER.
ARE YOU SERIOUS?
NEVER MORE.
MICHAEL. I HAVEN'T WASHED MY HAIR IN A WEEK!
WELL, IT'S NOT LIKE I'M HITTING ON YOU.
©B Trudeau

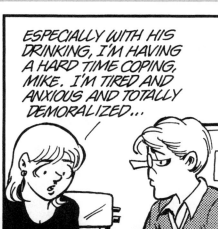

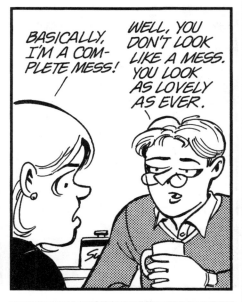

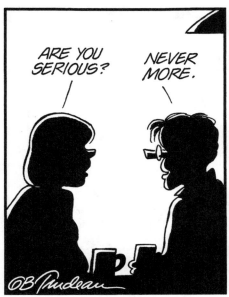

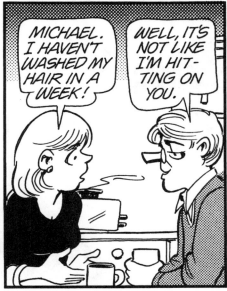

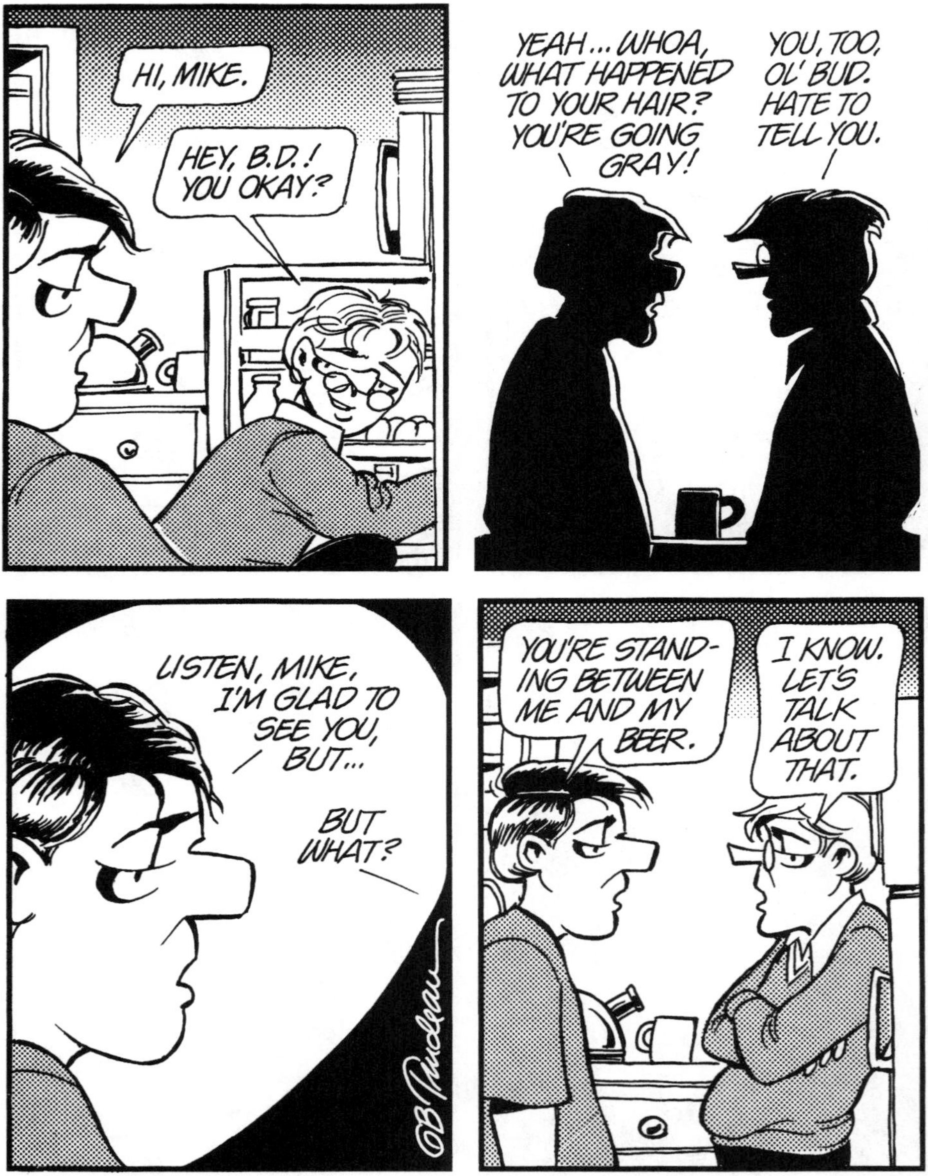
HI, MIKE.
HEY, B.D.! YOU OKAY?
YEAH... WHOA, WHAT HAPPENED TO YOUR HAIR? YOU'RE GOING GRAY!
YOU, TOO, OL' BUD. HATE TO TELL YOU.
LISTEN, MIKE, I'M GLAD TO SEE YOU, BUT...
BUT WHAT?
YOU'RE STANDING BETWEEN ME AND MY BEER.
I KNOW. LET'S TALK ABOUT THAT.
©B Trudeau

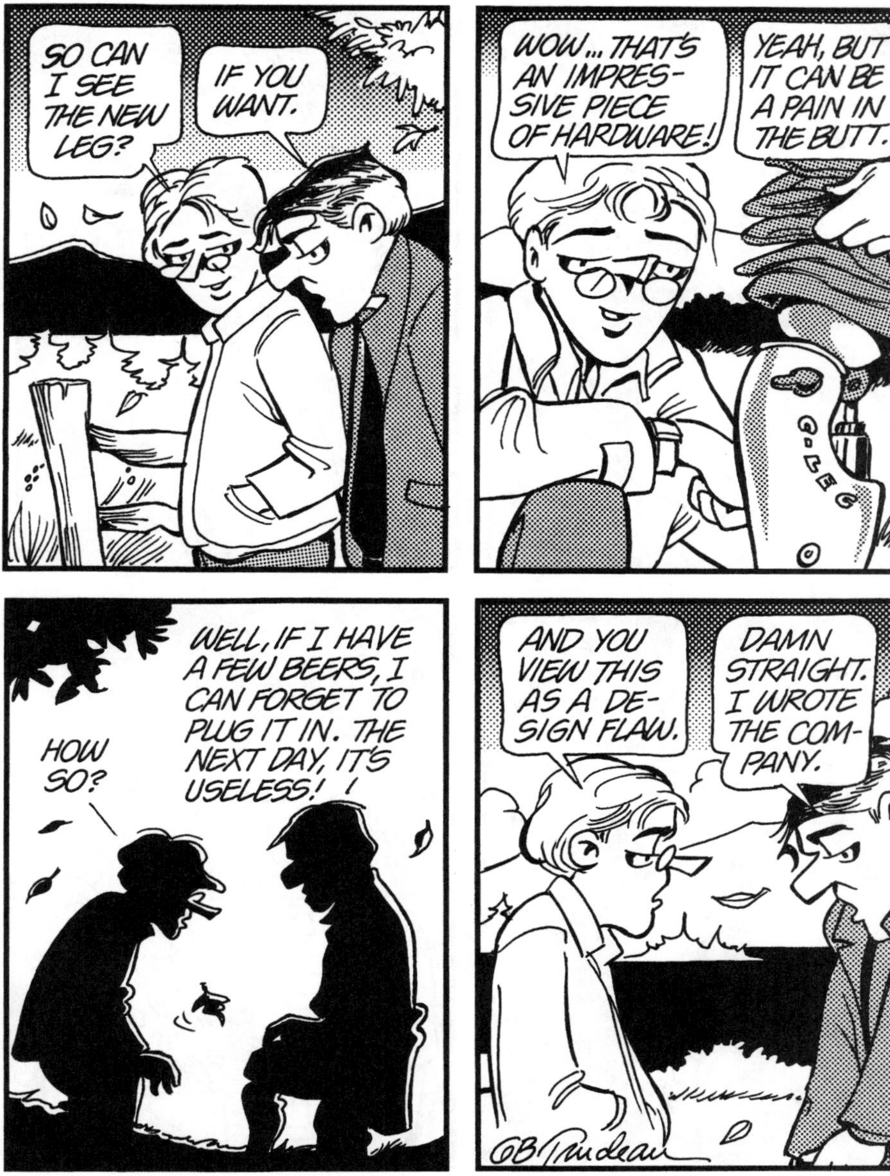
SO CAN I SEE THE NEW LEG?
IF YOU WANT.
WOW... THAT'S AN IMPRESSIVE PIECE OF HARDWARE!
YEAH, BUT IT CAN BE A PAIN IN THE BUTT.
G-LEG
HOW SO?
WELL, IF I HAVE A FEW BEERS, I CAN FORGET TO PLUG IT IN. THE NEXT DAY, IT'S USELESS!
AND YOU VIEW THIS AS A DESIGN FLAW.
DAMN STRAIGHT. I WROTE THE COMPANY.
©B Trudeau

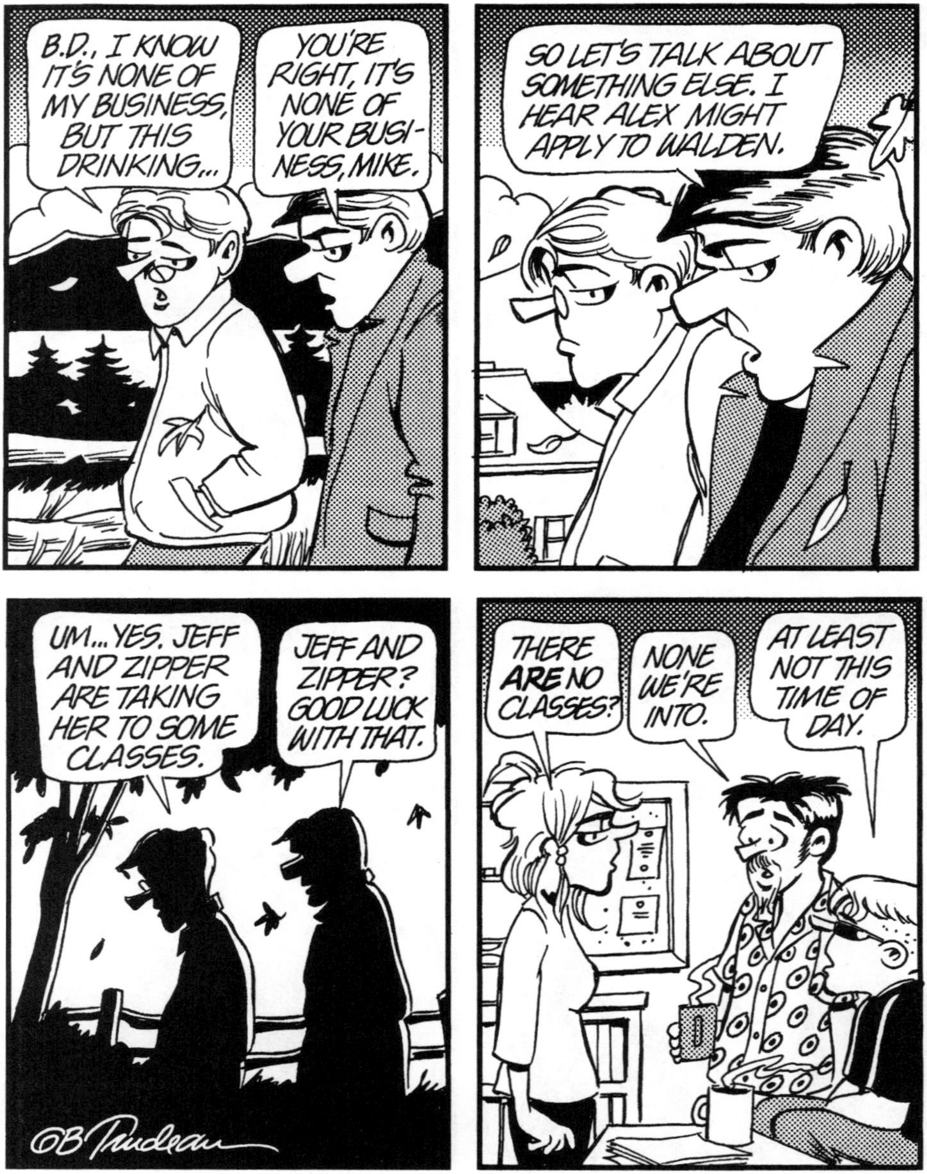
B.D., I KNOW IT'S NONE OF MY BUSINESS, BUT THIS DRINKING...
YOU'RE RIGHT, IT'S NONE OF YOUR BUSINESS, MIKE.
SO LET'S TALK ABOUT SOMETHING ELSE. I HEAR ALEX MIGHT APPLY TO WALDEN.
UM... YES. JEFF AND ZIPPER ARE TAKING HER TO SOME CLASSES.
JEFF AND ZIPPER? GOOD LUCK WITH THAT.
THERE ARE NO CLASSES?
NONE WE'RE INTO.
AT LEAST NOT THIS TIME OF DAY.
©B Trudeau

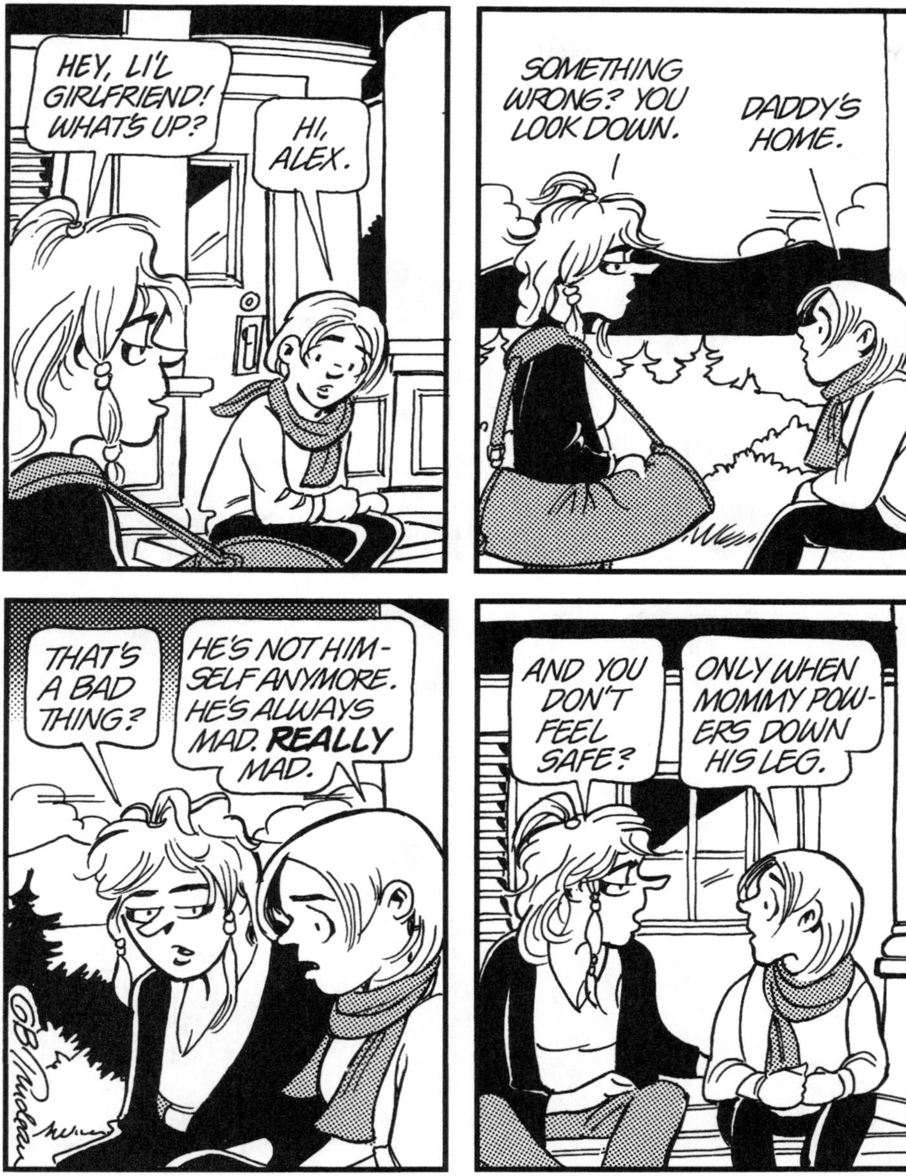
HEY, LI'L GIRLFRIEND! WHAT'S UP?
HI, ALEX.
SOMETHING WRONG? YOU LOOK DOWN.
DADDY'S HOME.
THAT'S A BAD THING?
HE'S NOT HIMSELF ANYMORE. HE'S ALWAYS MAD. **REALLY** MAD.
AND YOU DON'T FEEL SAFE?
ONLY WHEN MOMMY POWERS DOWN HIS LEG.
©B. Trudeau

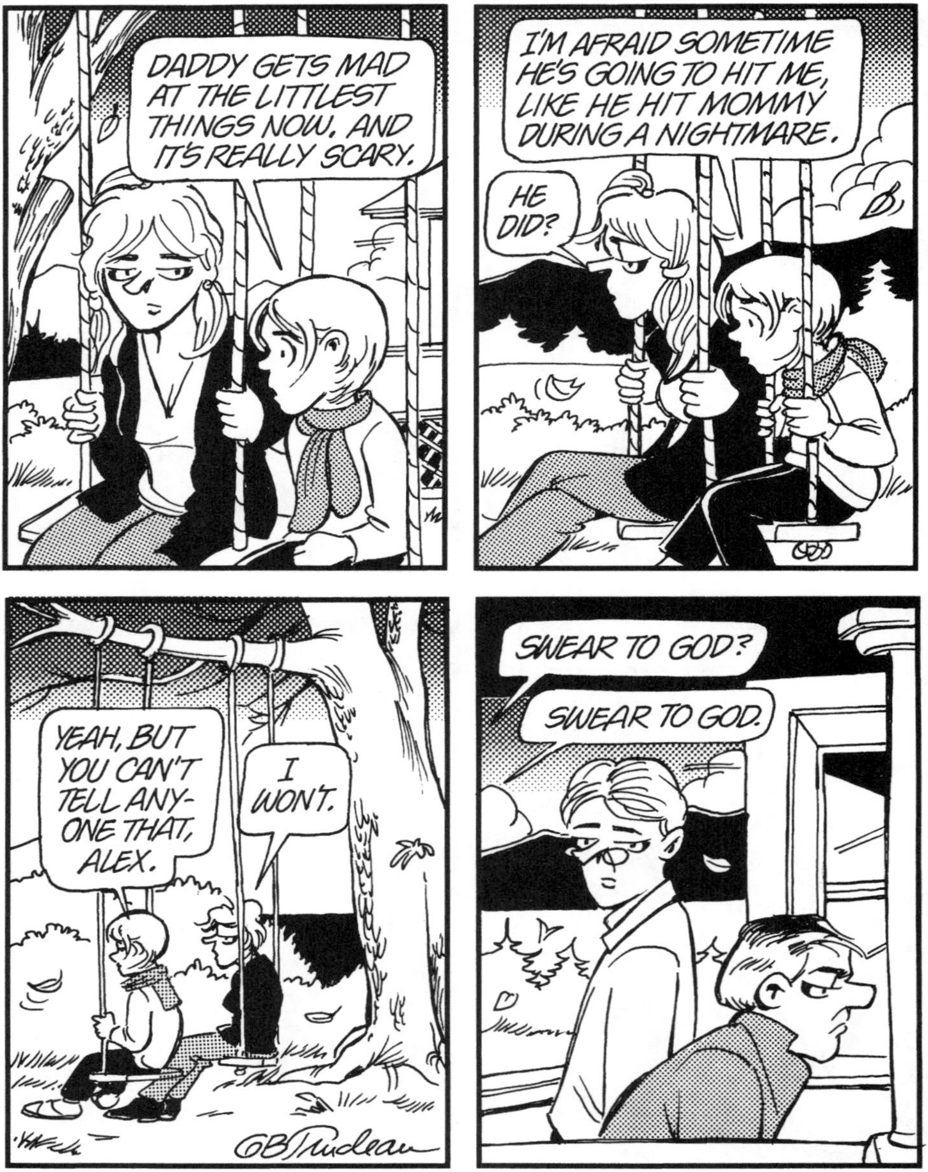
DADDY GETS MAD AT THE LITTLEST THINGS NOW, AND IT'S REALLY SCARY.
I'M AFRAID SOMETIME HE'S GOING TO HIT ME, LIKE HE HIT MOMMY DURING A NIGHTMARE.
HE DID?
YEAH, BUT YOU CAN'T TELL ANYONE THAT, ALEX.
I WON'T.
SWEAR TO GOD?
SWEAR TO GOD.

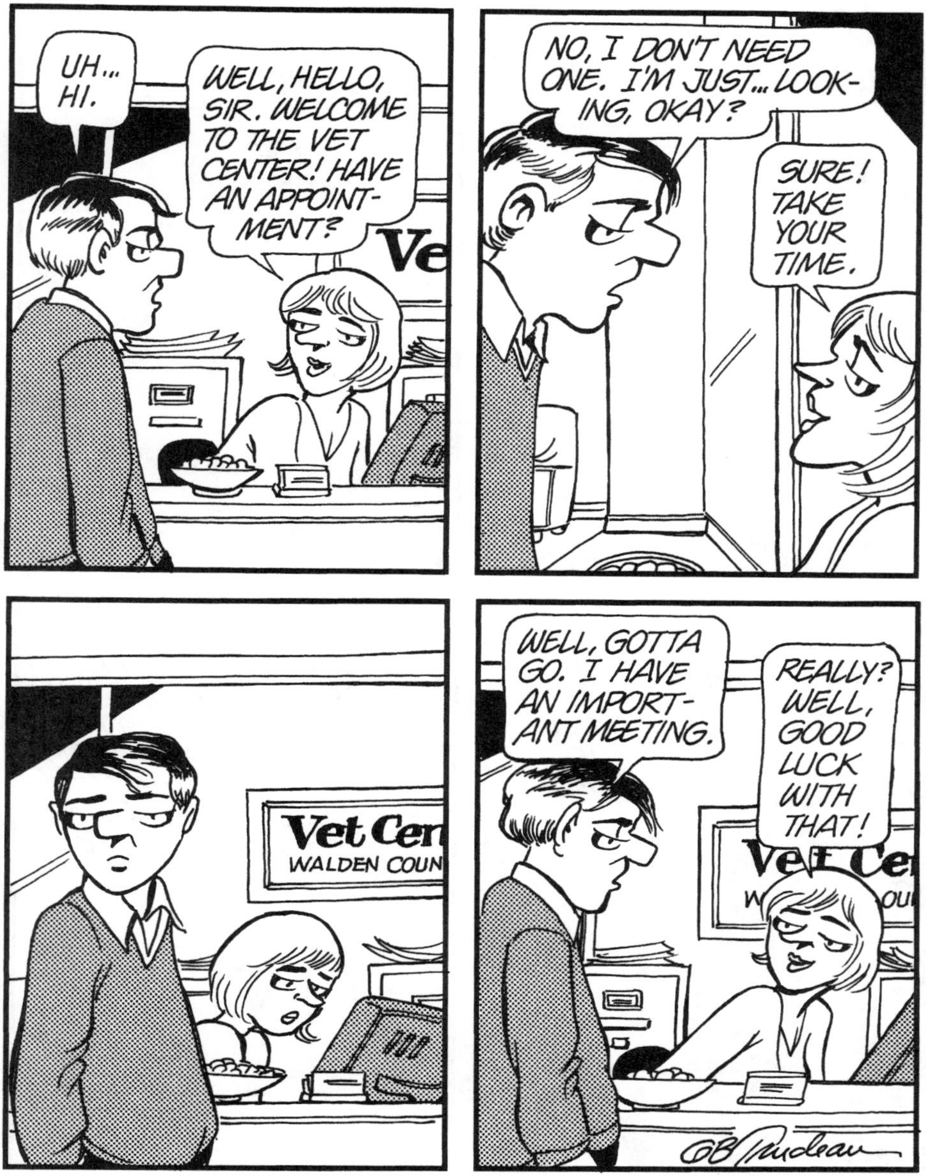
UH... HI.
WELL, HELLO, SIR. WELCOME TO THE VET CENTER! HAVE AN APPOINT-MENT?
Ve
NO, I DON'T NEED ONE. I'M JUST... LOOK-ING, OKAY?
SURE! TAKE YOUR TIME.
Vet Cen
WALDEN COUN
WELL, GOTTA GO. I HAVE AN IMPORT-ANT MEETING.
REALLY? WELL, GOOD LUCK WITH THAT!
GB Trudeau

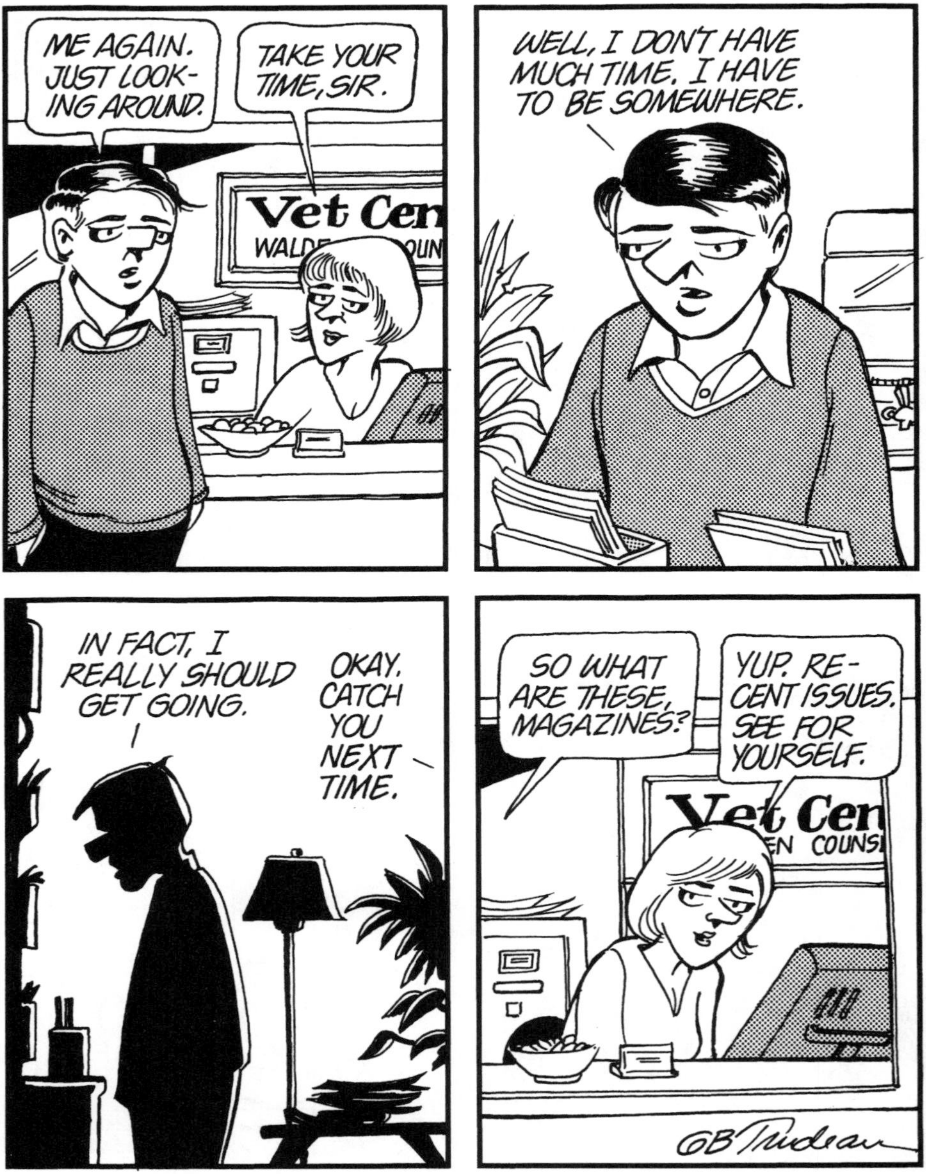
ME AGAIN. JUST LOOK-ING AROUND.
TAKE YOUR TIME, SIR.
Vet Cen
WALD
OUN
WELL, I DON'T HAVE MUCH TIME. I HAVE TO BE SOMEWHERE.
IN FACT, I REALLY SHOULD GET GOING.
OKAY. CATCH YOU NEXT TIME.
SO WHAT ARE THESE, MAGAZINES?
YUP. RE-CENT ISSUES. SEE FOR YOURSELF.
Vet Cen
EN COUNS
GB Trudeau

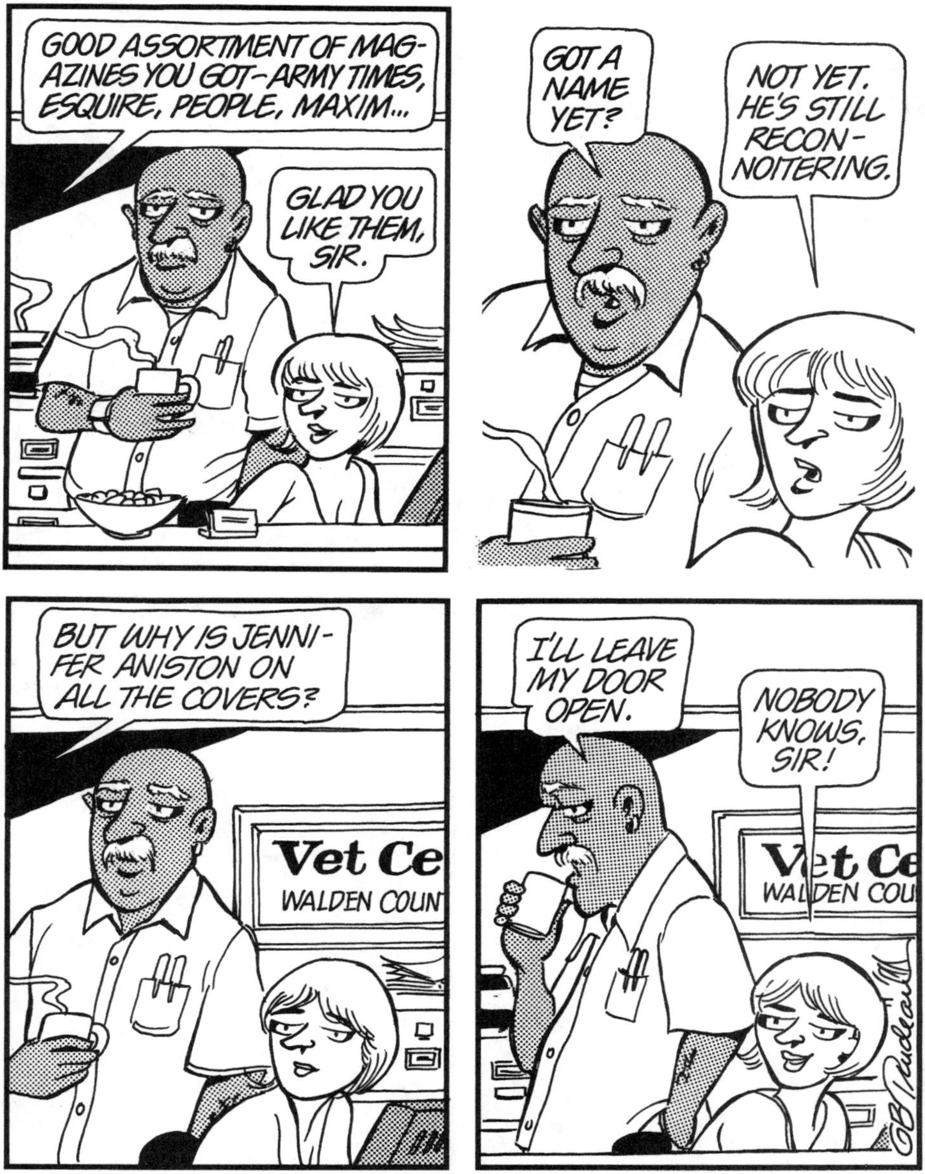
GOOD ASSORTMENT OF MAGAZINES YOU GOT-ARMY TIMES, ESQUIRE, PEOPLE, MAXIM...
GLAD YOU LIKE THEM, SIR.
GOT A NAME YET?
NOT YET. HE'S STILL RECONNOITERING.
BUT WHY IS JENNIFER ANISTON ON ALL THE COVERS?
Vet Ce
WALDEN COUNT
I'LL LEAVE MY DOOR OPEN.
NOBODY KNOWS, SIR!
Vet Ce
WALDEN COU
GBTrudeau

HEY, BRO. HELP YOU WITH ANY-THING?
UH,...NO. JUST LOOKING AROUND.
Vet
COOL. I'M ELIAS, A COUNSELOR HERE. AND AN AK AMP, JUST LIKE YOU.
HOW'D YOU KNOW THAT?
Vet
TAKES ONE TO KNOW ONE. READY TO TALK?
ABOUT WHAT?
Vet
OKAY. MAYBE LATER.
WHAT, LIKE YOU'RE TOO BUSY?
GB Trudeau

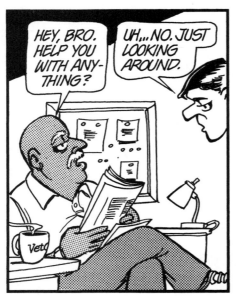

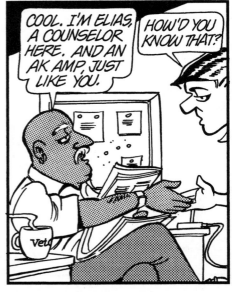

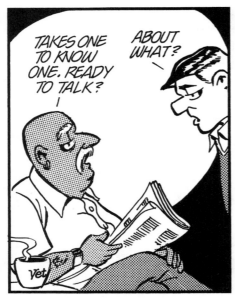

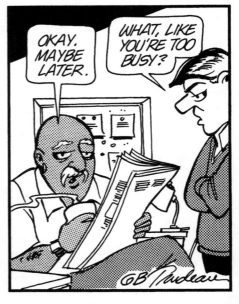

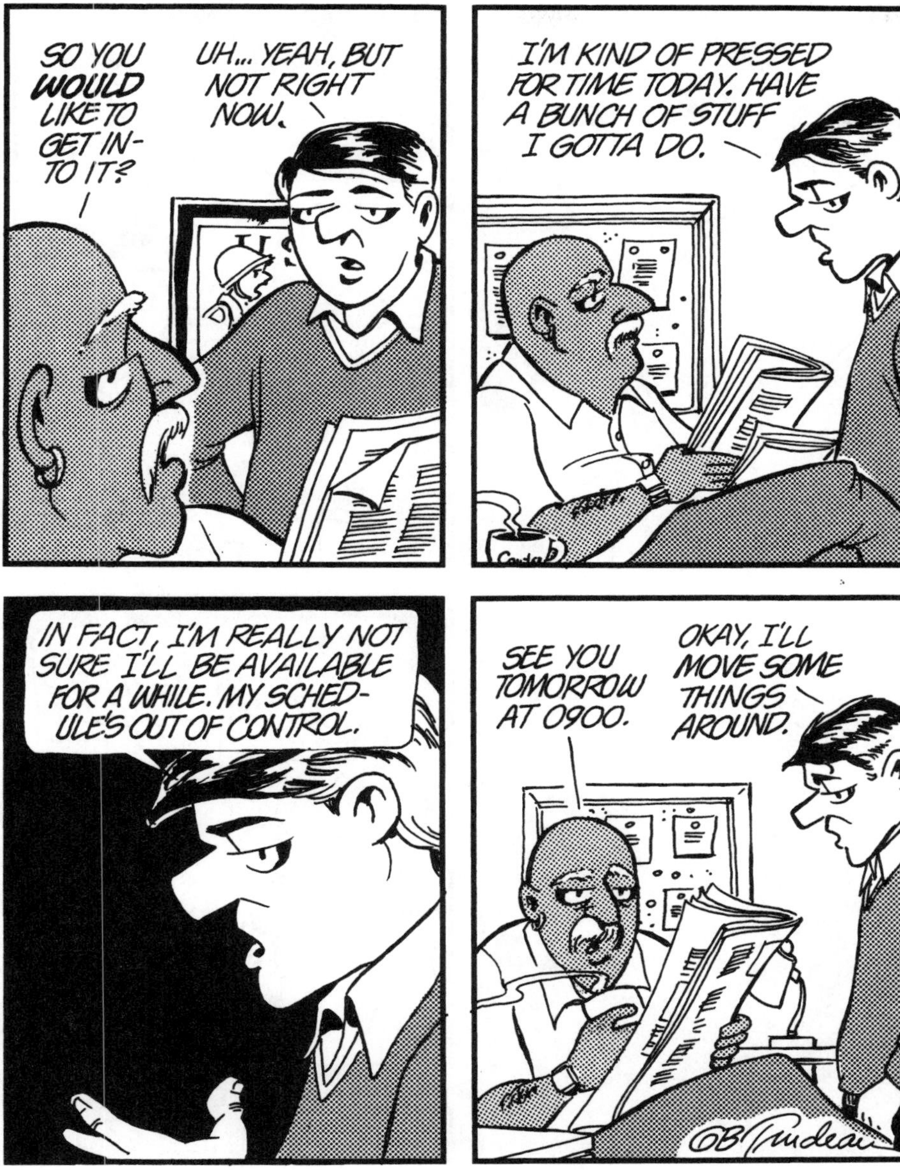
SO YOU WOULD LIKE TO GET INTO IT?
UH... YEAH, BUT NOT RIGHT NOW.
I'M KIND OF PRESSED FOR TIME TODAY. HAVE A BUNCH OF STUFF I GOTTA DO.
IN FACT, I'M REALLY NOT SURE I'LL BE AVAILABLE FOR A WHILE. MY SCHEDULE'S OUT OF CONTROL.
OKAY, I'LL MOVE SOME THINGS AROUND.
SEE YOU TOMORROW AT 0900.
GB Trudeau

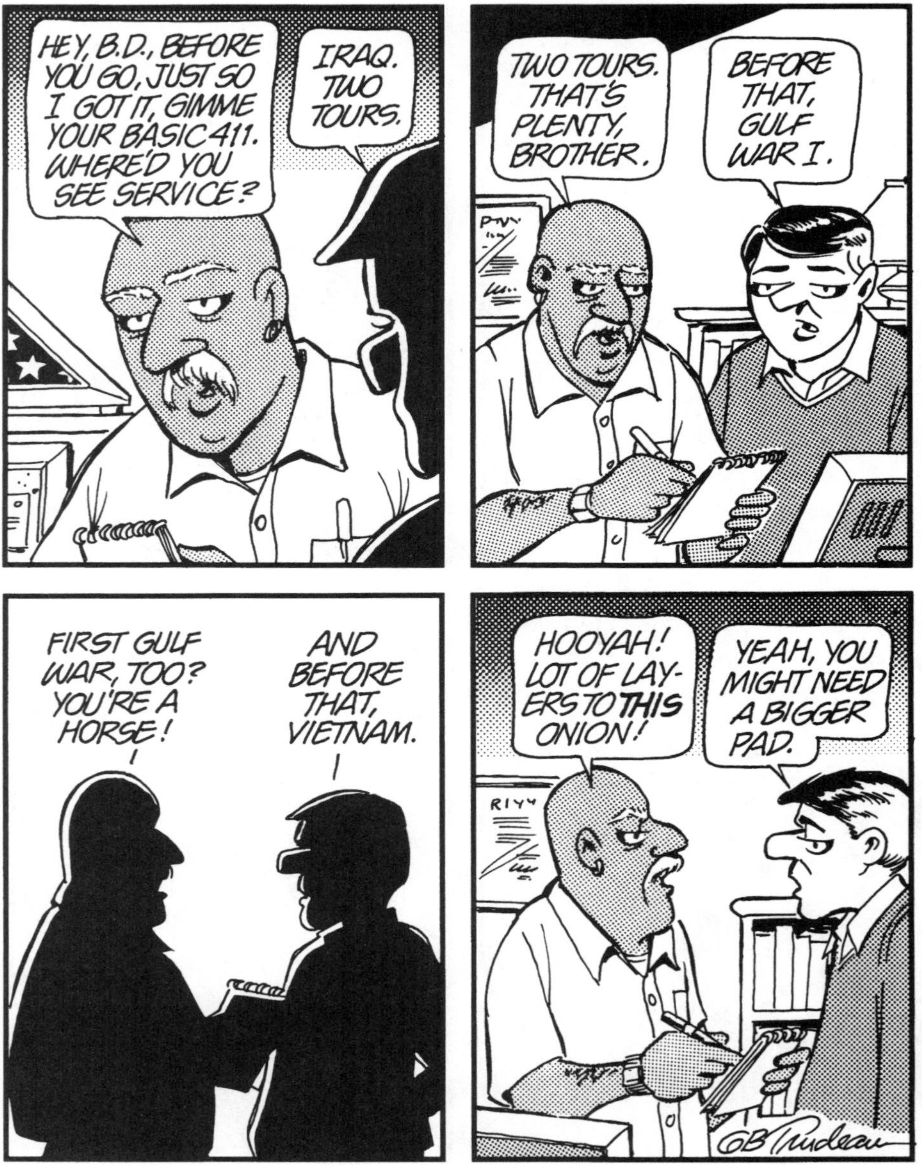
HEY, B.D., BEFORE YOU GO, JUST SO I GOT IT, GIMME YOUR BASIC 411. WHERE'D YOU SEE SERVICE?
IRAQ. TWO TOURS.
TWO TOURS. THAT'S PLENTY, BROTHER.
BEFORE THAT, GULF WAR I.
FIRST GULF WAR, TOO? YOU'RE A HORSE!
AND BEFORE THAT, VIETNAM.
HOOYAH! LOT OF LAYERS TO THIS ONION!
YEAH, YOU MIGHT NEED A BIGGER PAD.
©B Trudeau

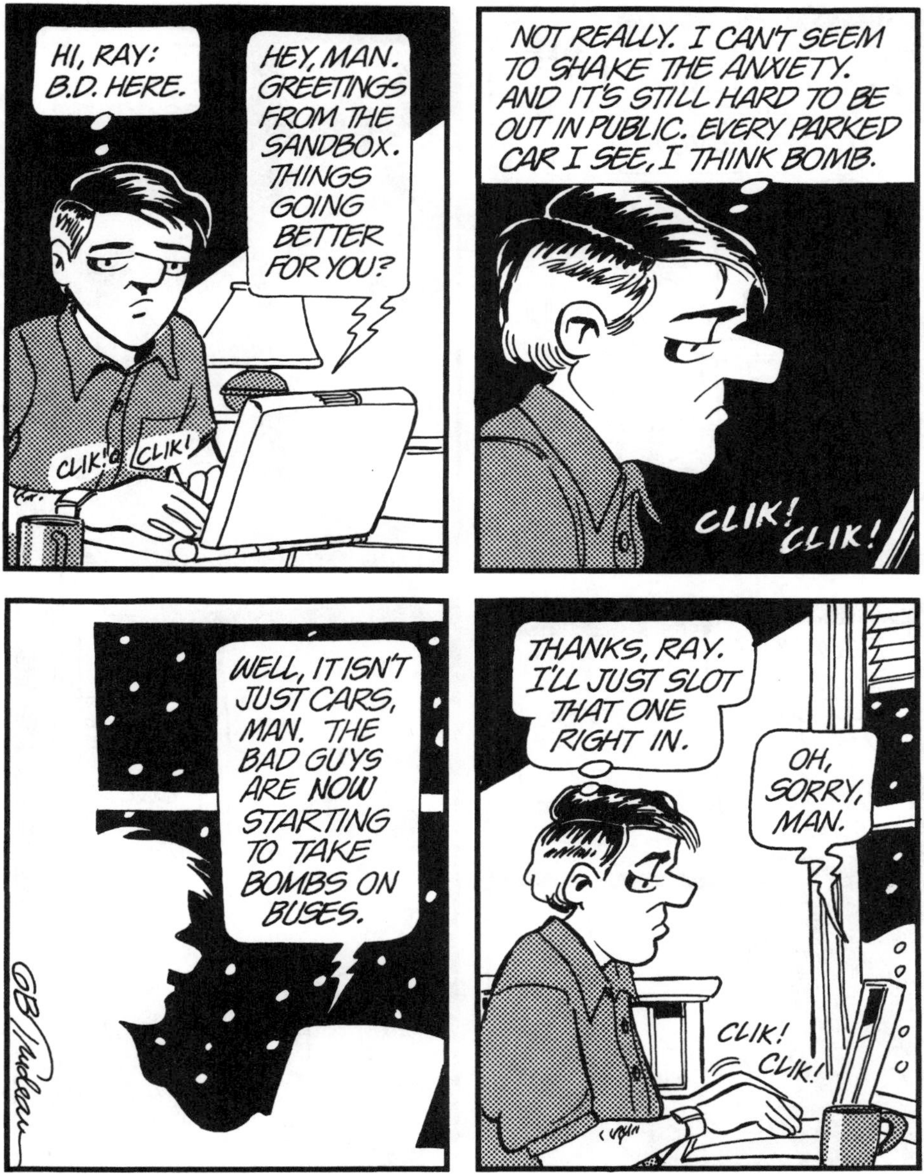
HI, RAY: B.D. HERE.
HEY, MAN. GREETINGS FROM THE SANDBOX. THINGS GOING BETTER FOR YOU?
CLIK! CLIK!
NOT REALLY. I CAN'T SEEM TO SHAKE THE ANXIETY. AND IT'S STILL HARD TO BE OUT IN PUBLIC. EVERY PARKED CAR I SEE, I THINK BOMB.
CLIK! CLIK!
WELL, IT ISN'T JUST CARS, MAN. THE BAD GUYS ARE NOW STARTING TO TAKE BOMBS ON BUSES.
THANKS, RAY. I'LL JUST SLOT THAT ONE RIGHT IN.
OH, SORRY, MAN.
CLIK! CLIK!

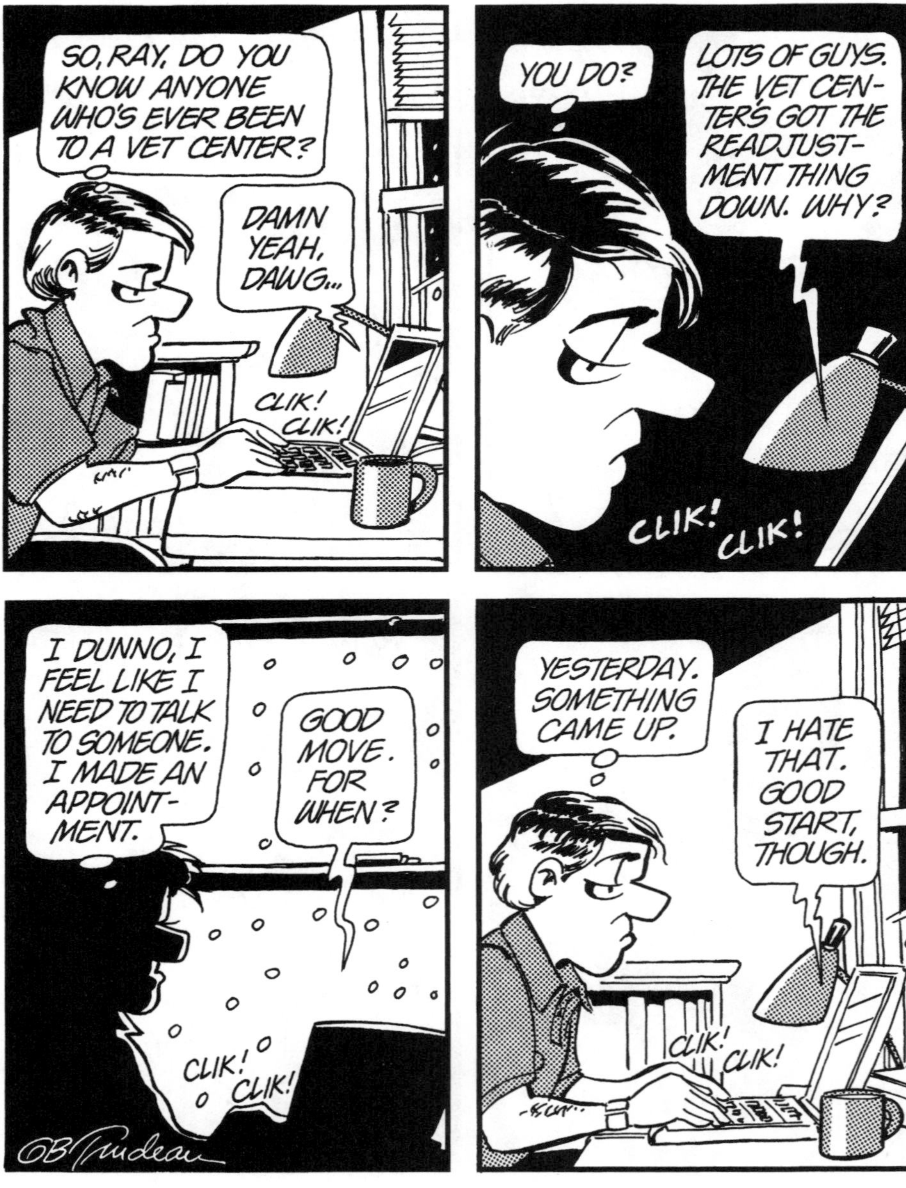
SO, RAY, DO YOU KNOW ANYONE WHO'S EVER BEEN TO A VET CENTER?
DAMN YEAH, DAWG...
CLIK! CLIK!
YOU DO?
LOTS OF GUYS. THE VET CENTER'S GOT THE READJUSTMENT THING DOWN. WHY?
CLIK! CLIK!
I DUNNO, I FEEL LIKE I NEED TO TALK TO SOMEONE. I MADE AN APPOINTMENT.
GOOD MOVE. FOR WHEN?
CLIK! CLIK!
YESTERDAY. SOMETHING CAME UP.
I HATE THAT. GOOD START, THOUGH.
CLIK! CLIK!
GB Trudeau

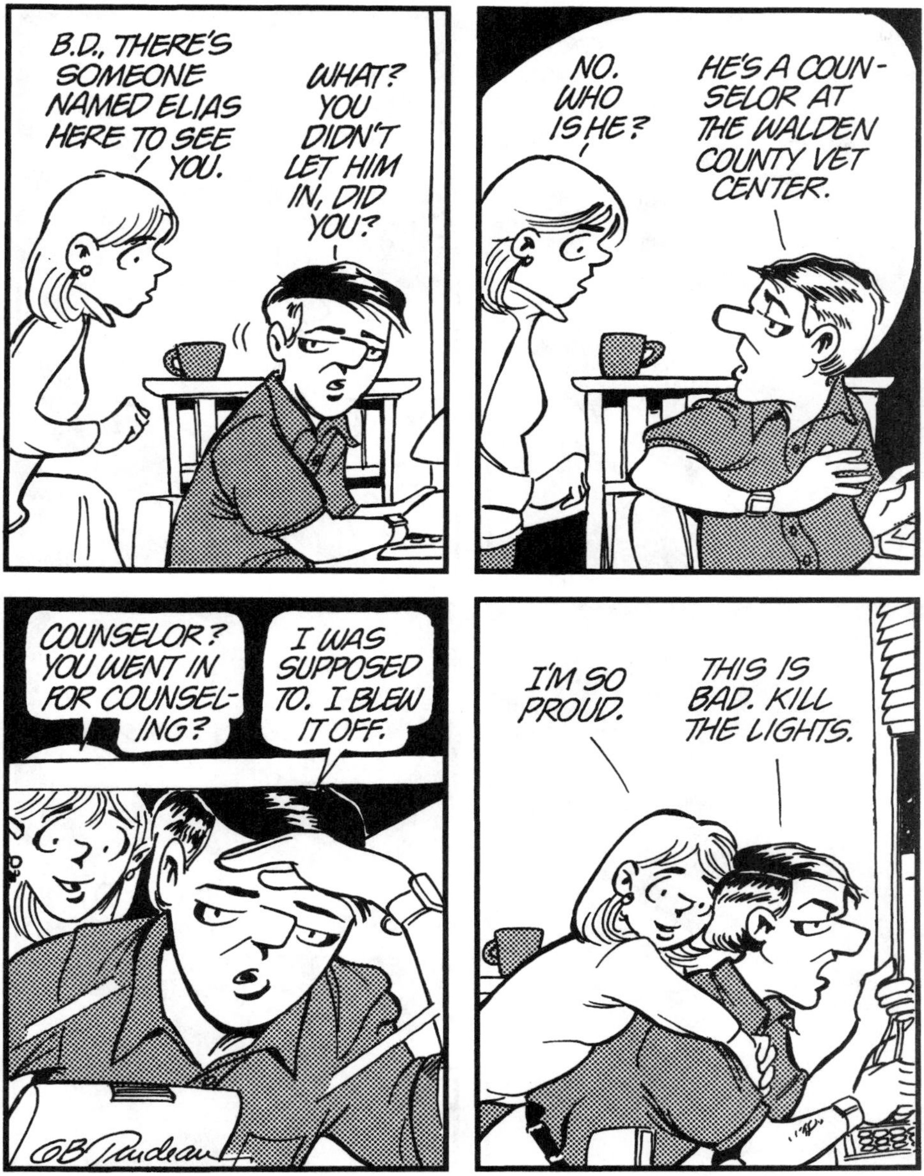
B.D., THERE'S SOMEONE NAMED ELIAS HERE TO SEE YOU.
WHAT? YOU DIDN'T LET HIM IN, DID YOU?
NO. WHO IS HE?
HE'S A COUN-SELOR AT THE WALDEN COUNTY VET CENTER.
COUNSELOR? YOU WENT IN FOR COUNSEL-ING?
I WAS SUPPOSED TO. I BLEW IT OFF.
I'M SO PROUD.
THIS IS BAD. KILL THE LIGHTS.
GB Trudeau

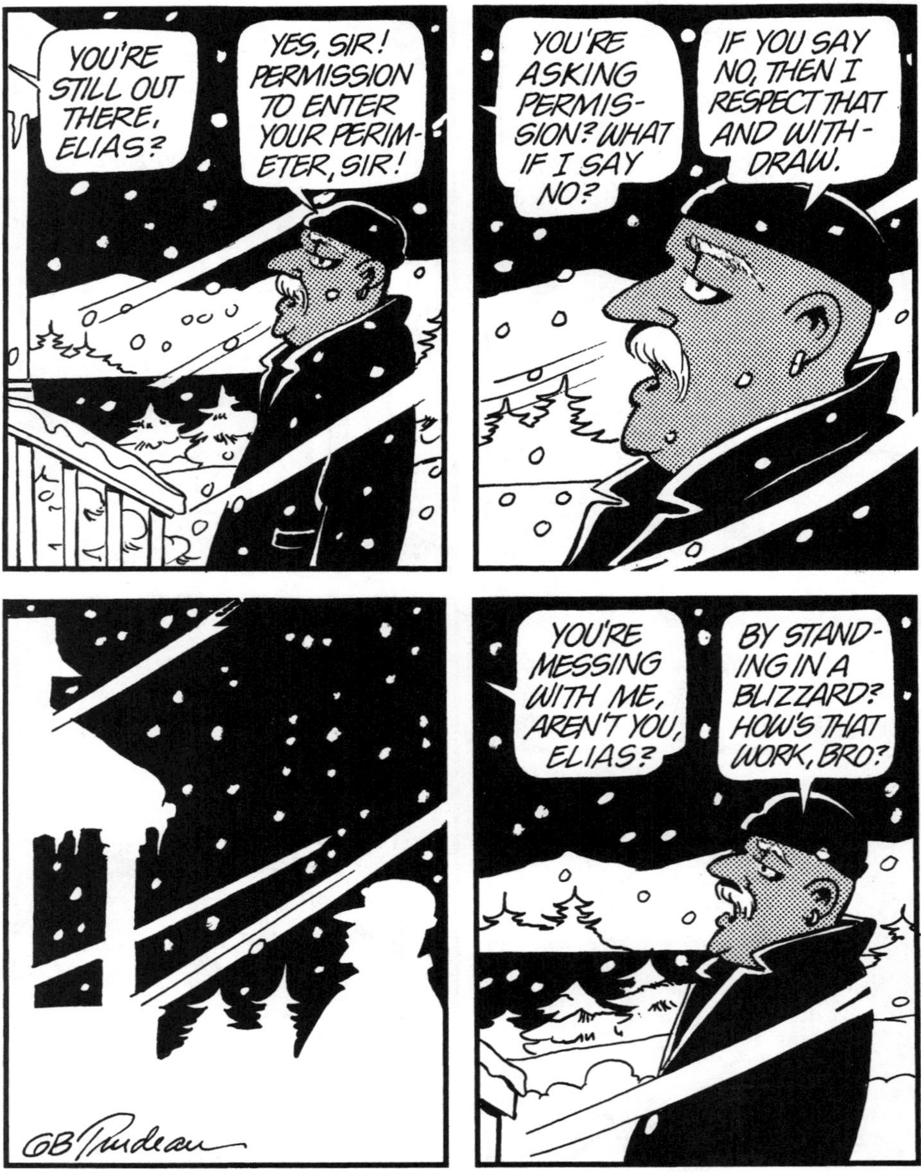
YOU'RE STILL OUT THERE, ELIAS?
YES, SIR! PERMISSION TO ENTER YOUR PERIMETER, SIR!
YOU'RE ASKING PERMISSION? WHAT IF I SAY NO?
IF YOU SAY NO, THEN I RESPECT THAT AND WITHDRAW.
YOU'RE MESSING WITH ME, AREN'T YOU, ELIAS?
BY STANDING IN A BLIZZARD? HOW'S THAT WORK, BRO?
GB Trudeau

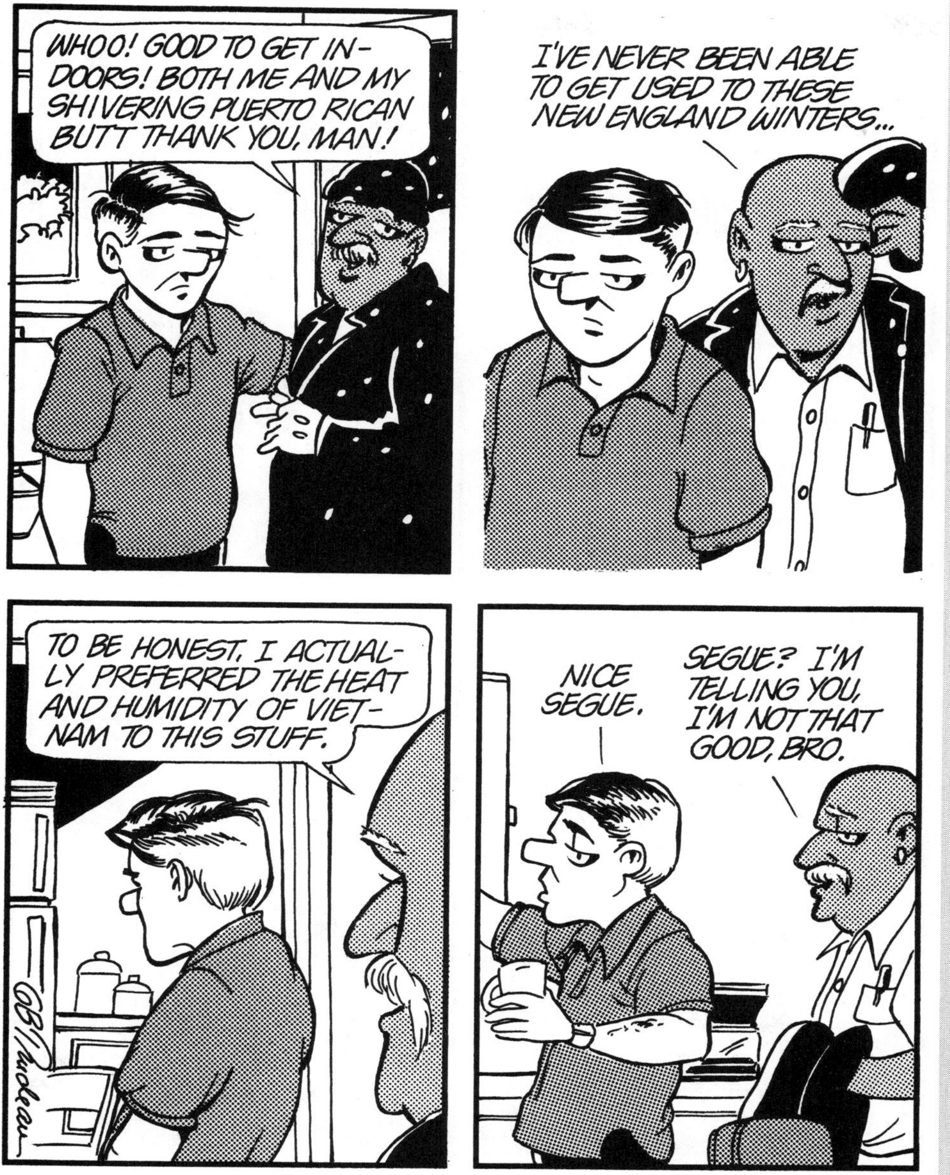
WHOO! GOOD TO GET INDOORS! BOTH ME AND MY SHIVERING PUERTO RICAN BUTT THANK YOU, MAN!
I'VE NEVER BEEN ABLE TO GET USED TO THESE NEW ENGLAND WINTERS...
TO BE HONEST, I ACTUALLY PREFERRED THE HEAT AND HUMIDITY OF VIETNAM TO THIS STUFF.
NICE SEGUE.
SEGUE? I'M TELLING YOU, I'M NOT THAT GOOD, BRO.
GBTrudeau

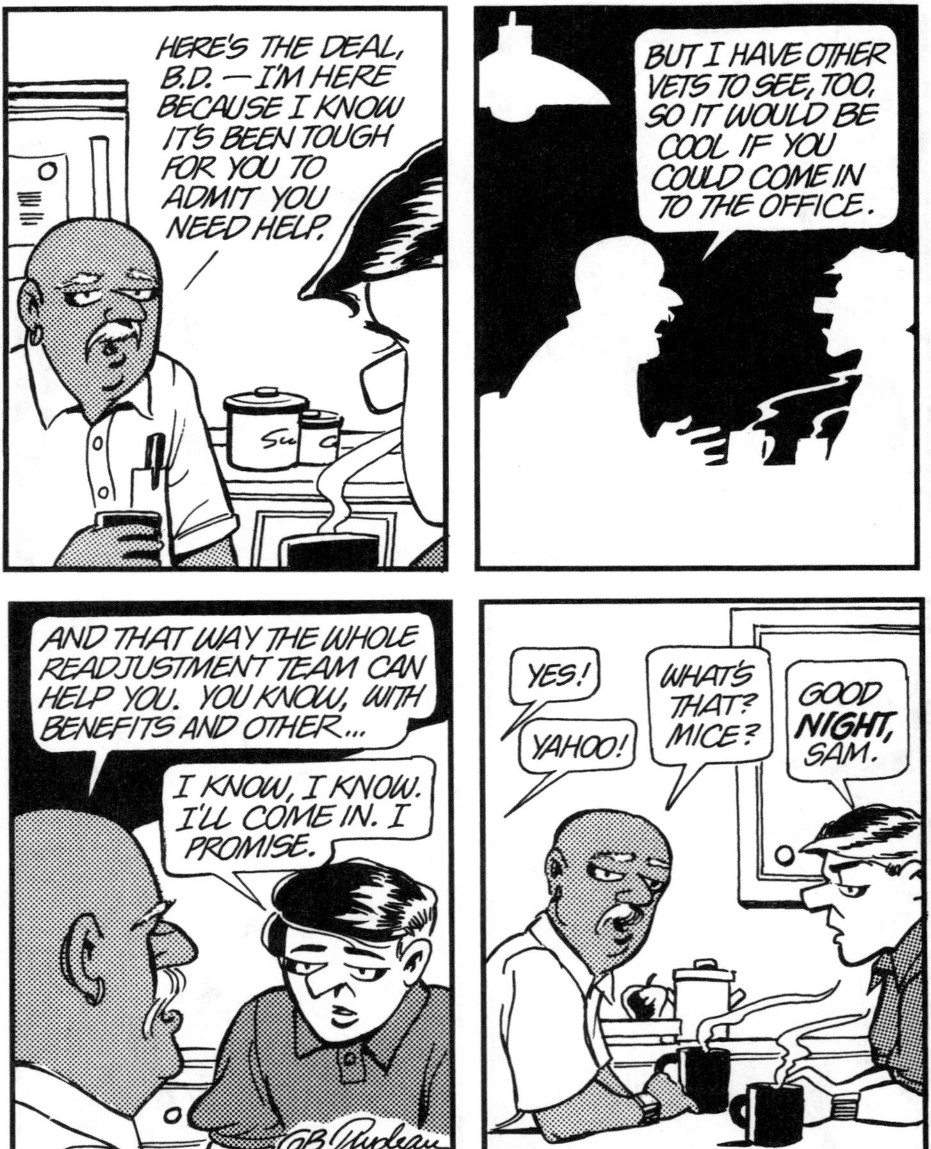
HERE'S THE DEAL, B.D. — I'M HERE BECAUSE I KNOW IT'S BEEN TOUGH FOR YOU TO ADMIT YOU NEED HELP.
BUT I HAVE OTHER VETS TO SEE, TOO, SO IT WOULD BE COOL IF YOU COULD COME IN TO THE OFFICE.
AND THAT WAY THE WHOLE READJUSTMENT TEAM CAN HELP YOU. YOU KNOW, WITH BENEFITS AND OTHER...
I KNOW, I KNOW. I'LL COME IN. I PROMISE.
YES!
YAHOO!
WHAT'S THAT? MICE?
GOOD NIGHT, SAM.

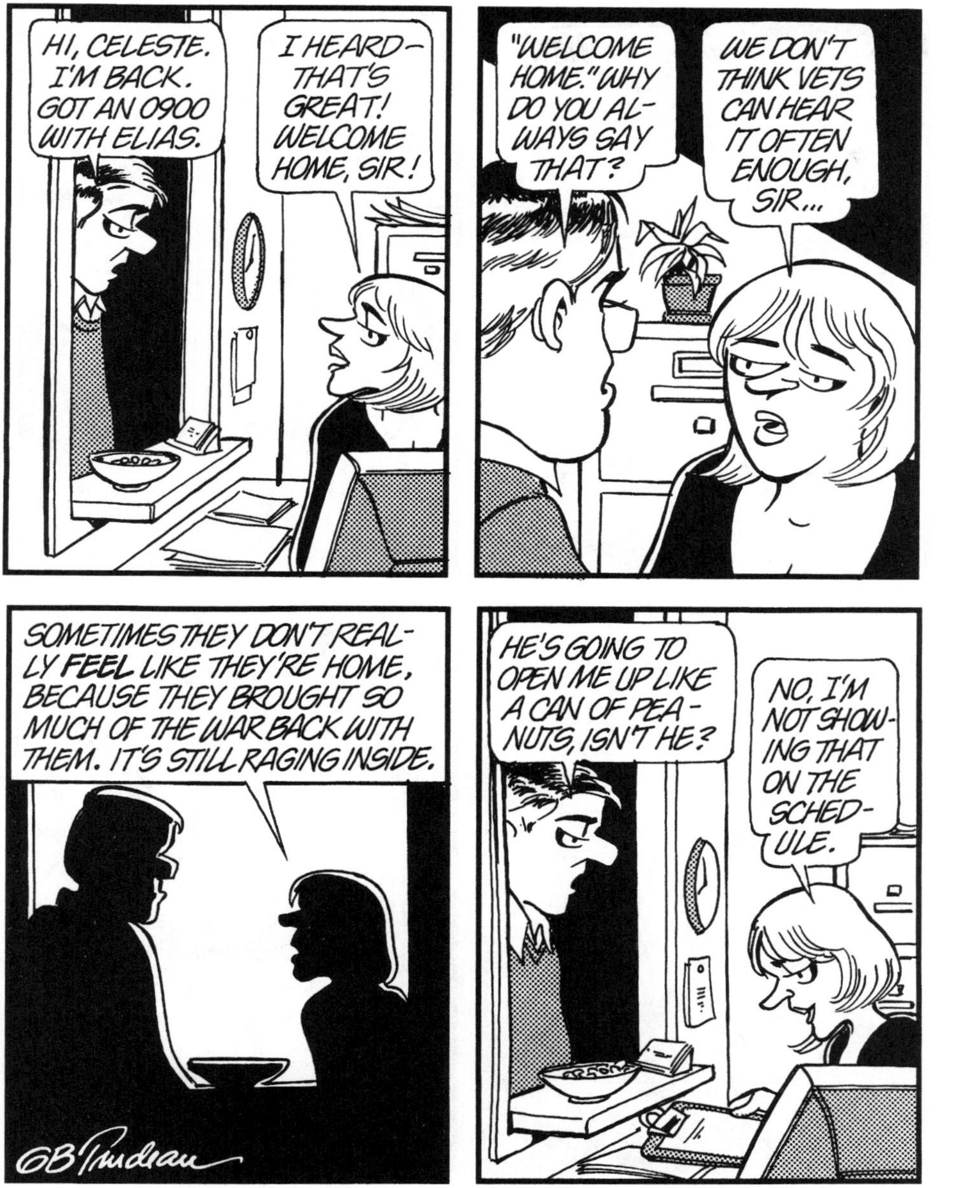
HI, CELESTE. I'M BACK. GOT AN 0900 WITH ELIAS.
I HEARD— THAT'S GREAT! WELCOME HOME, SIR!
"WELCOME HOME." WHY DO YOU ALWAYS SAY THAT?
WE DON'T THINK VETS CAN HEAR IT OFTEN ENOUGH, SIR...
SOMETIMES THEY DON'T REALLY **FEEL** LIKE THEY'RE HOME, BECAUSE THEY BROUGHT SO MUCH OF THE WAR BACK WITH THEM. IT'S STILL RAGING INSIDE.
GB Trudeau
HE'S GOING TO OPEN ME UP LIKE A CAN OF PEANUTS, ISN'T HE?
NO, I'M NOT SHOWING THAT ON THE SCHEDULE.

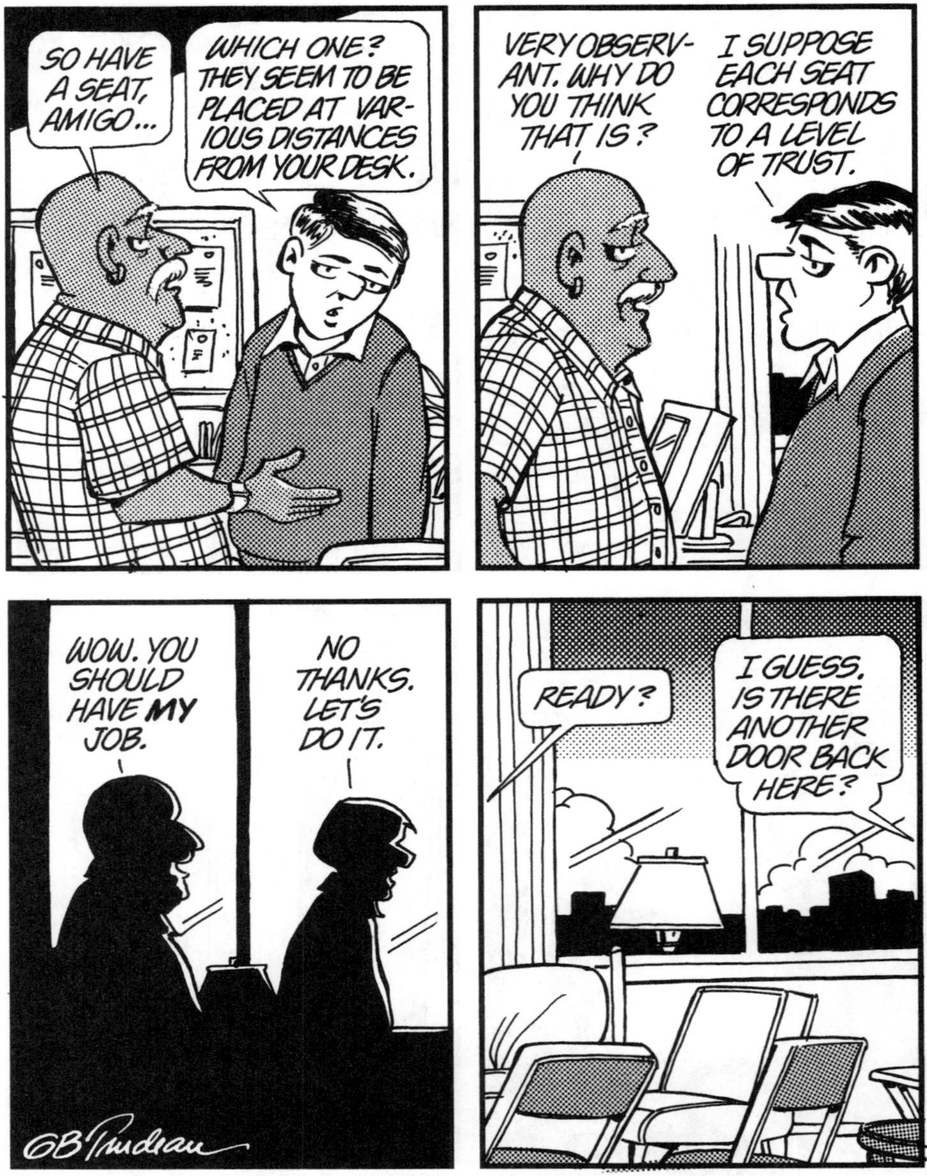
SO HAVE A SEAT, AMIGO...
WHICH ONE? THEY SEEM TO BE PLACED AT VARIOUS DISTANCES FROM YOUR DESK.
VERY OBSERVANT. WHY DO YOU THINK THAT IS?
I SUPPOSE EACH SEAT CORRESPONDS TO A LEVEL OF TRUST.
WOW. YOU SHOULD HAVE **MY** JOB.
NO THANKS. LET'S DO IT.
READY?
I GUESS. IS THERE ANOTHER DOOR BACK HERE?
GB Trudeau

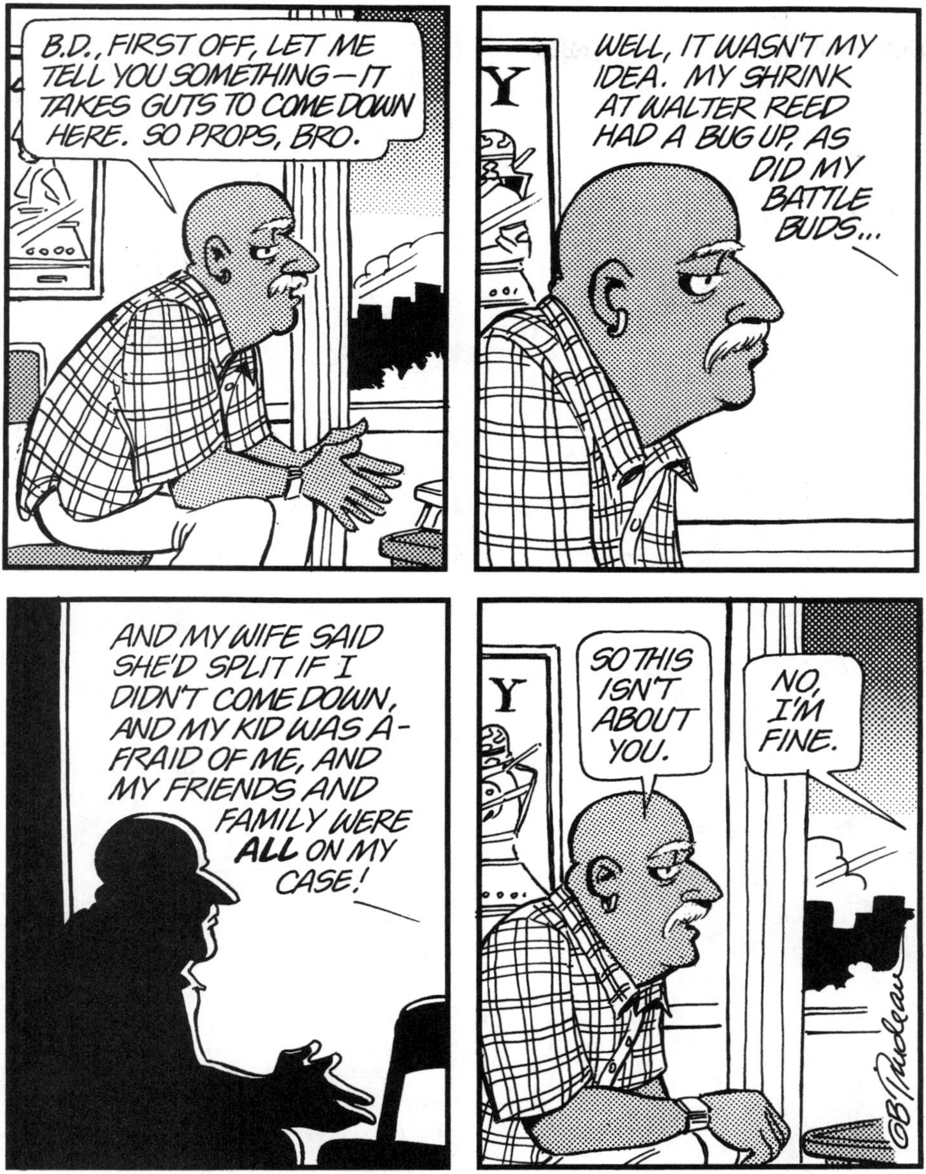
B.D., FIRST OFF, LET ME TELL YOU SOMETHING — IT TAKES GUTS TO COME DOWN HERE. SO PROPS, BRO.
WELL, IT WASN'T MY IDEA. MY SHRINK AT WALTER REED HAD A BUG UP, AS DID MY BATTLE BUDS...
AND MY WIFE SAID SHE'D SPLIT IF I DIDN'T COME DOWN, AND MY KID WAS AFRAID OF ME, AND MY FRIENDS AND FAMILY WERE **ALL** ON MY CASE!
SO THIS ISN'T ABOUT YOU.
NO, I'M FINE.
©B Trudeau

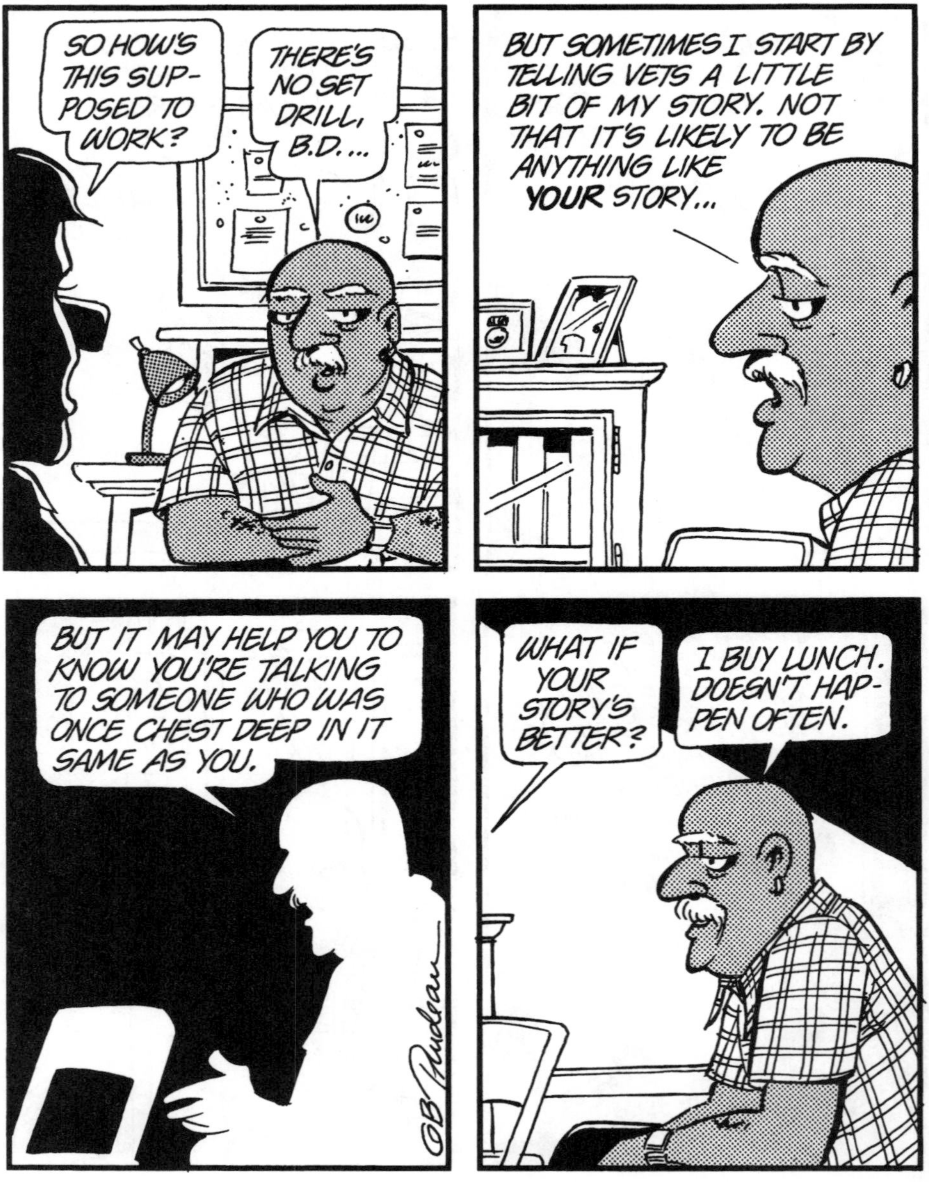
SO HOW'S THIS SUP-POSED TO WORK?
THERE'S NO SET DRILL, B.D....
BUT SOMETIMES I START BY TELLING VETS A LITTLE BIT OF MY STORY. NOT THAT IT'S LIKELY TO BE ANYTHING LIKE **YOUR** STORY...
BUT IT MAY HELP YOU TO KNOW YOU'RE TALKING TO SOMEONE WHO WAS ONCE CHEST DEEP IN IT SAME AS YOU.
WHAT IF YOUR STORY'S BETTER?
I BUY LUNCH. DOESN'T HAP-PEN OFTEN.
GB Trudeau

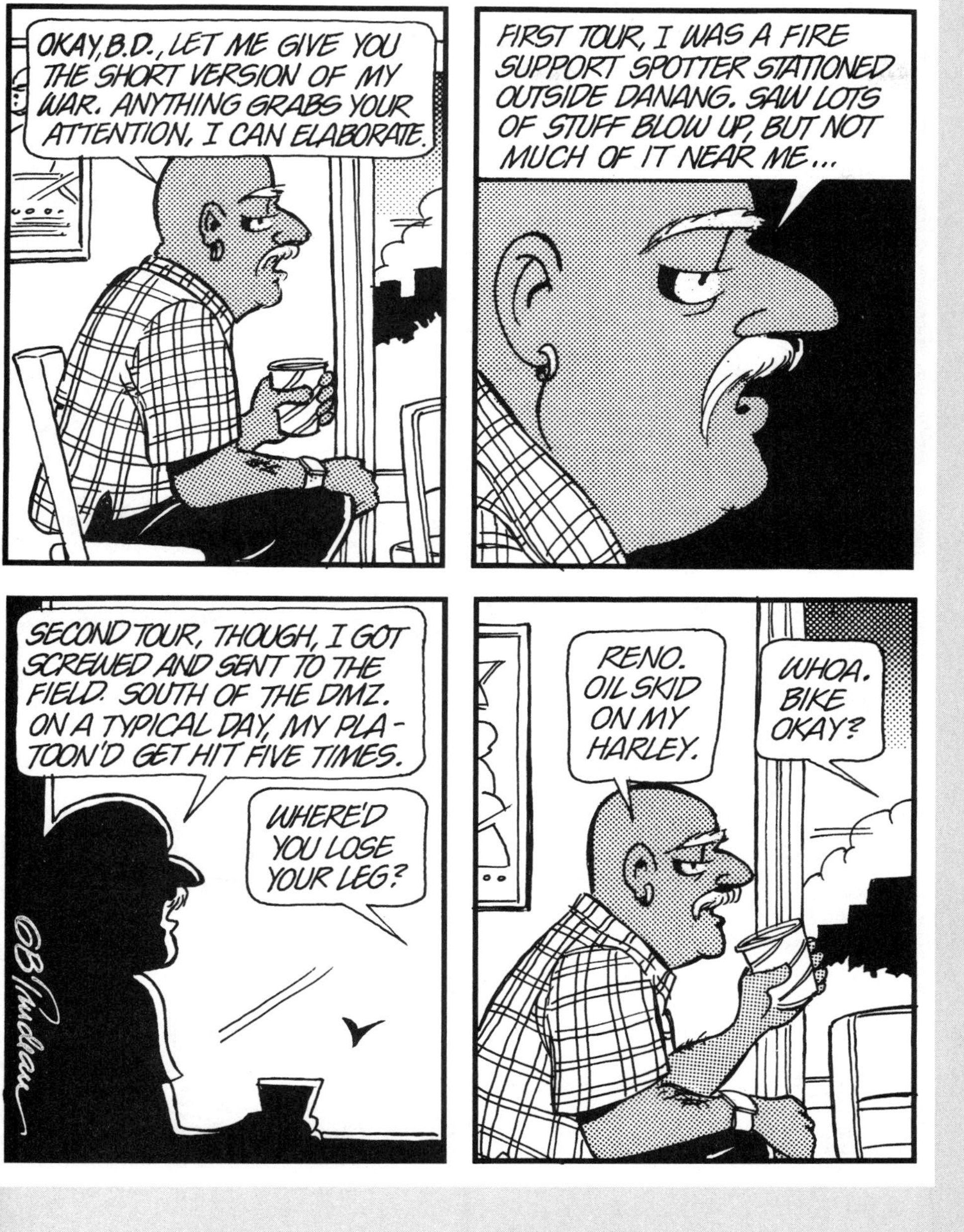
OKAY, B.D., LET ME GIVE YOU THE SHORT VERSION OF MY WAR. ANYTHING GRABS YOUR ATTENTION, I CAN ELABORATE.
FIRST TOUR, I WAS A FIRE SUPPORT SPOTTER STATIONED OUTSIDE DANANG. SAW LOTS OF STUFF BLOW UP, BUT NOT MUCH OF IT NEAR ME...
SECOND TOUR, THOUGH, I GOT SCREWED AND SENT TO THE FIELD. SOUTH OF THE DMZ. ON A TYPICAL DAY, MY PLA-TOON'D GET HIT FIVE TIMES.
WHERE'D YOU LOSE YOUR LEG?
RENO. OIL SKID ON MY HARLEY.
WHOA. BIKE OKAY?
©B Trudeau

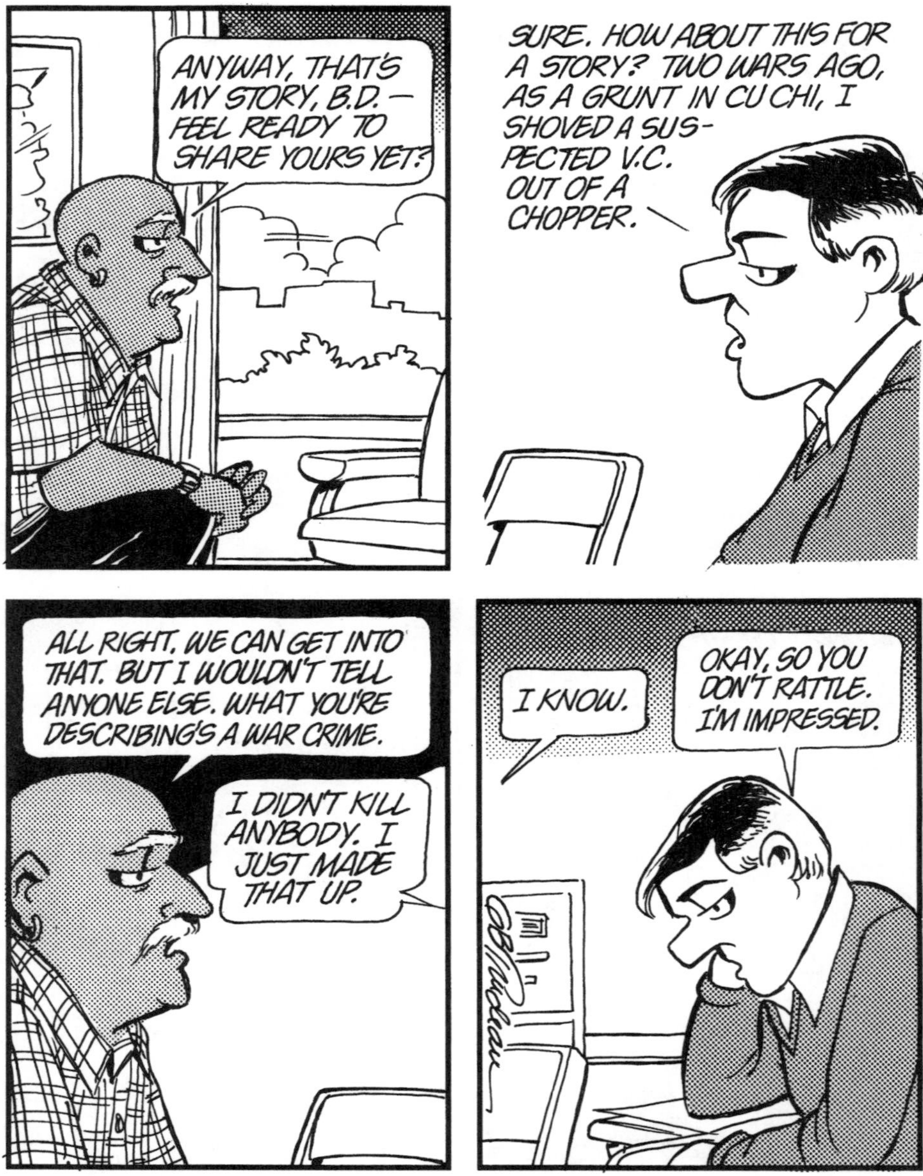
ANYWAY, THAT'S MY STORY, B.D.— FEEL READY TO SHARE YOURS YET?
SURE. HOW ABOUT THIS FOR A STORY? TWO WARS AGO, AS A GRUNT IN CU CHI, I SHOVED A SUS-PECTED V.C. OUT OF A CHOPPER.
ALL RIGHT, WE CAN GET INTO THAT. BUT I WOULDN'T TELL ANYONE ELSE. WHAT YOU'RE DESCRIBING'S A WAR CRIME.
I DIDN'T KILL ANYBODY. I JUST MADE THAT UP.
OKAY, SO YOU DON'T RATTLE. I'M IMPRESSED.
I KNOW.

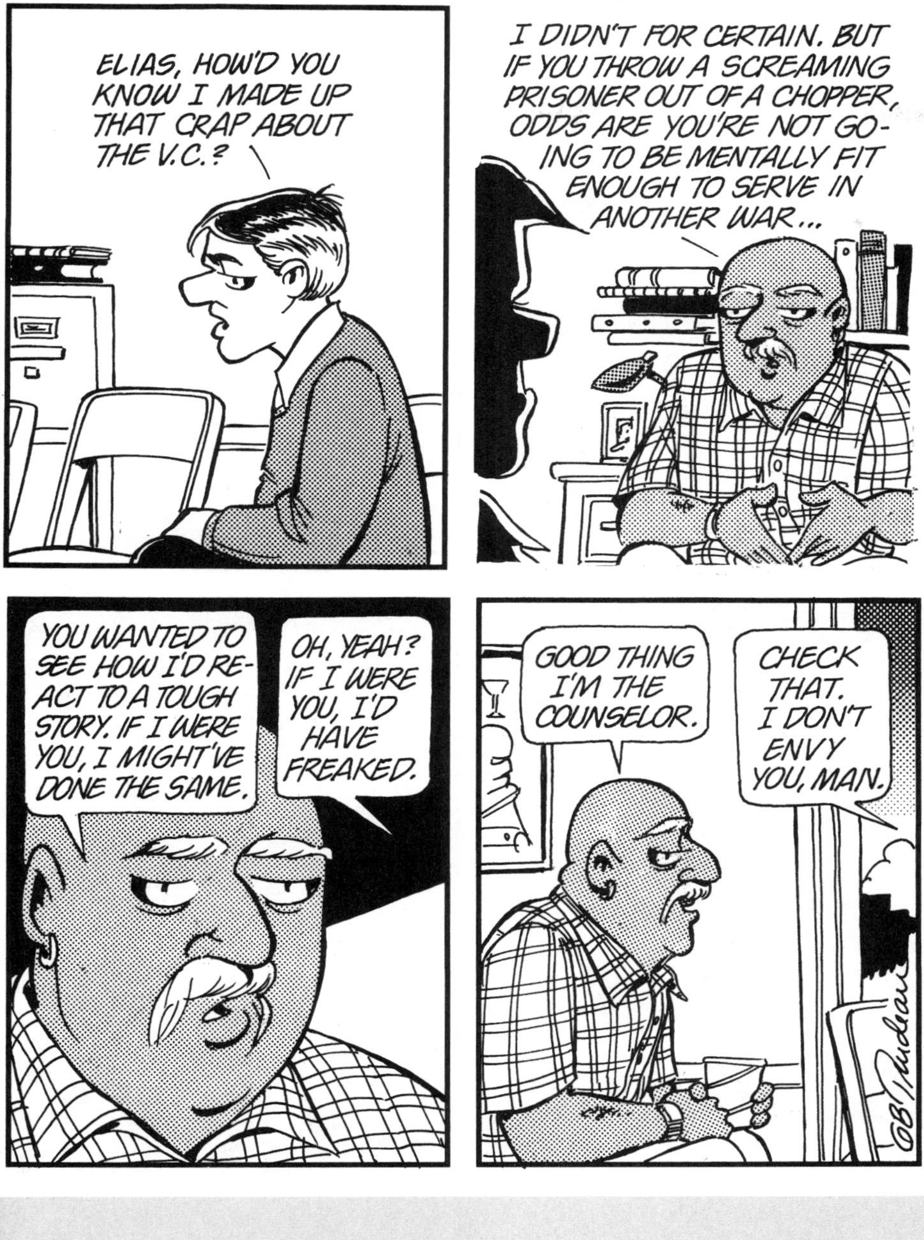
ELIAS, HOW'D YOU KNOW I MADE UP THAT CRAP ABOUT THE V.C.?
I DIDN'T FOR CERTAIN. BUT IF YOU THROW A SCREAMING PRISONER OUT OF A CHOPPER, ODDS ARE YOU'RE NOT GOING TO BE MENTALLY FIT ENOUGH TO SERVE IN ANOTHER WAR...
YOU WANTED TO SEE HOW I'D REACT TO A TOUGH STORY. IF I WERE YOU, I MIGHT'VE DONE THE SAME.
OH, YEAH? IF I WERE YOU, I'D HAVE FREAKED.
GOOD THING I'M THE COUNSELOR.
CHECK THAT. I DON'T ENVY YOU, MAN.
GBTrudeau

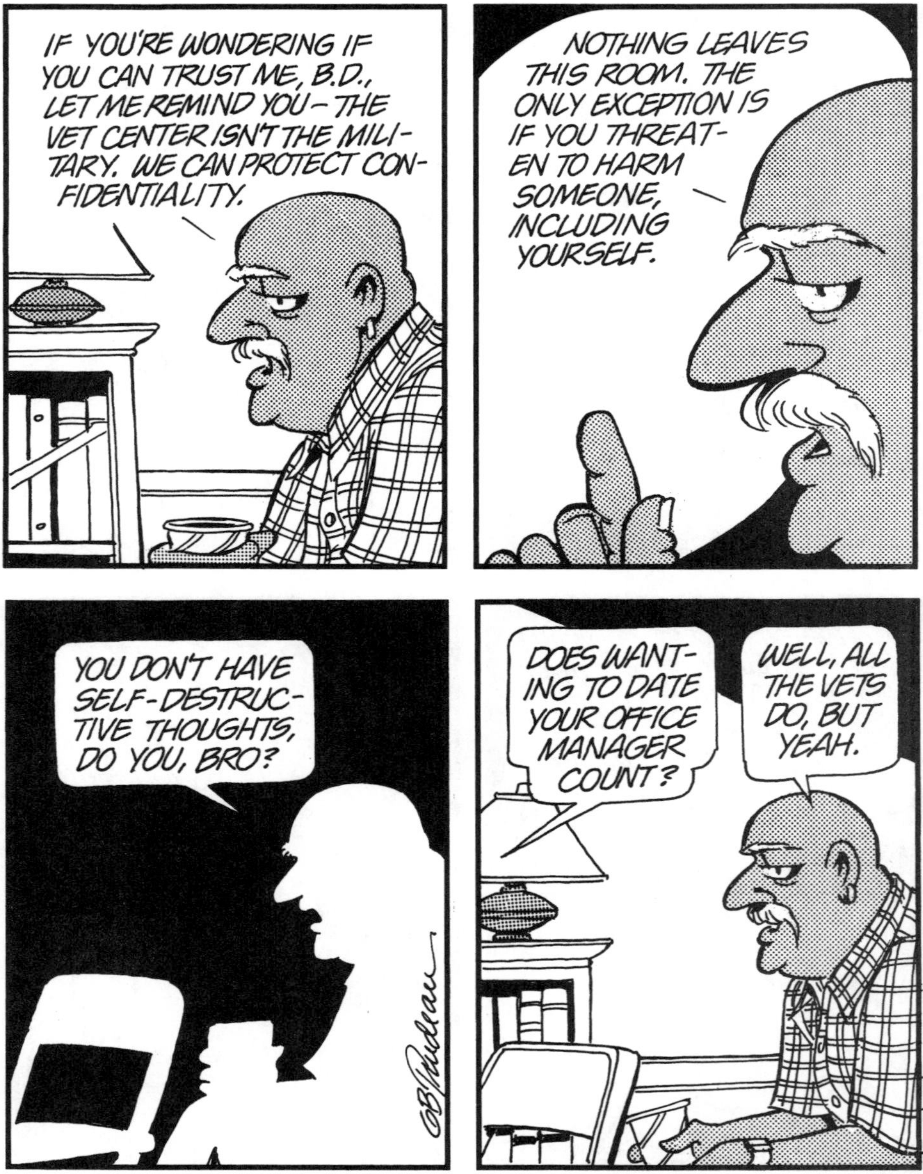
IF YOU'RE WONDERING IF YOU CAN TRUST ME, B.D., LET ME REMIND YOU—THE VET CENTER ISN'T THE MILITARY. WE CAN PROTECT CONFIDENTIALITY.
NOTHING LEAVES THIS ROOM. THE ONLY EXCEPTION IS IF YOU THREATEN TO HARM SOMEONE, INCLUDING YOURSELF.
YOU DON'T HAVE SELF-DESTRUCTIVE THOUGHTS, DO YOU, BRO?
DOES WANTING TO DATE YOUR OFFICE MANAGER COUNT?
WELL, ALL THE VETS DO, BUT YEAH.

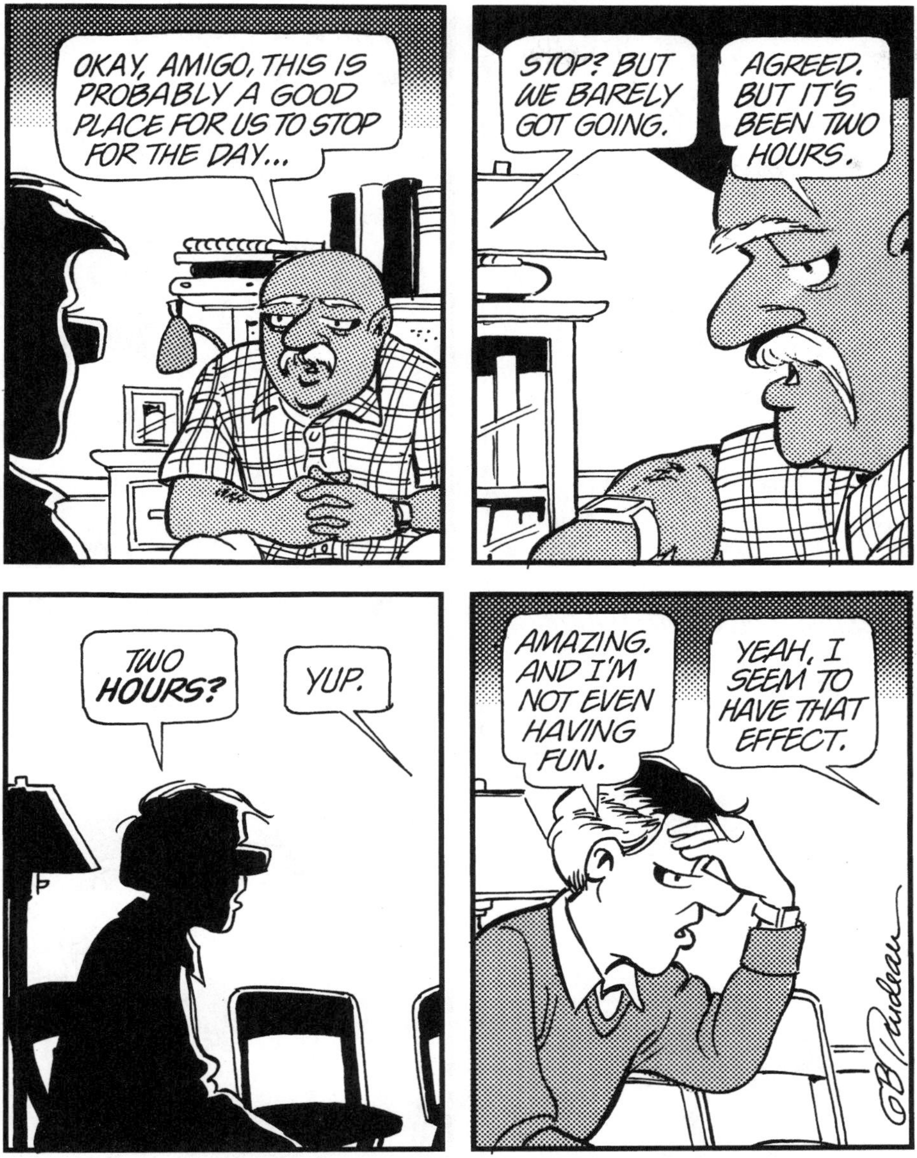
OKAY, AMIGO, THIS IS PROBABLY A GOOD PLACE FOR US TO STOP FOR THE DAY...
STOP? BUT WE BARELY GOT GOING.
AGREED. BUT IT'S BEEN TWO HOURS.
TWO **HOURS?**
YUP.
AMAZING. AND I'M NOT EVEN HAVING FUN.
YEAH, I SEEM TO HAVE THAT EFFECT.
©B Trudeau

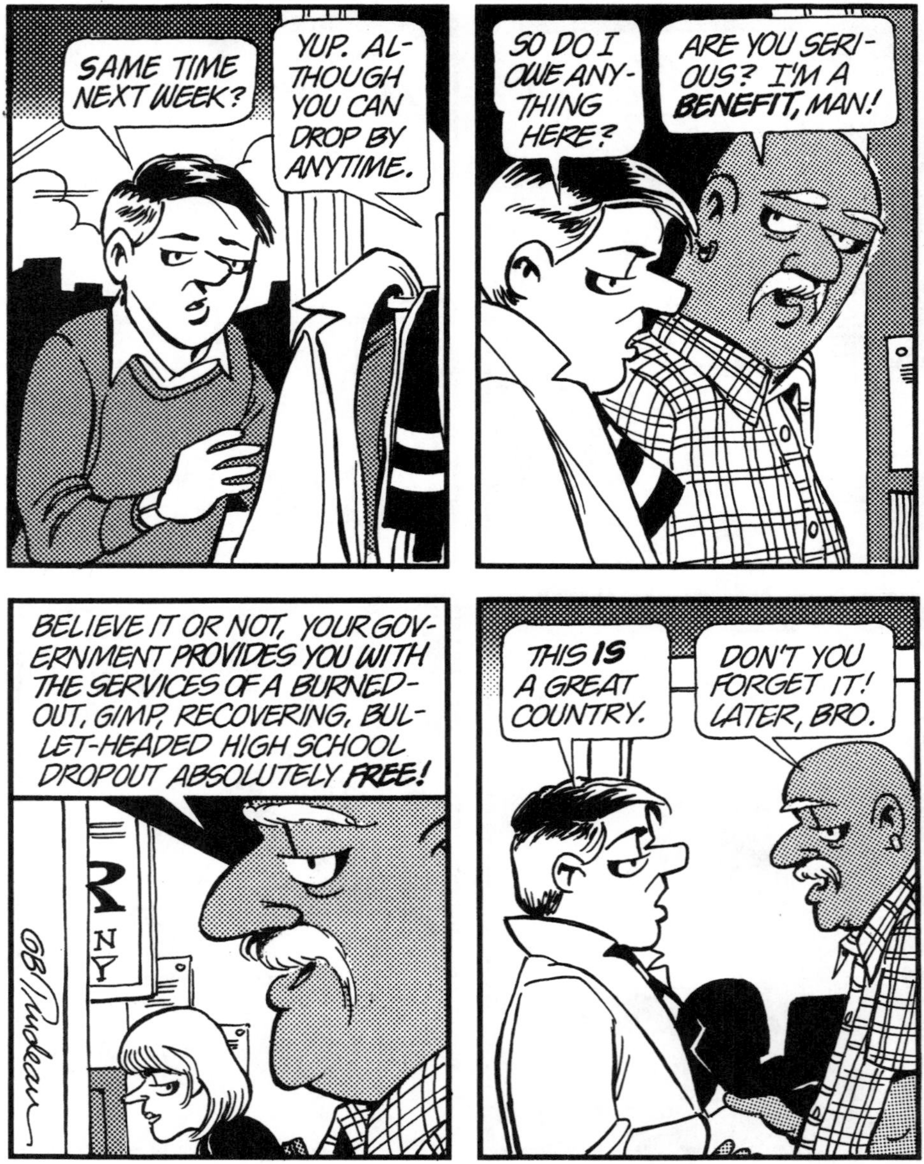
SAME TIME NEXT WEEK?
YUP. ALTHOUGH YOU CAN DROP BY ANYTIME.
SO DO I OWE ANYTHING HERE?
ARE YOU SERIOUS? I'M A **BENEFIT,** MAN!
BELIEVE IT OR NOT, YOUR GOVERNMENT PROVIDES YOU WITH THE SERVICES OF A BURNED-OUT, GIMP, RECOVERING, BULLET-HEADED HIGH SCHOOL DROPOUT ABSOLUTELY **FREE!**
THIS **IS** A GREAT COUNTRY.
DON'T YOU FORGET IT! LATER, BRO.

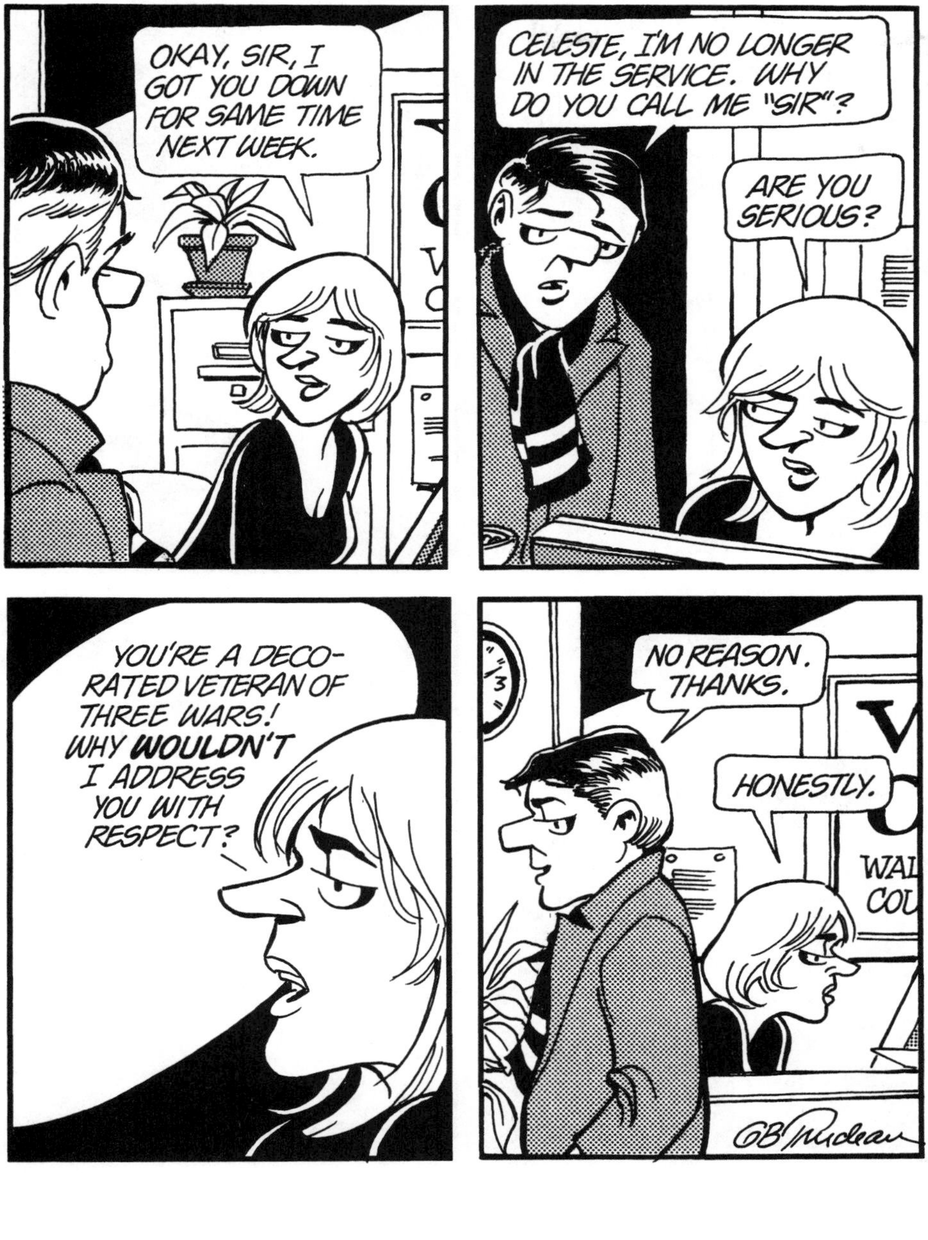
OKAY, SIR, I GOT YOU DOWN FOR SAME TIME NEXT WEEK.
CELESTE, I'M NO LONGER IN THE SERVICE. WHY DO YOU CALL ME "SIR"?
ARE YOU SERIOUS?
YOU'RE A DECORATED VETERAN OF THREE WARS! WHY **WOULDN'T** I ADDRESS YOU WITH RESPECT?
NO REASON. THANKS.
HONESTLY.
GBTrudeau

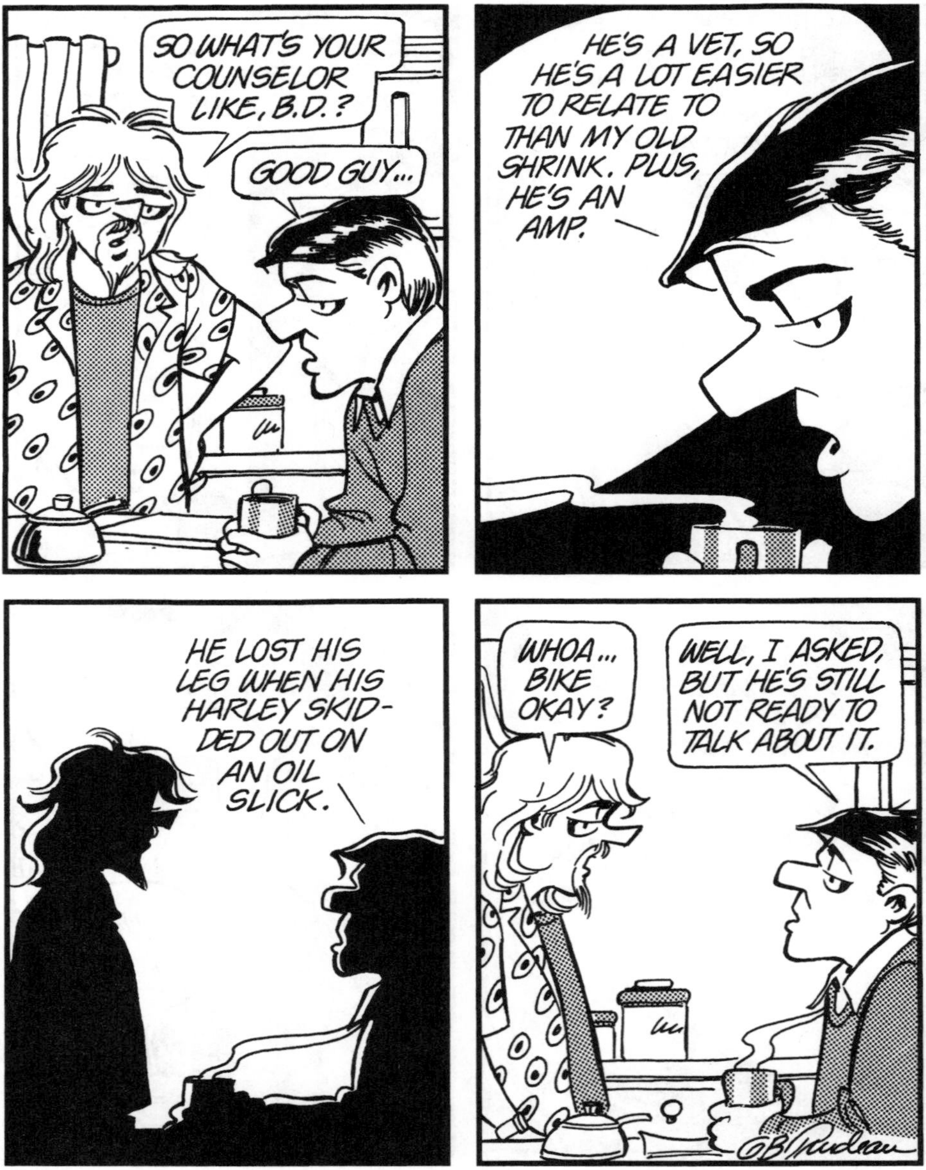
SO WHAT'S YOUR COUNSELOR LIKE, B.D.?
GOOD GUY...
HE'S A VET, SO HE'S A LOT EASIER TO RELATE TO THAN MY OLD SHRINK. PLUS, HE'S AN AMP.
HE LOST HIS LEG WHEN HIS HARLEY SKID-DED OUT ON AN OIL SLICK.
WHOA... BIKE OKAY?
WELL, I ASKED, BUT HE'S STILL NOT READY TO TALK ABOUT IT.

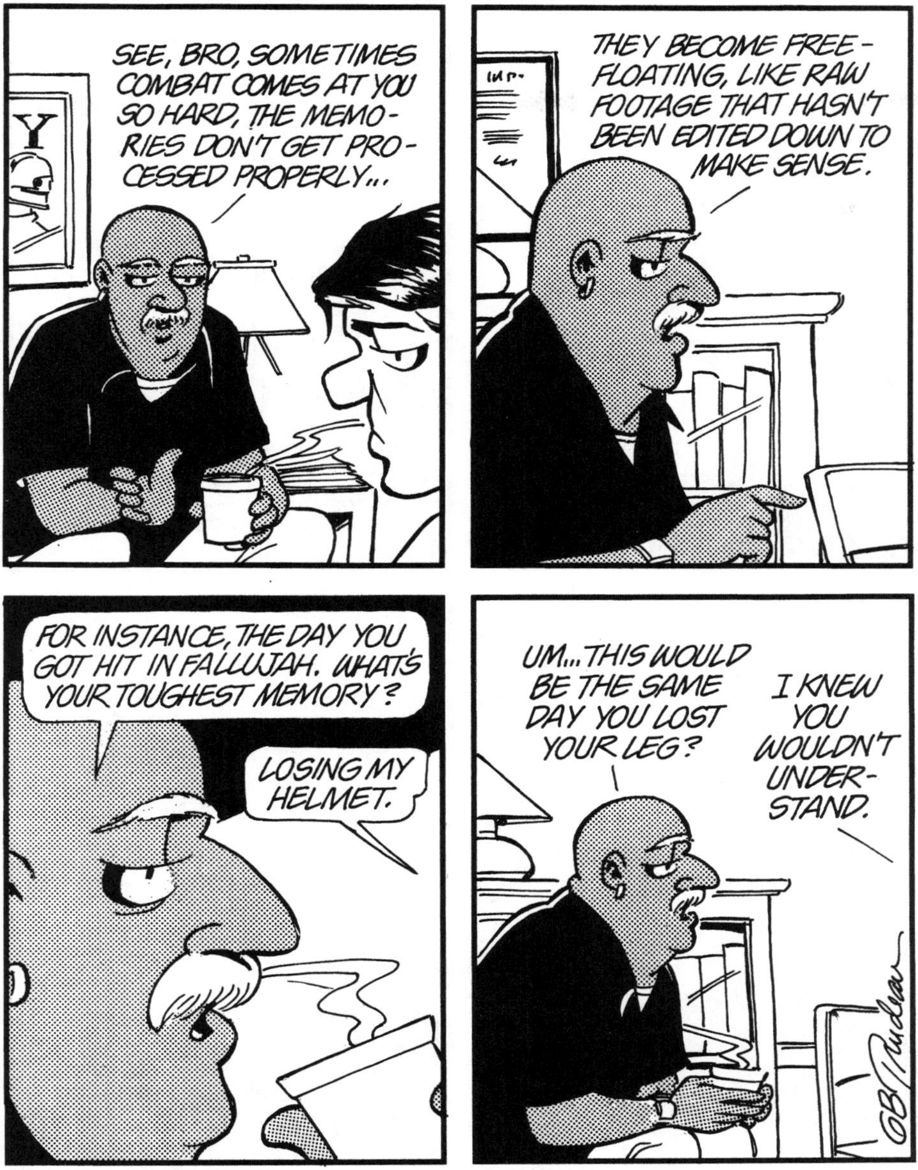
SEE, BRO, SOMETIMES COMBAT COMES AT YOU SO HARD, THE MEMORIES DON'T GET PROCESSED PROPERLY...
THEY BECOME FREE-FLOATING, LIKE RAW FOOTAGE THAT HASN'T BEEN EDITED DOWN TO MAKE SENSE.
FOR INSTANCE, THE DAY YOU GOT HIT IN FALLUJAH. WHAT'S YOUR TOUGHEST MEMORY?
LOSING MY HELMET.
UM... THIS WOULD BE THE SAME DAY YOU LOST YOUR LEG?
I KNEW YOU WOULDN'T UNDERSTAND.
GBTrudeau

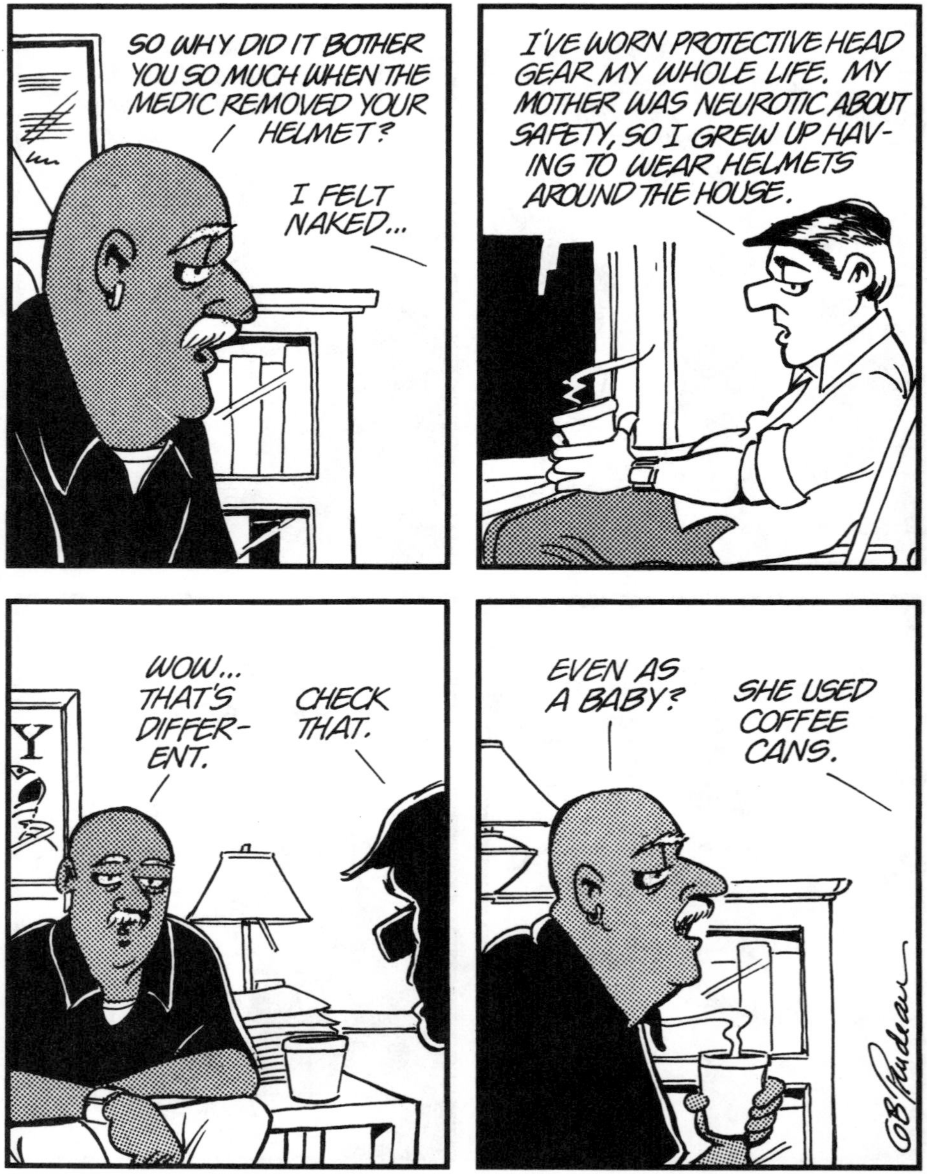
SO WHY DID IT BOTHER YOU SO MUCH WHEN THE MEDIC REMOVED YOUR HELMET?
I FELT NAKED...
I'VE WORN PROTECTIVE HEAD GEAR MY WHOLE LIFE. MY MOTHER WAS NEUROTIC ABOUT SAFETY, SO I GREW UP HAVING TO WEAR HELMETS AROUND THE HOUSE.
WOW... THAT'S DIFFERENT.
CHECK THAT.
EVEN AS A BABY?
SHE USED COFFEE CANS.
GBTrudeau

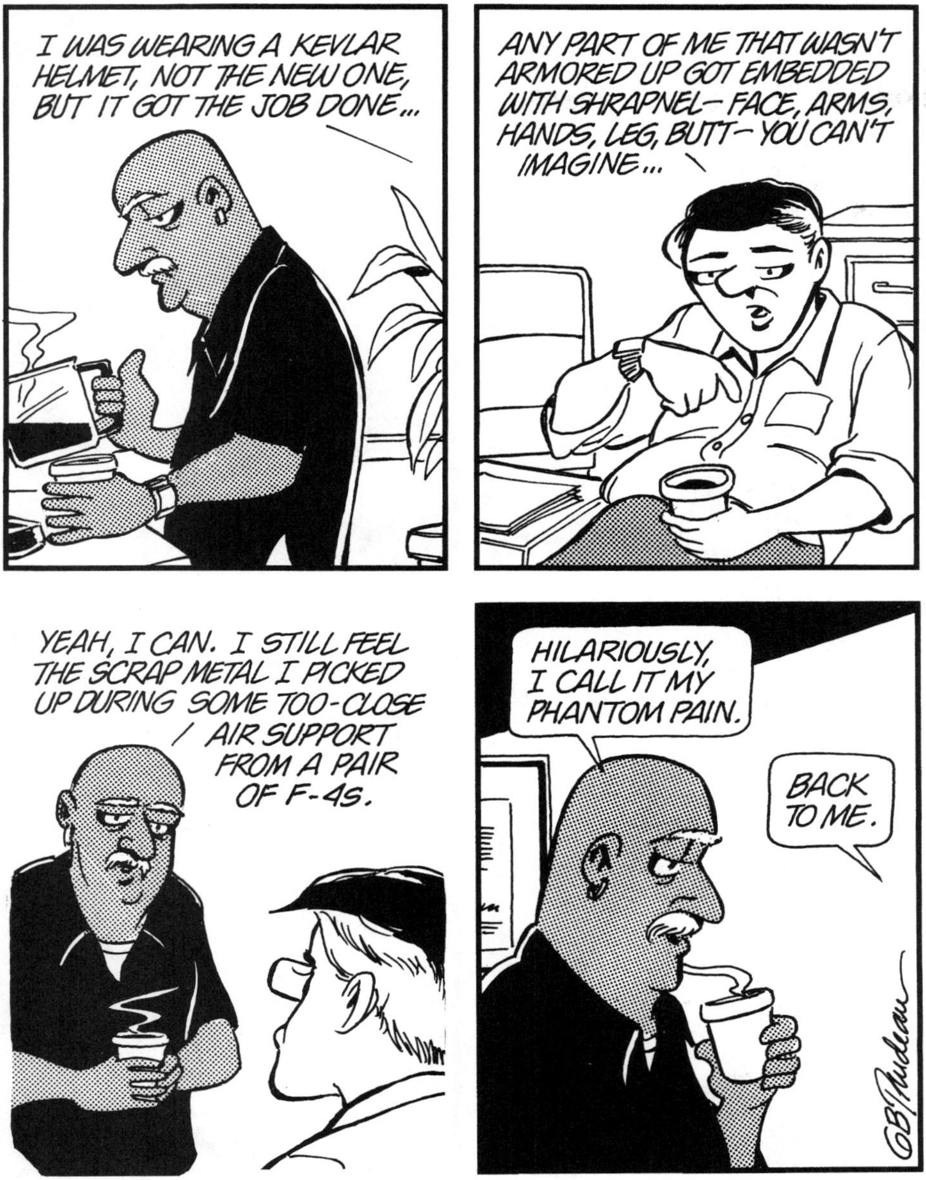
I WAS WEARING A KEVLAR HELMET, NOT THE NEW ONE, BUT IT GOT THE JOB DONE...
ANY PART OF ME THAT WASN'T ARMORED UP GOT EMBEDDED WITH SHRAPNEL– FACE, ARMS, HANDS, LEG, BUTT– YOU CAN'T IMAGINE...
YEAH, I CAN. I STILL FEEL THE SCRAP METAL I PICKED UP DURING SOME TOO-CLOSE AIR SUPPORT FROM A PAIR OF F-4s.
HILARIOUSLY, I CALL IT MY PHANTOM PAIN.
BACK TO ME.
©B Trudeau

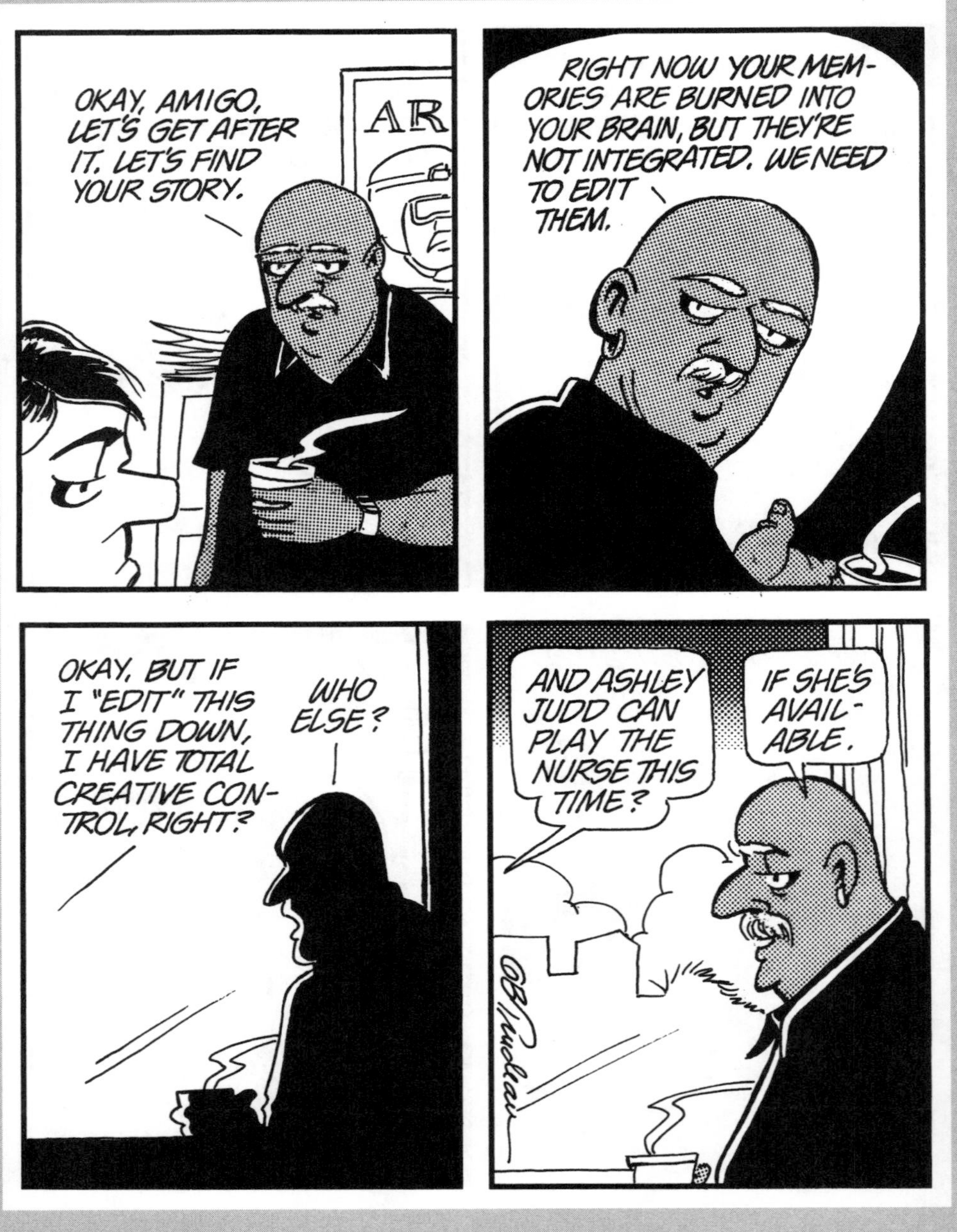
OKAY, AMIGO, LET'S GET AFTER IT. LET'S FIND YOUR STORY.
AR
RIGHT NOW YOUR MEMORIES ARE BURNED INTO YOUR BRAIN, BUT THEY'RE NOT INTEGRATED. WE NEED TO EDIT THEM.
OKAY, BUT IF I "EDIT" THIS THING DOWN, I HAVE TOTAL CREATIVE CONTROL, RIGHT?
WHO ELSE?
AND ASHLEY JUDD CAN PLAY THE NURSE THIS TIME?
IF SHE'S AVAILABLE.

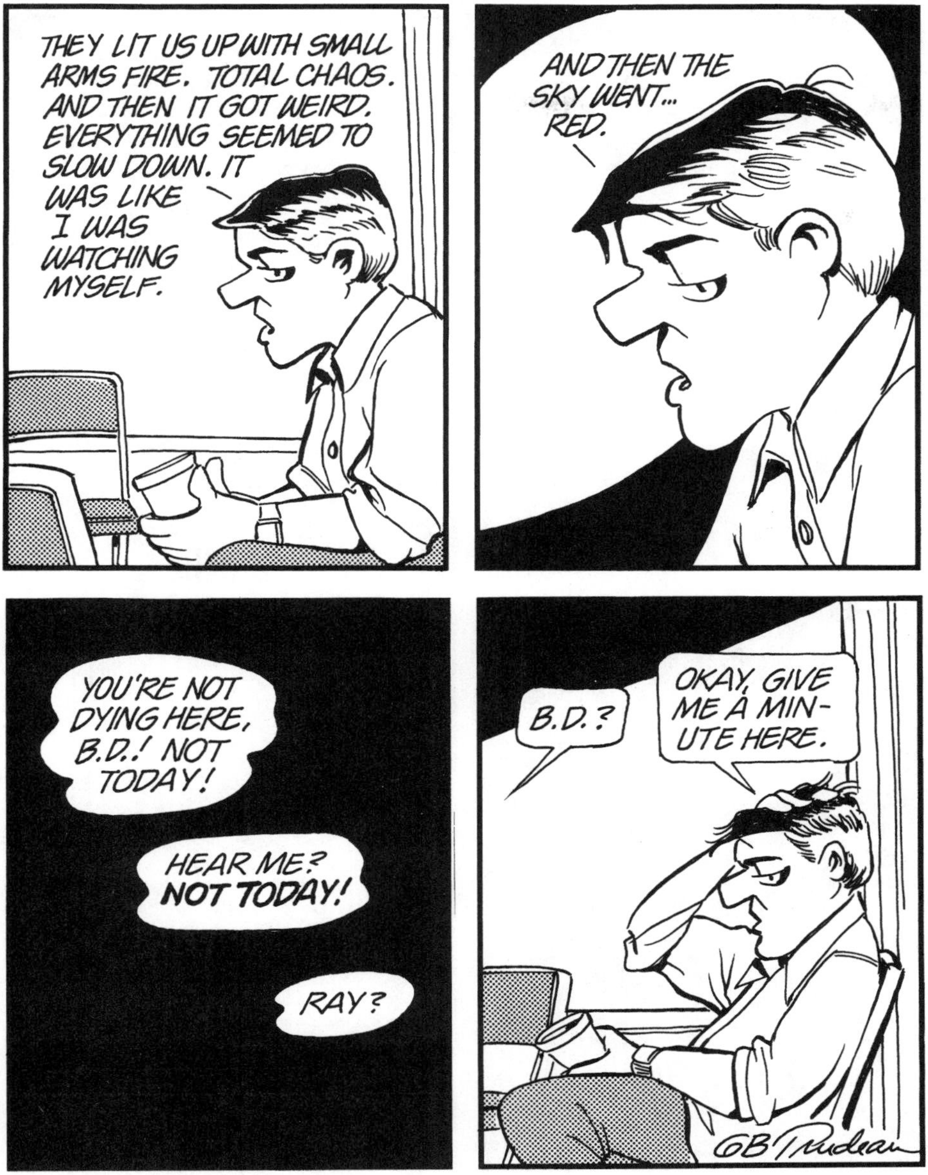
THEY LIT US UP WITH SMALL ARMS FIRE. TOTAL CHAOS. AND THEN IT GOT WEIRD. EVERYTHING SEEMED TO SLOW DOWN. IT WAS LIKE I WAS WATCHING MYSELF.
AND THEN THE SKY WENT... RED.
YOU'RE NOT DYING HERE, B.D.! NOT TODAY!
HEAR ME? **NOT TODAY!**
RAY?
B.D.?
OKAY, GIVE ME A MIN-UTE HERE.
GB Trudeau

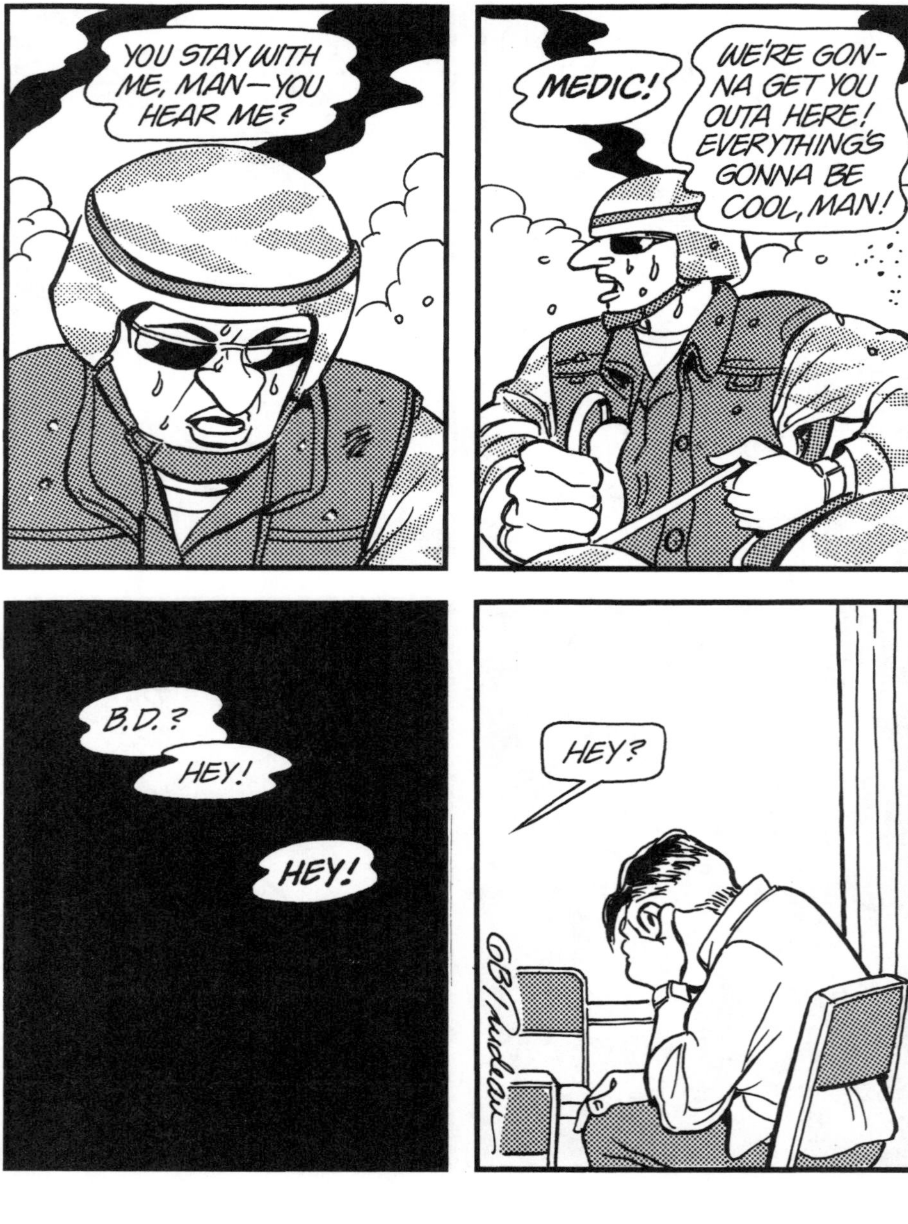
YOU STAY WITH ME, MAN—YOU HEAR ME?
MEDIC!
WE'RE GON-NA GET YOU OUTA HERE! EVERYTHING'S GONNA BE COOL, MAN!
B.D.?
HEY!
HEY!
HEY?
GBTrudeau

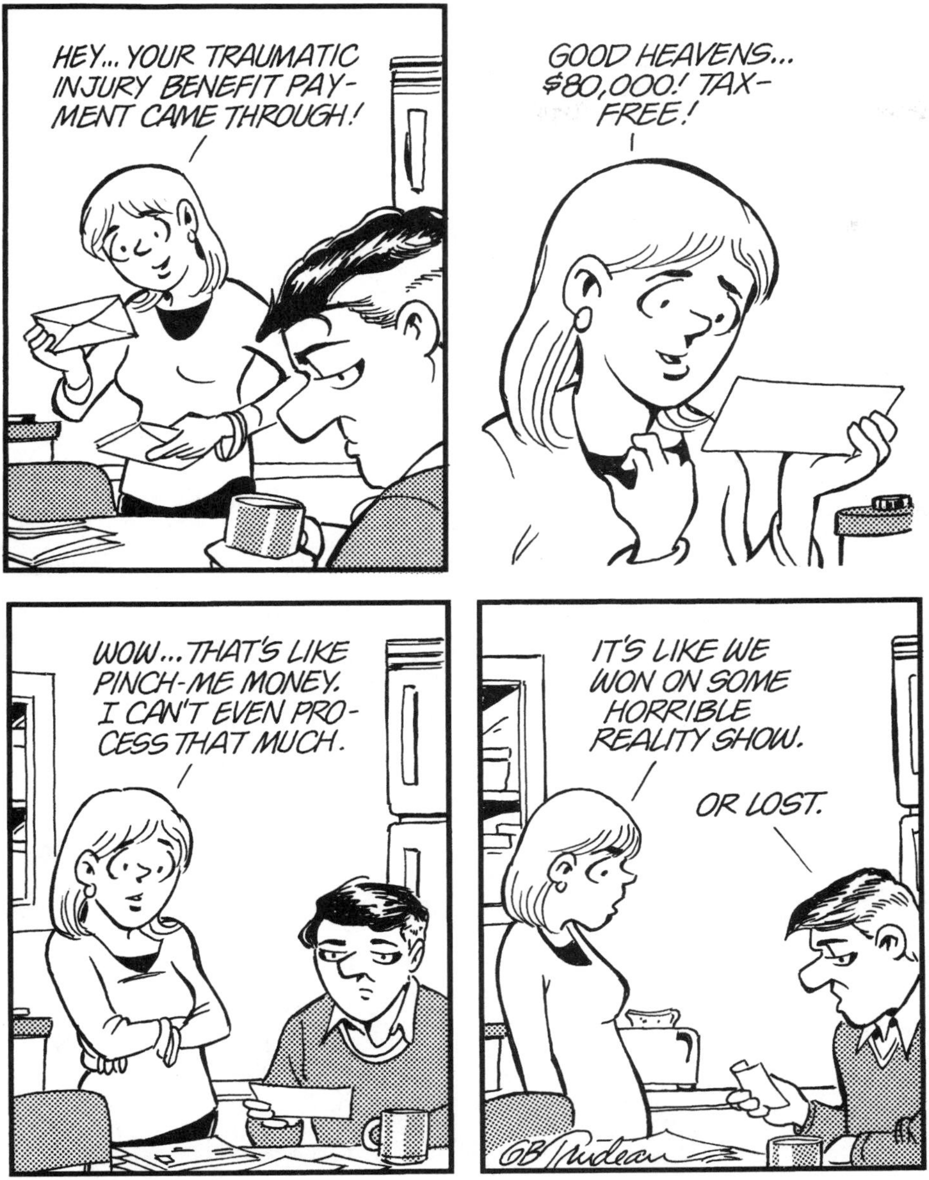
HEY... YOUR TRAUMATIC INJURY BENEFIT PAY-MENT CAME THROUGH!
GOOD HEAVENS... $80,000! TAX-FREE!
WOW... THAT'S LIKE PINCH-ME MONEY. I CAN'T EVEN PRO-CESS THAT MUCH.
IT'S LIKE WE WON ON SOME HORRIBLE REALITY SHOW.
OR LOST.
GB Trudeau

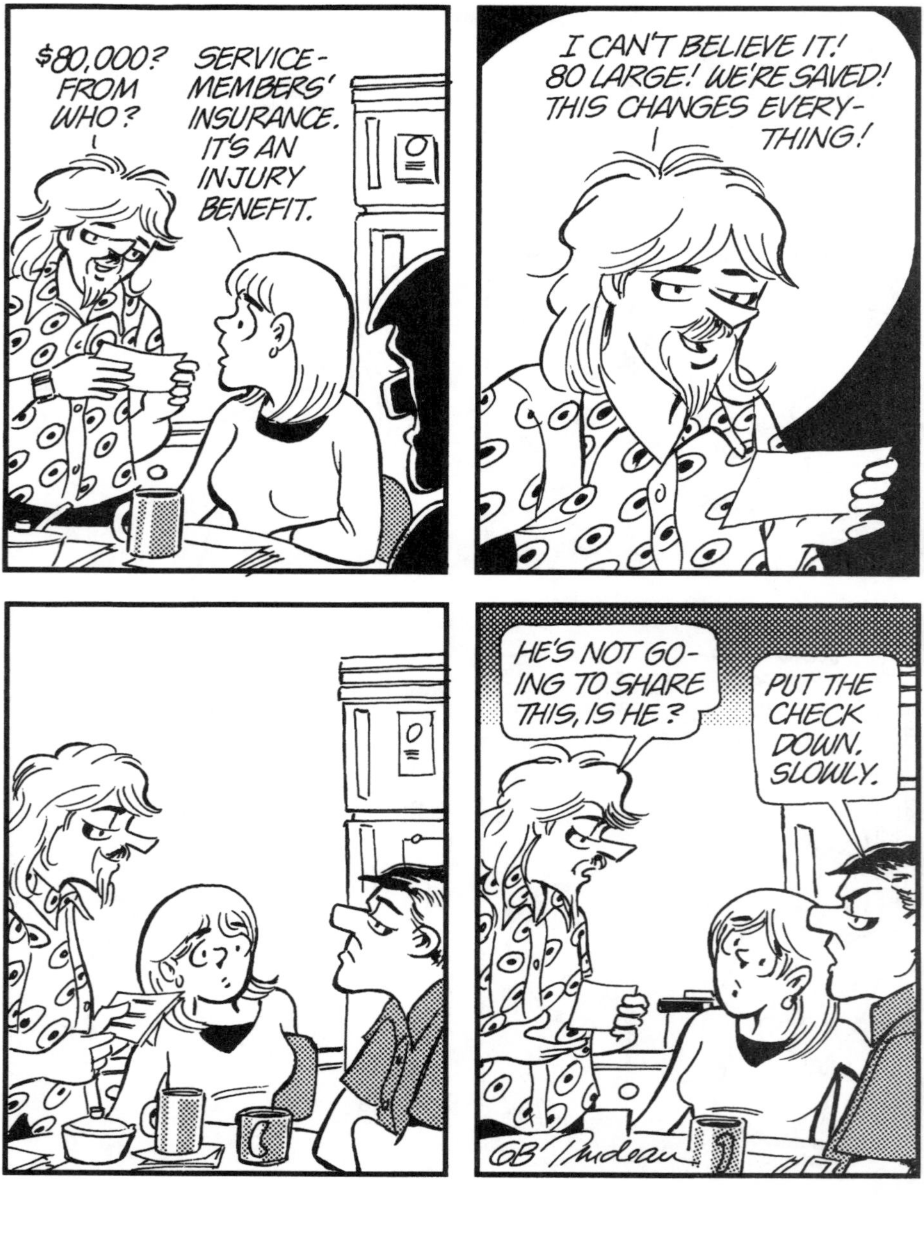
$80,000? FROM WHO?
SERVICE-MEMBERS' INSURANCE. IT'S AN INJURY BENEFIT.
I CAN'T BELIEVE IT! 80 LARGE! WE'RE SAVED! THIS CHANGES EVERY-THING!
HE'S NOT GO-ING TO SHARE THIS, IS HE?
PUT THE CHECK DOWN. SLOWLY.
GB Trudeau

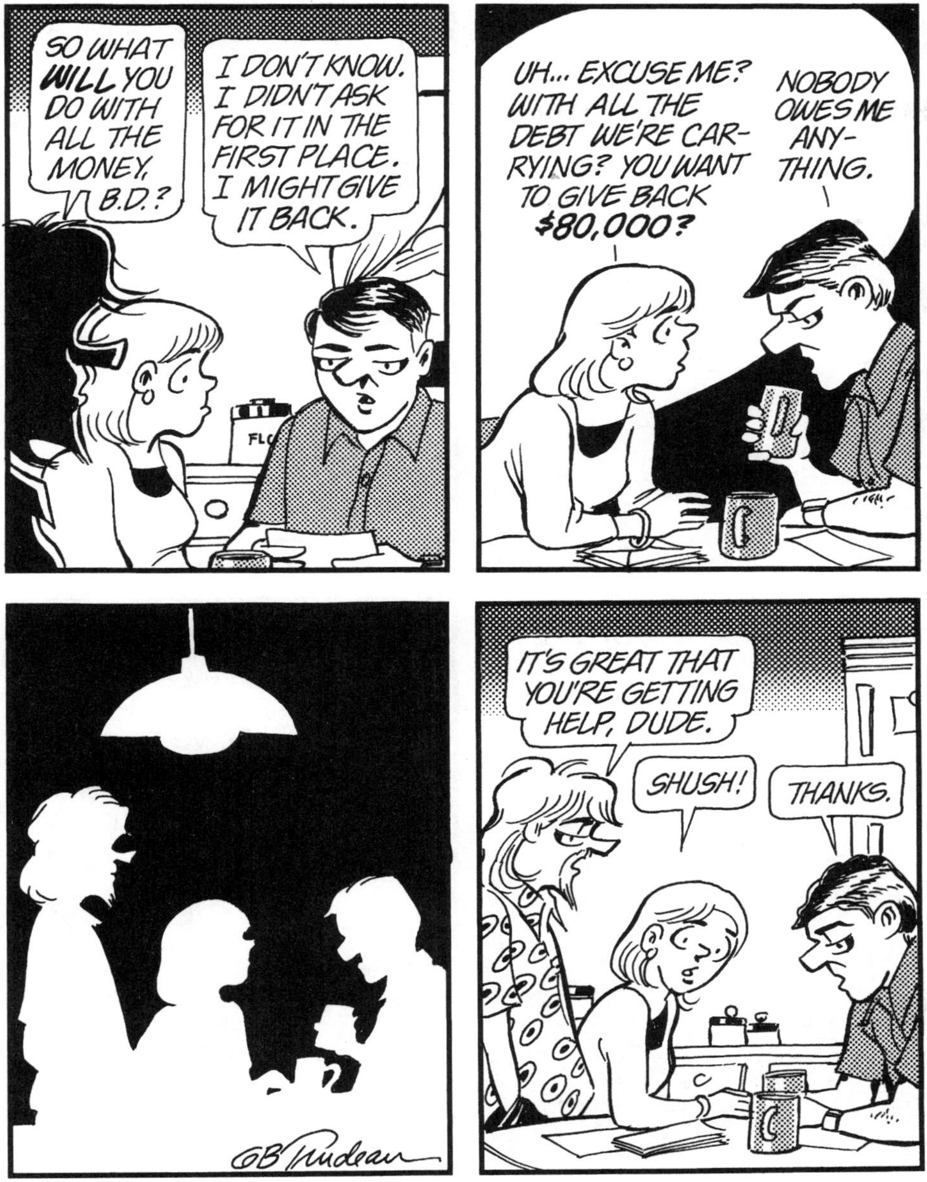
SO WHAT WILL YOU DO WITH ALL THE MONEY, B.D.?
I DON'T KNOW. I DIDN'T ASK FOR IT IN THE FIRST PLACE. I MIGHT GIVE IT BACK.
UH... EXCUSE ME? WITH ALL THE DEBT WE'RE CARRYING? YOU WANT TO GIVE BACK $80,000?
NOBODY OWES ME ANYTHING.
IT'S GREAT THAT YOU'RE GETTING HELP, DUDE.
SHUSH!
THANKS.
GB Trudeau

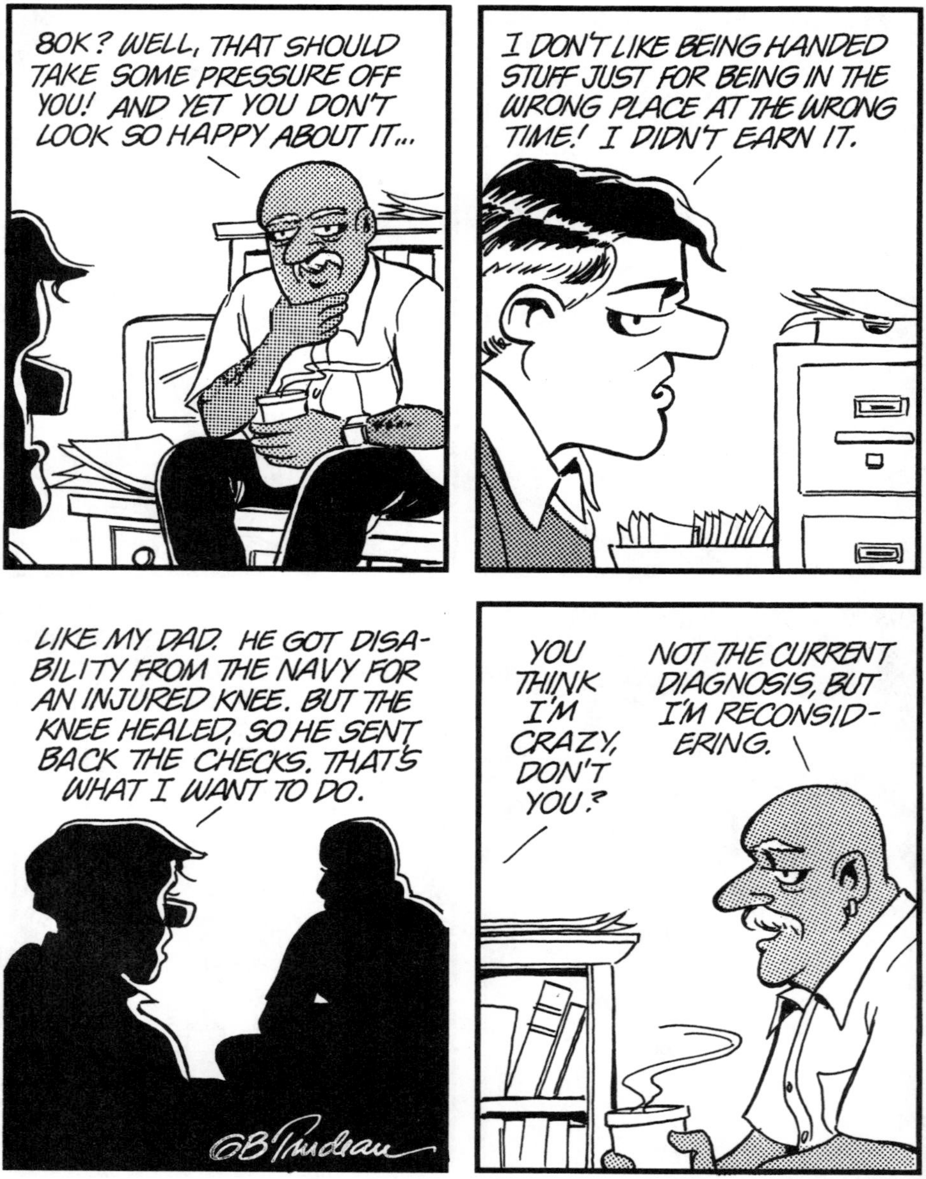
80K? WELL, THAT SHOULD TAKE SOME PRESSURE OFF YOU! AND YET YOU DON'T LOOK SO HAPPY ABOUT IT...
I DON'T LIKE BEING HANDED STUFF JUST FOR BEING IN THE WRONG PLACE AT THE WRONG TIME! I DIDN'T EARN IT.
LIKE MY DAD. HE GOT DISABILITY FROM THE NAVY FOR AN INJURED KNEE. BUT THE KNEE HEALED, SO HE SENT BACK THE CHECKS. THAT'S WHAT I WANT TO DO.
©B Trudeau
YOU THINK I'M CRAZY, DON'T YOU?
NOT THE CURRENT DIAGNOSIS, BUT I'M RECONSIDERING.

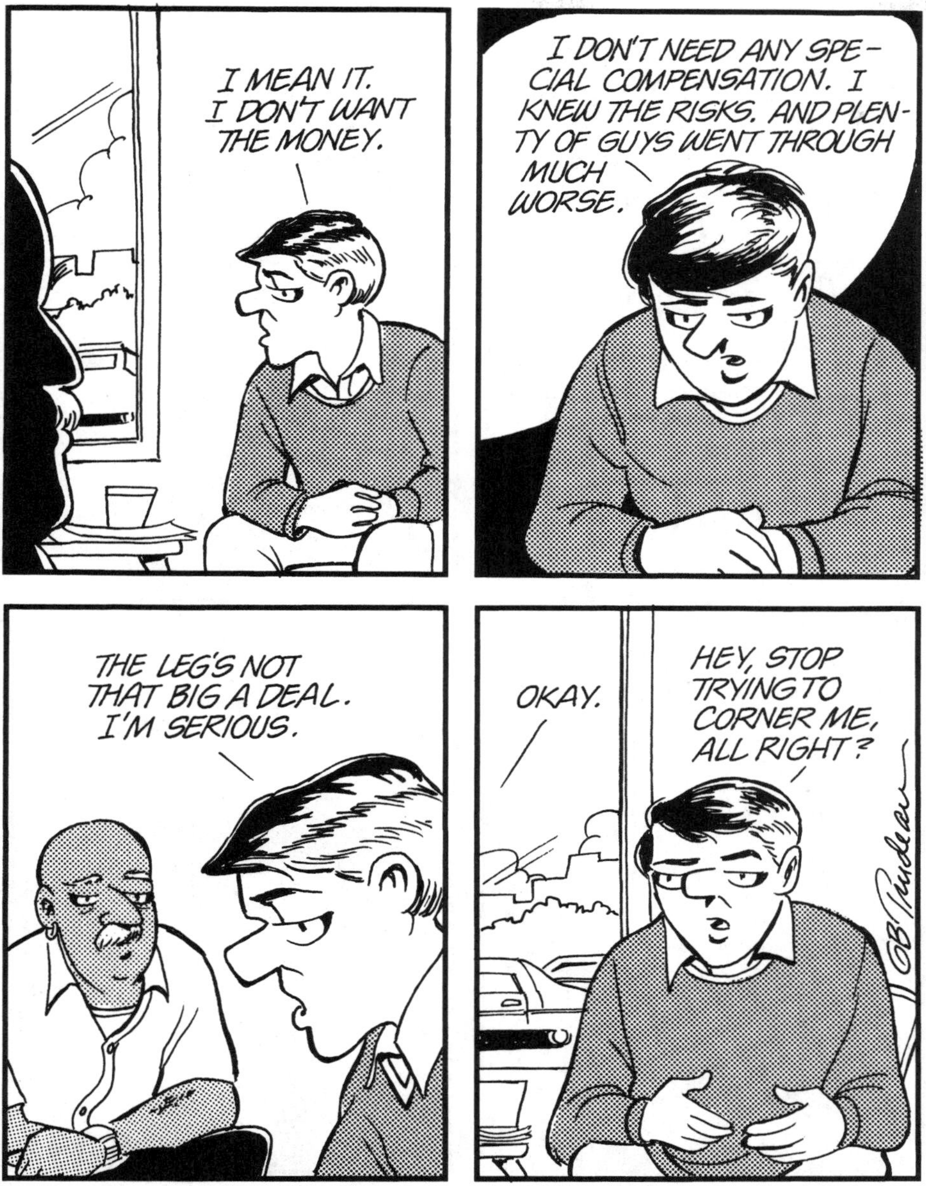
I MEAN IT. I DON'T WANT THE MONEY.
I DON'T NEED ANY SPE- CIAL COMPENSATION. I KNEW THE RISKS. AND PLEN- TY OF GUYS WENT THROUGH MUCH WORSE.
THE LEG'S NOT THAT BIG A DEAL. I'M SERIOUS.
OKAY.
HEY, STOP TRYING TO CORNER ME, ALL RIGHT?
GB Trudeau

LOOK, B.D., THE MONEY IS YOUR FAMILY'S FUTURE. WE NEED TO TALK ABOUT IT SOME MORE BEFORE YOU DO ANY-THING.
SO DEPOSIT THE CHECK FOR NOW. YOU CAN ALWAYS RETURN IT LATER, OKAY?
YEAH, OKAY.
I HAVE YOUR WORD ON THIS?
I SAID YES.
IN THE MEANTIME, MY WIFE AND I COULD USE A NEW WASHER-DRYER.
WHY DO I COME HERE?
©B. Trudeau

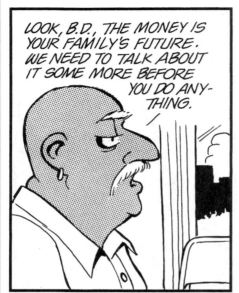

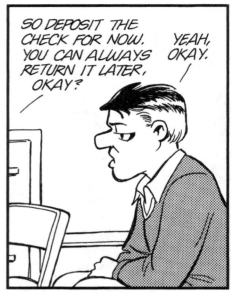

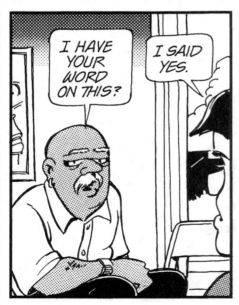

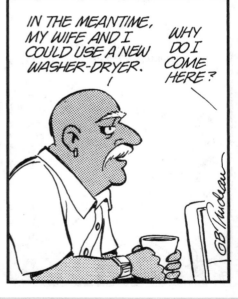

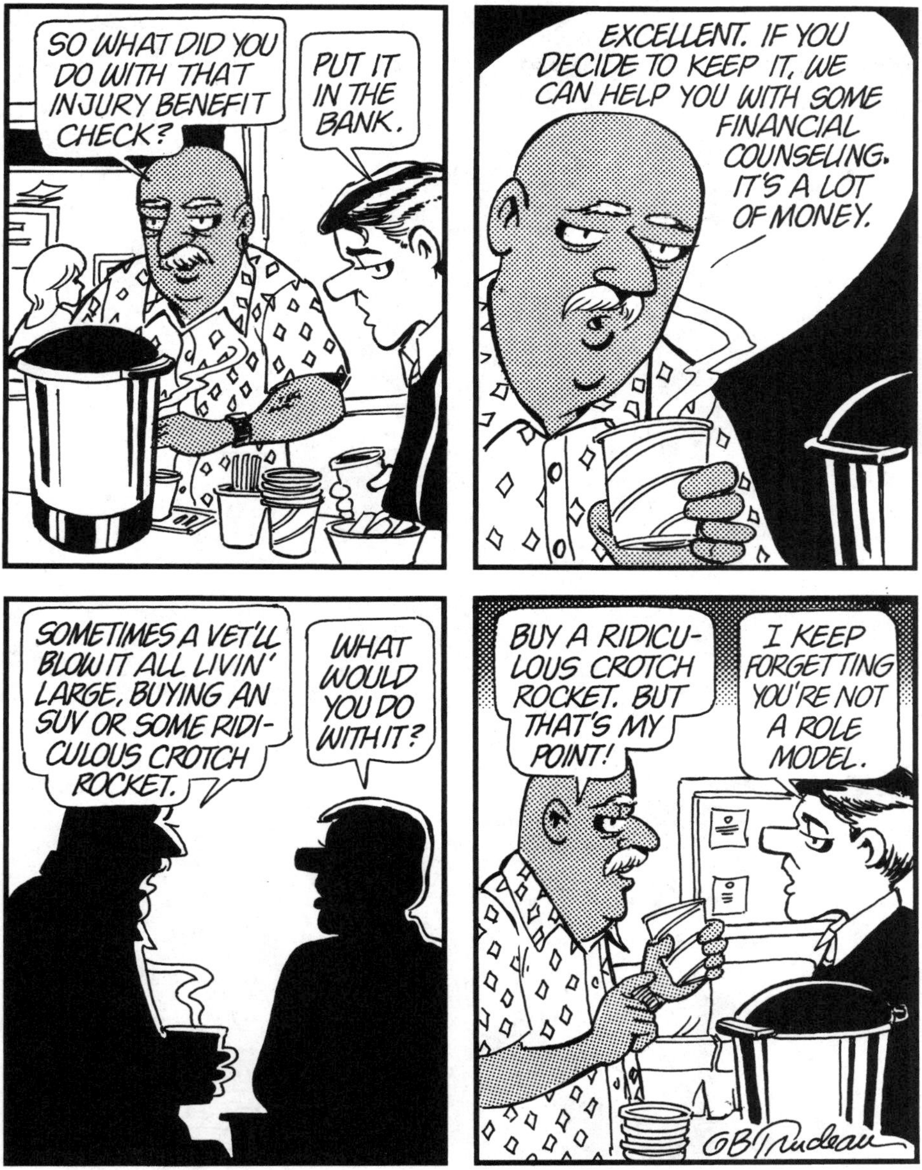
SO WHAT DID YOU DO WITH THAT INJURY BENEFIT CHECK?
PUT IT IN THE BANK.
EXCELLENT. IF YOU DECIDE TO KEEP IT, WE CAN HELP YOU WITH SOME FINANCIAL COUNSELING. IT'S A LOT OF MONEY.
SOMETIMES A VET'LL BLOW IT ALL LIVIN' LARGE, BUYING AN SUV OR SOME RIDICULOUS CROTCH ROCKET.
WHAT WOULD YOU DO WITH IT?
BUY A RIDICULOUS CROTCH ROCKET. BUT THAT'S MY POINT!
I KEEP FORGETTING YOU'RE NOT A ROLE MODEL.
GB Trudeau

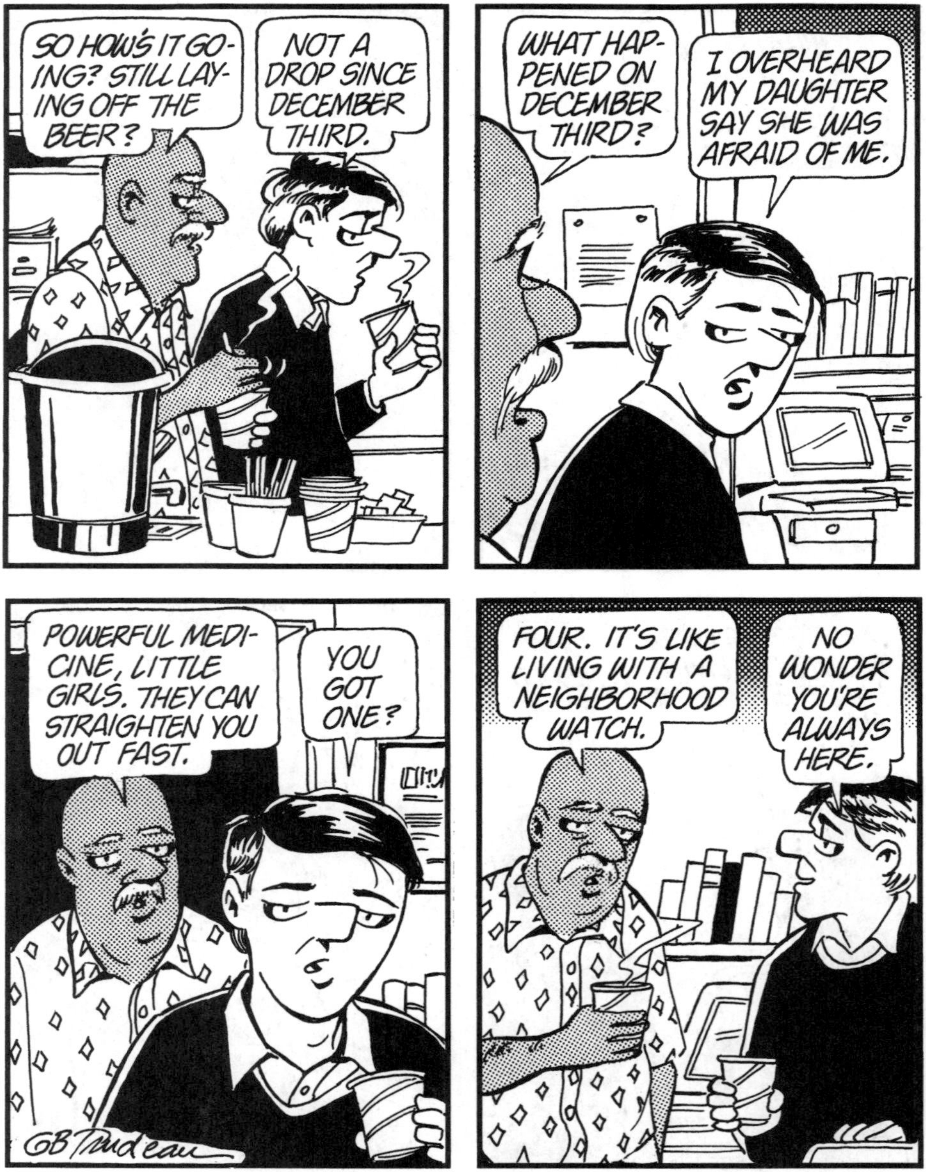
SO HOW'S IT GO-ING? STILL LAY-ING OFF THE BEER?
NOT A DROP SINCE DECEMBER THIRD.
WHAT HAP-PENED ON DECEMBER THIRD?
I OVERHEARD MY DAUGHTER SAY SHE WAS AFRAID OF ME.
POWERFUL MEDI-CINE, LITTLE GIRLS. THEY CAN STRAIGHTEN YOU OUT FAST.
YOU GOT ONE?
FOUR. IT'S LIKE LIVING WITH A NEIGHBORHOOD WATCH.
NO WONDER YOU'RE ALWAYS HERE.
GB Trudeau

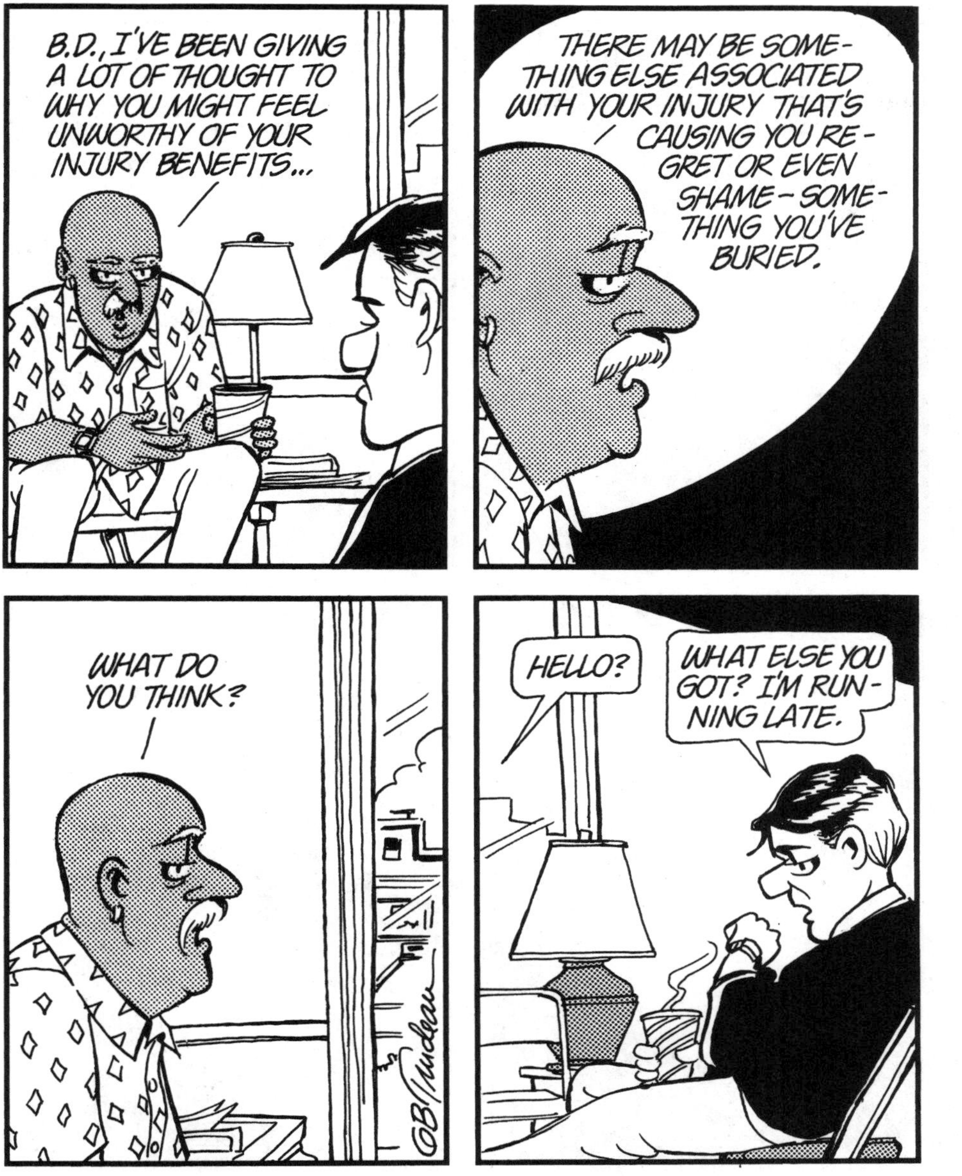
B.D., I'VE BEEN GIVING A LOT OF THOUGHT TO WHY YOU MIGHT FEEL UNWORTHY OF YOUR INJURY BENEFITS...
THERE MAY BE SOMETHING ELSE ASSOCIATED WITH YOUR INJURY THAT'S CAUSING YOU REGRET OR EVEN SHAME–SOMETHING YOU'VE BURIED.
WHAT DO YOU THINK?
HELLO?
WHAT ELSE YOU GOT? I'M RUNNING LATE.
GBTrudeau

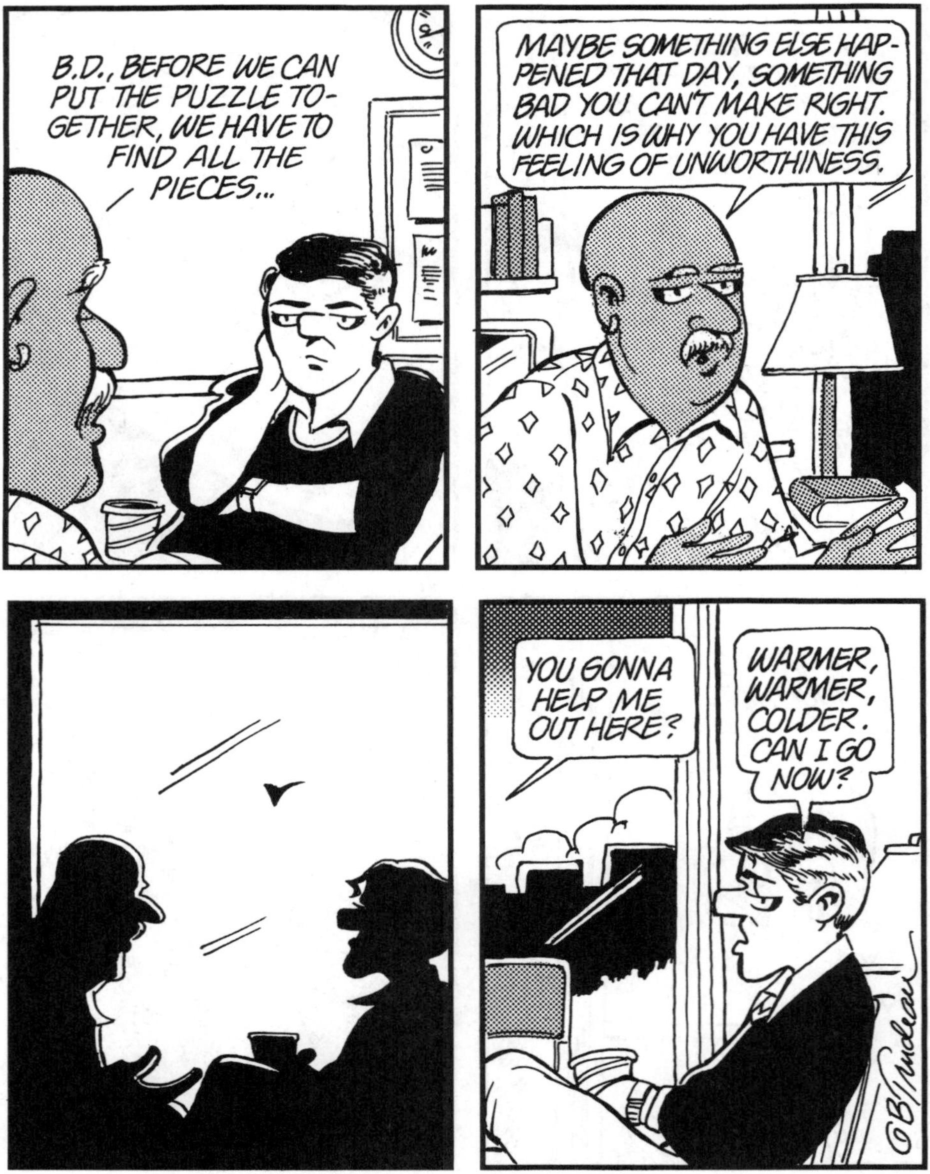
B.D., BEFORE WE CAN PUT THE PUZZLE TOGETHER, WE HAVE TO FIND ALL THE PIECES...
MAYBE SOMETHING ELSE HAPPENED THAT DAY, SOMETHING BAD YOU CAN'T MAKE RIGHT. WHICH IS WHY YOU HAVE THIS FEELING OF UNWORTHINESS.
YOU GONNA HELP ME OUT HERE?
WARMER, WARMER, COLDER. CAN I GO NOW?
©B/Trudeau

I DON'T WANT TO TALK ABOUT THIS ANYMORE!
THIS IS KEY, B.D.—I MEAN, YOU LEFT A LEG ON THE BATTLEFIELD...
YEAH, WELL, THAT'S NOT THE ONLY THING I LEFT ON THE BATTLEFIELD!
OKAY, THAT PROBABLY MEANS SOMETHING, DOESN'T IT?
YOU THINK?
GB Trudeau

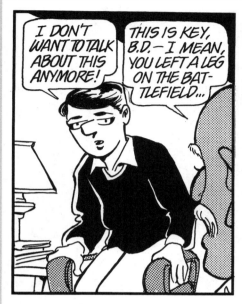

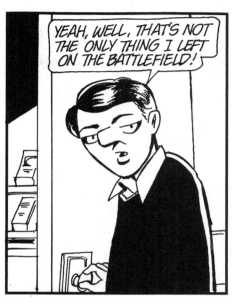

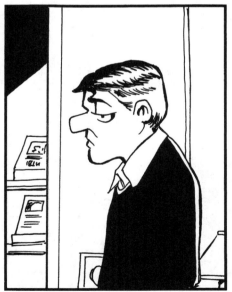

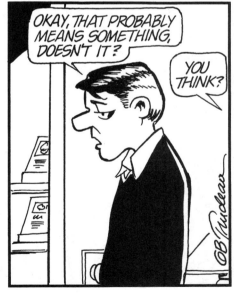

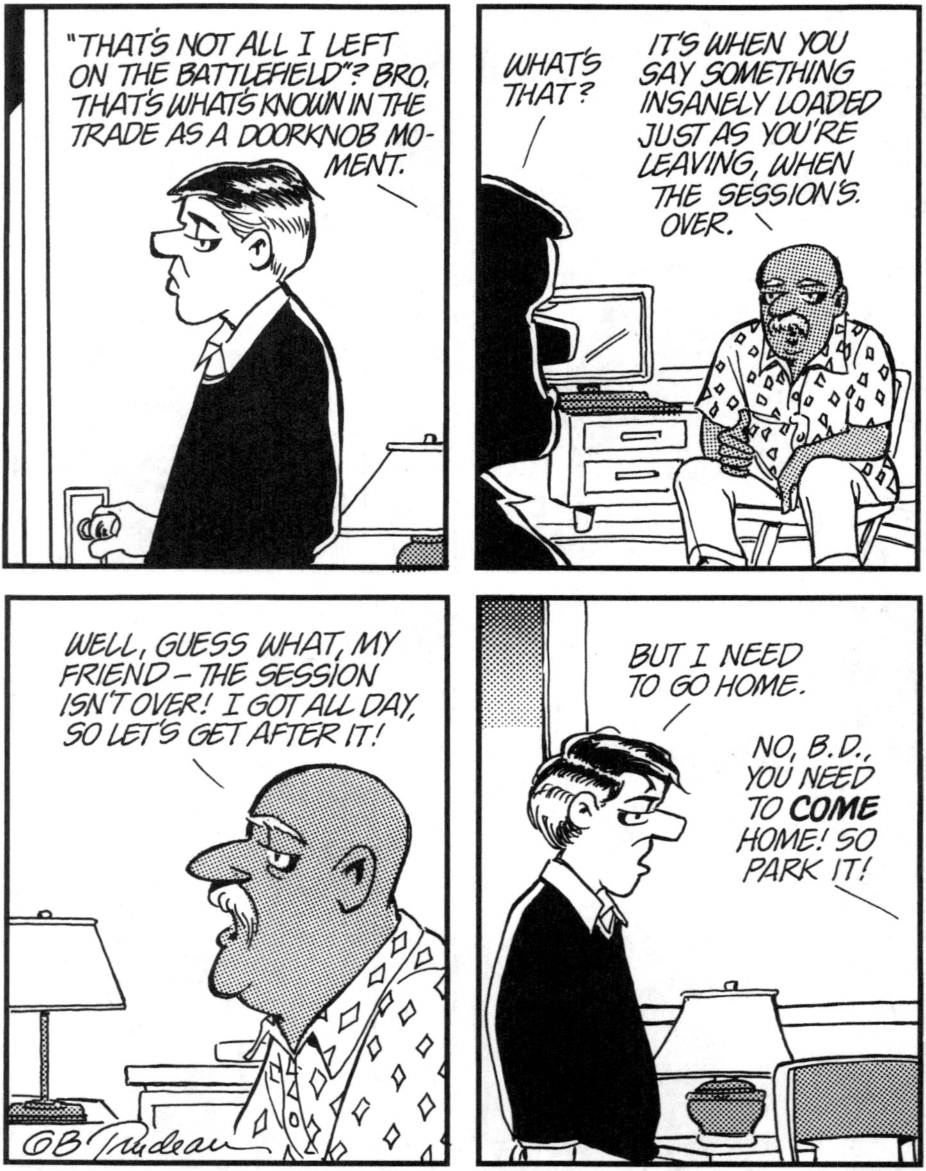
"THAT'S NOT ALL I LEFT ON THE BATTLEFIELD"? BRO, THAT'S WHAT'S KNOWN IN THE TRADE AS A DOORKNOB MOMENT.
WHAT'S THAT?
IT'S WHEN YOU SAY SOMETHING INSANELY LOADED JUST AS YOU'RE LEAVING, WHEN THE SESSION'S OVER.
WELL, GUESS WHAT, MY FRIEND – THE SESSION ISN'T OVER! I GOT ALL DAY, SO LET'S GET AFTER IT!
BUT I NEED TO GO HOME.
NO, B.D., YOU NEED TO **COME** HOME! SO PARK IT!
©B Trudeau

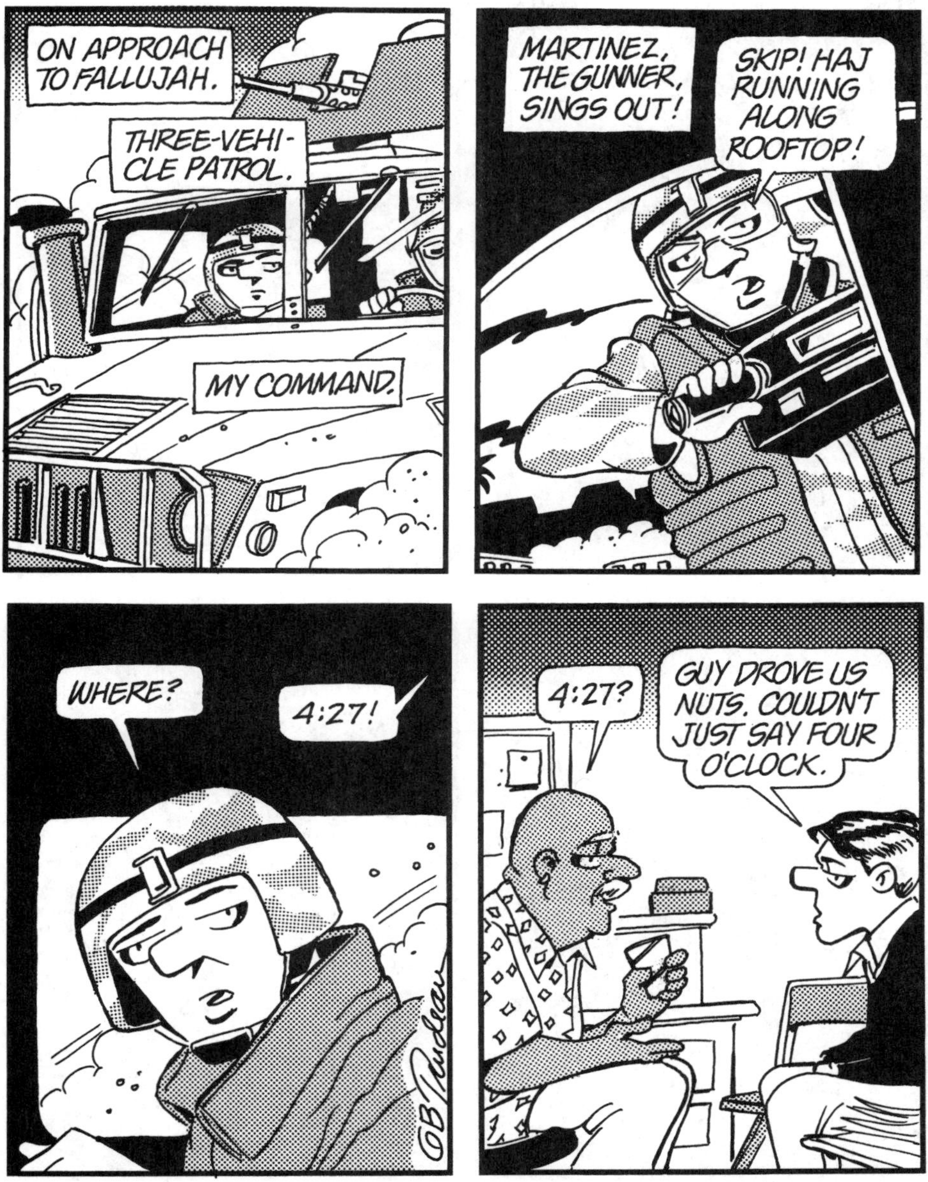

ON APPROACH TO FALLUJAH.
THREE-VEHICLE PATROL.
MY COMMAND.
MARTINEZ, THE GUNNER, SINGS OUT!
SKIP! HAJ RUNNING ALONG ROOFTOP!
WHERE?
4:27!
4:27?
GUY DROVE US NUTS. COULDN'T JUST SAY FOUR O'CLOCK.
©B Trudeau

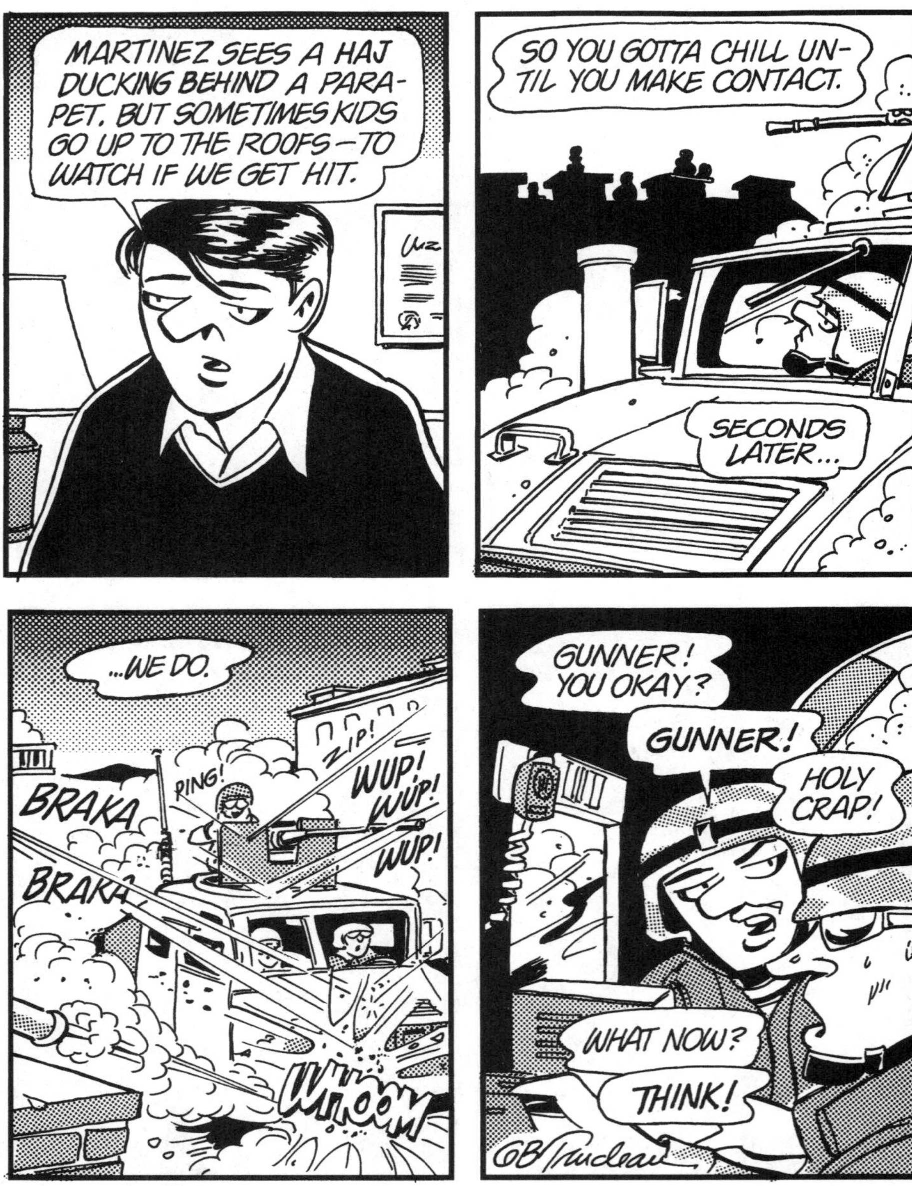
MARTINEZ SEES A HAJ DUCKING BEHIND A PARAPET. BUT SOMETIMES KIDS GO UP TO THE ROOFS—TO WATCH IF WE GET HIT.
SO YOU GOTTA CHILL UNTIL YOU MAKE CONTACT.
SECONDS LATER...
...WE DO.
ZIP!
PING!
WUP! WUP!
WUP!
BRAKA
BRAKA
WHOOM
GUNNER! YOU OKAY?
GUNNER!
HOLY CRAP!
WHAT NOW?
THINK!
GB Trudeau

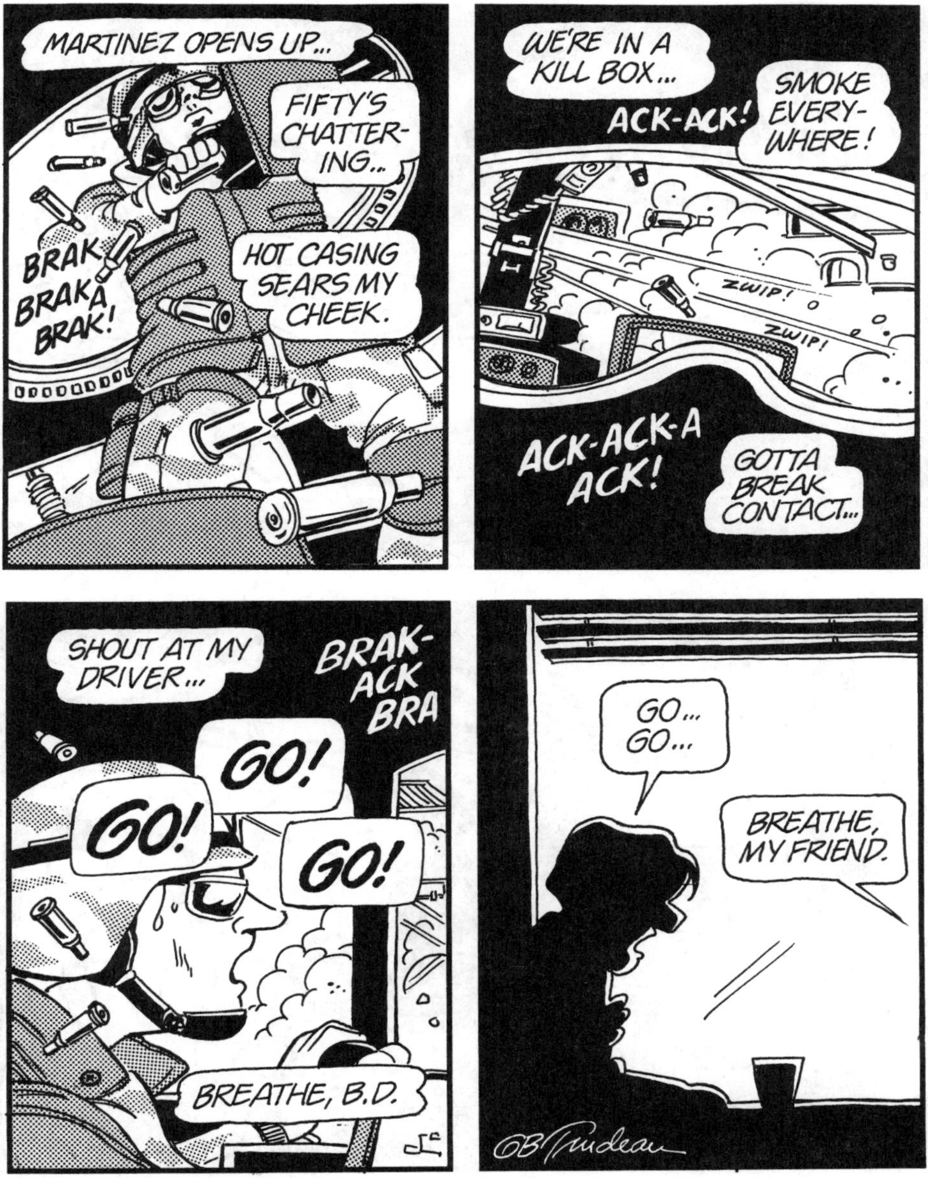
MARTINEZ OPENS UP...
FIFTY'S CHATTER-ING...
BRAK BRAK A BRAK!
HOT CASING SEARS MY CHEEK.
WE'RE IN A KILL BOX...
ACK-ACK!
SMOKE EVERY-WHERE!
ZWIP!
ZWIP!
ACK-ACK-A ACK!
GOTTA BREAK CONTACT...
SHOUT AT MY DRIVER...
BRAK-ACK BRA
GO!
GO!
GO!
BREATHE, B.D.
GO... GO...
BREATHE, MY FRIEND.
GB Trudeau

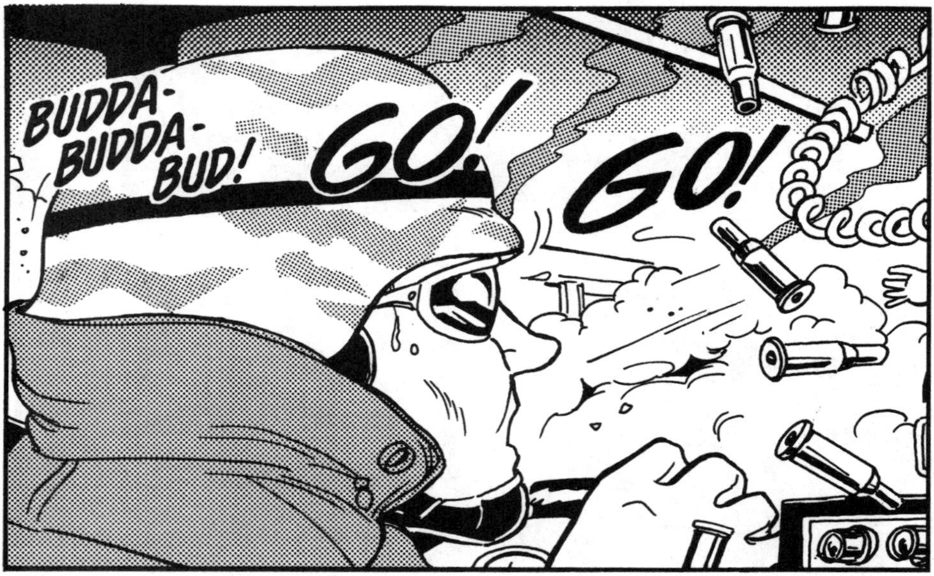
BUDDA-
BUDDA-
BUD!
GO!
GO!

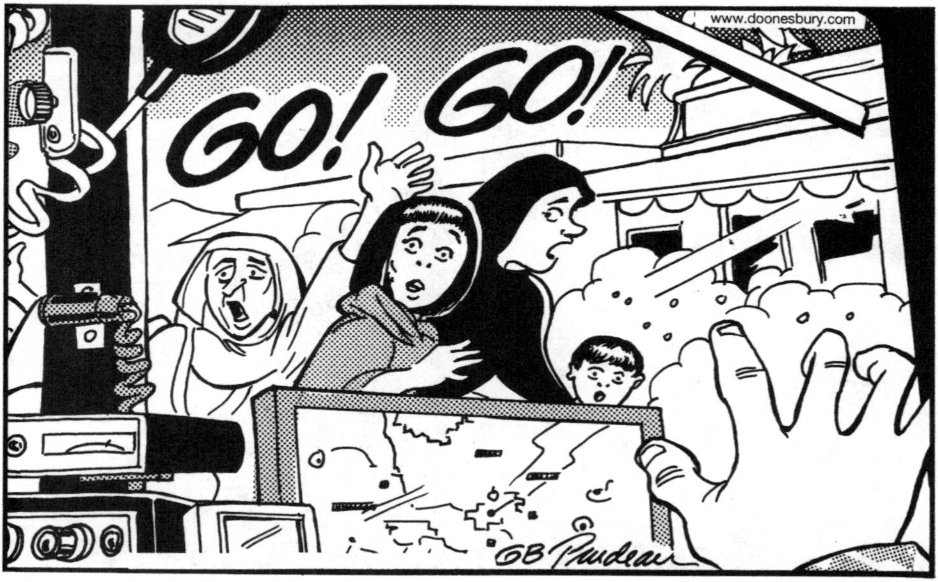
www.doonesbury.com
GO! GO!
GB Trudeau

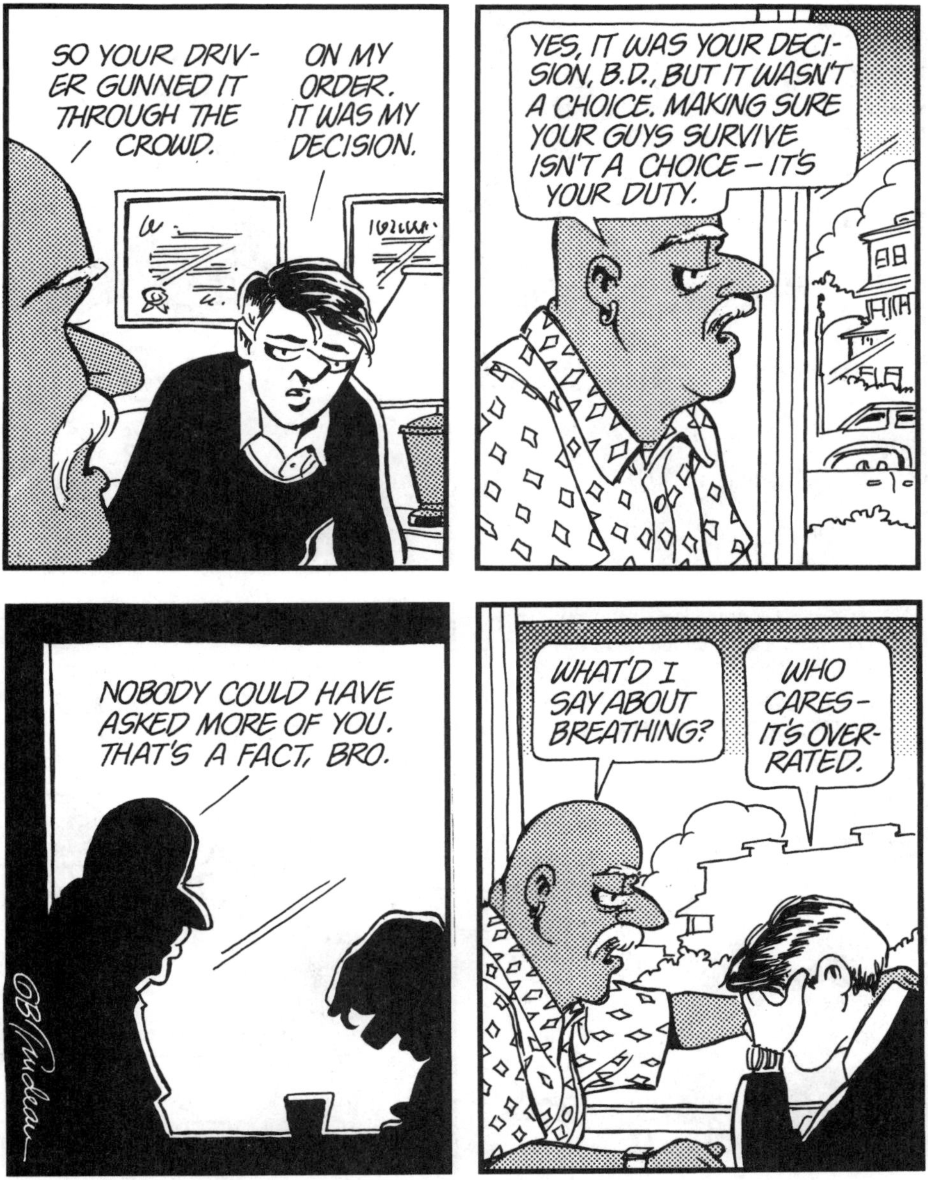
SO YOUR DRIVER GUNNED IT THROUGH THE CROWD.
ON MY ORDER. IT WAS MY DECISION.
YES, IT WAS YOUR DECISION, B.D., BUT IT WASN'T A CHOICE. MAKING SURE YOUR GUYS SURVIVE ISN'T A CHOICE – IT'S YOUR DUTY.
NOBODY COULD HAVE ASKED MORE OF YOU. THAT'S A FACT, BRO.
WHAT'D I SAY ABOUT BREATHING?
WHO CARES – IT'S OVERRATED.

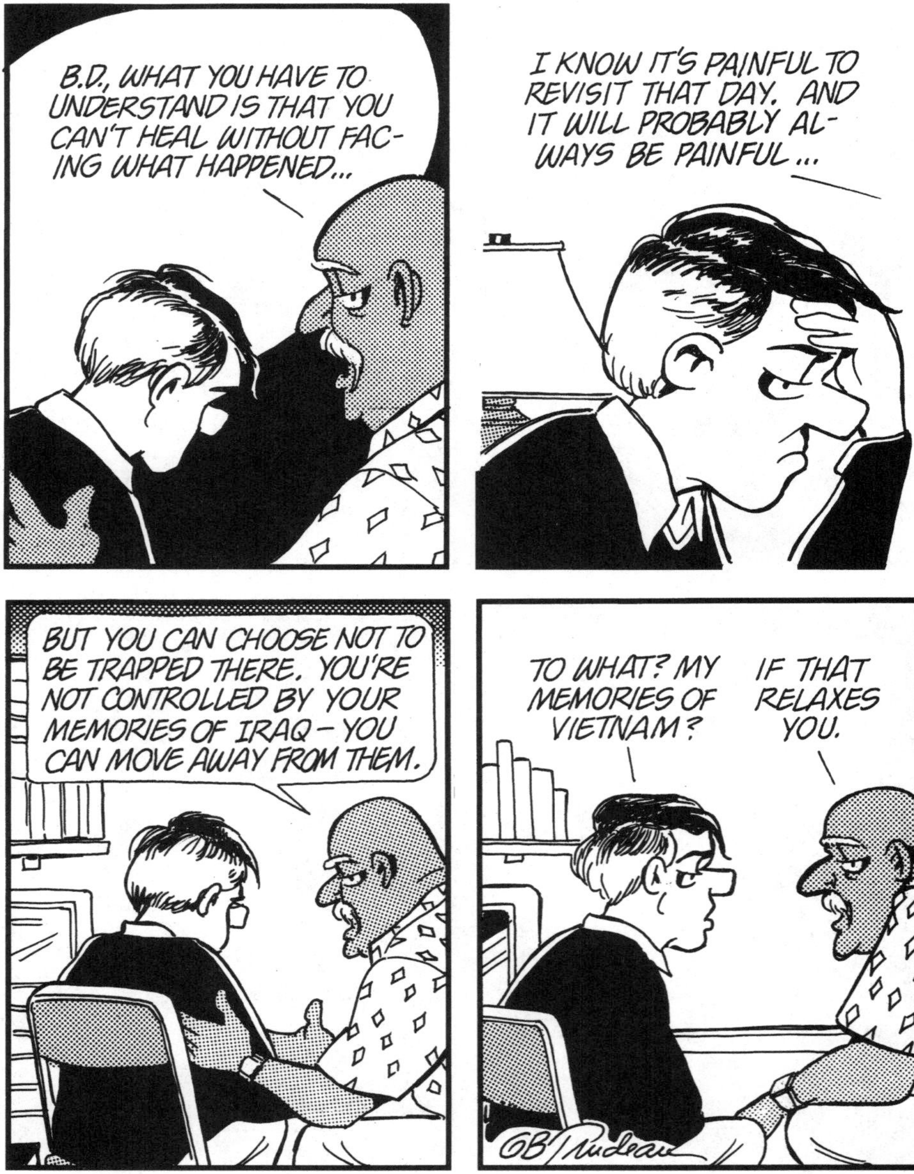
B.D., WHAT YOU HAVE TO UNDERSTAND IS THAT YOU CAN'T HEAL WITHOUT FACING WHAT HAPPENED...
I KNOW IT'S PAINFUL TO REVISIT THAT DAY. AND IT WILL PROBABLY ALWAYS BE PAINFUL...
BUT YOU CAN CHOOSE NOT TO BE TRAPPED THERE. YOU'RE NOT CONTROLLED BY YOUR MEMORIES OF IRAQ – YOU CAN MOVE AWAY FROM THEM.
TO WHAT? MY MEMORIES OF VIETNAM?
IF THAT RELAXES YOU.
GB Trudeau

FISHER HOUSE

because A Family's Love is Good Medicine

www.fisherhouse.org

A Fisher House is a "home away from home" for families of patients receiving medical care at major military and VA medical centers. As of this printing, there are thirty-three Fisher Houses located on seventeen military installations and seven VA medical centers, with another five houses in design. The program began in 1990 and has offered more than two million days of lodging to more than seventy thousand families.

The Fisher House Foundation donates Fisher Houses to the U.S. Government. They have full-time salaried managers but depend on volunteers and voluntary support to enhance daily operations and program expansion.

Through the generosity of the American public, the foundation has expanded its programs to meet the needs of our service men and women who have been wounded. The foundation uses donated frequent-flier miles to provide airline travel to reunite families of the wounded and to enable our wounded heroes to go home to convalesce. They also help cover the cost of alternative lodging when the Fisher Houses are full.

For further information about these programs, to find out about volunteering, or to make a tax-deductible gift, go to their Web site at

www.fisherhouse.org.

You can also obtain information by writing them at

Executive Director
Fisher House Foundation, Inc.
1401 Rockville Pike, Suite 600
Rockville, MD 20852

Phone: (888) 294-8560
E-mail: info@fisherhouse.org